THE JESUIT MYSTIQUE

DOUGLAS LETSON
MICHAEL HIGGINS

An Imprint of Loyola Press
Chicago

An Imprint of Loyola Press
3441 N. Ashland Avenue
Chicago, Illinois 60657
Phone (800) 621-1008 FAX (312) 281-0555

Copublished with Macmillan Canada
A Division of Canada Publishing Corporation
Toronto, Canada

Readers will note some minor differences between U.S. and Canadian usage, for example, in spellings. Our editors accepted the Canadian version to expedite publication and to save costs by not having to reset the text. Savings were passed on to the reader.

United States Cataloging in Publication Data

Letson, Douglas Richard, 1939–
The Jesuit mystique / Douglas Letson, Michael Higgins.
p. cm.

Includes bibliographical references and index.
ISBN 0-8294-0865-7 (hardcover)

1. Jesuits—History. 2. Jesuits—History — 20th century. 3. Jesuits—Biography.
I. Higgins, Michael W. II. Title.

BX3706.2.L44 1995 271'.53—dc20 95-20288

1 2 3 4 5 99 98 97 96 95

Printed in Canada

To our fathers
Joseph Higgins
and
Ernie Letson

CONTENTS

ACKNOWLEDGEMENTS

The Jesuit Mystique has been some five years in composition, combined as it has been with our administrative and professorial obligations at the University of St. Jerome's College. These five years have provided us with the opportunity to meet, interview, and observe a representative cohort of today's Companions where they are actively engaged in their various ministries and, as a result, to experience first-hand the magic of the mystique that continues to energize the Society more than 450 years after its founding. These five years have also given us the opportunity to discuss, debate, research, and reflect on today's Jesuit and his indebtedness to yesterday's mentors. We are convinced that our effort to capture the ebb and flow of the mystique that has enveloped the Society of Jesus from its earliest days results in the depiction of a modern Company of dedicated Companions who not only embody the ideals of their founder, but who also transmit a Christian vision and a sense of hope for the church of tomorrow.

Jesuits are by nature a mobile society. As a result, many no longer live in the countries or occupy the positions they did at the time of their interview. Five years can be a long time in the posting of a Jesuit. Our list of interviews, therefore, notes only where and when the individuals were interviewed, and textual references tell which positions they held at the time of the interview. To be a Jesuit is to be open to new possibilities.

This long period of gestation has of necessity also left us indebted to our own company of companions. We are grateful indeed for the more than 100 Jesuits and associates of the Society of Jesus who have given so generously of their time to meet with us and to speak frankly about the Society they know and the work in which it is engaged. It is obviously impossible to echo all of their voices in the short space that this book provides, though each has influenced the shaping of our own conclusions. We are particularly grateful for those Jesuits and friends of the Society who so generously extended their hospitality to us when we were strangers in a foreign land, providing us sometimes with meals in the Society's dining areas and sometimes with lodgings in a Jesuit residence. Among them are Michael Campbell-Johnston in London; Dean Brackley in San Salvador and the Jesuit community in Santa Tecla, El Salvador; Wilfrid J. Usher at Stonyhurst; Michael Gallagher in Dublin; Jim Webb in Kingston, Jamaica; Stanislaw Obirek in Krakow; Winston Rye in Montreal; Hanz G. Wehner and Albert Keller in Munich; and various members of the International House in Rome. The Congregation of the Resurrection has extended similar hospitality to us, especially through the generosity of Bob Liddy in St. Louis, Missouri, and Bob Kurtz, Terry McGuire, and Sudie MacDonald at the Resurrectionist Mother House in Rome. We also thank Laetitia Bordes, for her friendly and useful assistance in acting as our interpreter in San Salvador as well as in Managua; Jacques Monet of the University of Sudbury who assisted us in tracking down research materials; the late papal biographer and religious affairs writer Peter Hebblethwaite who provided us with the benefit of his considerable wisdom; and Gary Draper and Carolyn Dirks, librarian and assistant librarian, respectively, at the University of St. Jerome's College, who spent many hours on our behalf in professional pursuit of elusive documents. And our special thanks to Alice Lemieux-Tapper, secretary to the president and dean at the University of St. Jerome's College, who devoted countless hours to carefully transcribing our numerous interview tapes—no easy task since they were sometimes quite technical, sometimes a trifle arcane to the uninitiated ear, and sometimes confusingly convivial.

We are especially grateful for the many photographs that help to cloak the Jesuit mystique in flesh and blood. José de Vera was particularly cooperative and most generous in so freely granting unlimited access to photographs housed at the Jesuit curia in Rome as part of the submissions provided for potential inclusion in the *Jesuit Yearbook*, the Society's annual chronicling of its international ministerial activities. We are, of course, indebted not only to Father de Vera but also to the many Jesuits who submitted the photographs to him. We have received blanket permission from Father de Vera to include photographs without being able to attain specific credit. J. A. Loftus, Jesuit professor of psychology at the University of St. Jerome's College, has also been most helpful in our search for photographic documentation.

Financial assistance to offset the cost of our research was provided through our personal professional development funds and the Academic Development Fund at the University of St. Jerome's College. Without this support, our on-site research would, of necessity, have been much more limited in its scope and this book far less lively in its presentation.

Finally, as always, our thanks to our wives, Krystyna Higgins and Donna Letson, who reviewed our manuscript with a careful eye and provided intelligent counsel, and who patiently endured long periods when we were away on research trips, lonely periods when we were at home but at work on our studies, and tedious periods when we were together but reflecting on our intellectual exploits.

University of St. Jerome's College
Waterloo, Ontario
January 31, 1995

PREFACE

WHY ANOTHER BOOK about the Jesuits?—a reasonable question, and one earnestly posed on a number of occasions over the course of our research into *The Jesuit Mystique*. The answer is embedded in questions of our own, questions we think are not only of interest in themselves but that are also instructive for our post-industrial society, seriously engaged as it is in its own pursuit of meaning. They are questions such as: Why have the Jesuits, the Companions of the Society of Jesus, been traditionally greeted with scorn or admiration, affection or hatred, open arms or the report of arms, outright suspicion or absolute trust? How does one define the essence of the Jesuit, that which distinguishes him from others who would walk in the footsteps of Jesus of Nazareth? What are his origins, and how does today's Companion compare with the post-Reformation Company whose path he also traces? What is there about the Society of Jesus that is clearly sustaining its diminished numbers through the ravages of an increasingly secular society laying waste to scores of smaller, less resilient congregations of men and women?

The Society of Jesus is important because, for all its human failings, for all of the eccentricities and inconsistencies of the Companions who constitute its ranks, in the incarnation of its vision the Jesuit Order courageously signs the possibility of a better society, of an earthly reign decidedly rooted in evangelical values, and of an ultimate victory of charity and compassion over cupidity and concupiscence.

The structure of *The Jesuit Mystique* springs from shared scholarly experience accumulated over the past fifteen years: collaborative research, talks, articles, and books based mostly on the conviction that ideas are best explored through the prism of human experience, through the voices of appropriate exemplars, and, therefore, through the medium of the biographer. Ignatius of Loyola, the founder of the Society of Jesus, is in a real sense never far from the heart of our exploration. He is the visionary and the man of the world to whom the Jesuits of every age have looked for direction, inspiration, guidance, and assurance. From the outset, therefore, Ignatius joins our exploratory pilgrimage into the Jesuit mystique, and he will never leave it since his charisma, his hard-nosed advice, and his *Spiritual Exercises* provide timeless beacons for every Jesuit's journey. As a result, in *The Jesuit Mystique* we have given Ignatius the opportunity to speak both through his letters and through his autobiography; we have erected the same platform for his closest friend, Francis Xavier, whose published correspondence provides a living voice from the earliest Jesuit missions; and we have handed the microphone to hosts of other Jesuits from the sixteenth to the twentieth century. It is in their voices that we catch the cadences of what we have dubbed the Jesuit mystique.

And that is why we have written *this* book, a book that is decidedly different in format and tone from any of which we are aware, but one that is wholly consistent with our own established scholarly history. *The Jesuit Mystique* is by design an invitation to engage the Society in an ongoing dialogue concerning the practical human imperative demanded by the written Word. Our pilgrimage has been stimulating, informative, instructive, sometimes inspiring, occasionally disappointing, and ultimately hopeful; we trust that our readers will find their pilgrimage with Ignatius's Company equally engaging.

I

Mystique in the Making: Historical Origins

From Courtier to General: 1491–1541

WHEN THE POPE of the Second Vatican Council (Vatican II, 1962–65), John XXIII, instructed the church to read the signs of the times and to respond meaningfully to them, he set in motion a consultative whirlwind that not only changed the face of the church in the modern world but also prompted a renewal of religious life, a renewal of those orders and congregations of professed men and women eager to do the work of the church "in perfect charity."[1]

The Council and its reading of the signs of the modern world triggered the 1974–75 32nd General Congregation of the Society of Jesus (the Jesuits), which was called specifically to examine the origins of the Society in search of its foundational reason for being, its charism. As a result of their deliberations, the Fathers of the Congregation promulgated a programme of social justice, an option for the poor, and a quest for perfect charity whose practical application resulted in the murder of scores of its members and spawned divisions within the Society not unlike those that developed within the church itself in the wake of Vatican II. An understanding of today's Society, therefore, begins with a search for its roots, its founding inspiration.

The company of men and the Society they formed, as well as the mystique that has enveloped that Society virtually from its inception, were fashioned by turbulent forces at work within the wider society; these men were driven by a deeply felt personal conviction about the need to transform the lives of the underprivileged in their society by putting the gospel imperatives into action. The consequences of that conviction have made the Society both a flashpoint for controversy and an agent of social reform from the Jesuits' pre-Society days to our own. It is these people, their personal passions, and the Company's struggles, their efforts to live in perfect charity that have given rise to the mystique of the Jesuit, a mystique that has been coincident with the word "Jesuit" from the drawing of the Society's first breath. By reflecting on the words of the practical visionaries—the men of learning and of action, men of the word and followers of Jesus, who have constituted the Company—and by focusing on their deeds, we will begin to know many of the Companions of Jesus, and in so doing we will come to appreciate the mystique that surrounds them still.

Like ours, the sixteenth-century Christian society in which the founding Jesuits lived, dreamed, and served was marked by huge discrepancies between the rich and the poor, the learned and the uneducated, the powerful and the weak; like ours, Ignatius's was also a world torn by military conflict and political strife. Unlike our twentieth-century post-Christian culture, however, Ignatius's society was deeply religious; indeed, the relationship between the state and the religion of the state was an intimate one: "the *cujus regio, ejus religio* [where one lives determines one's religion] was then, if not a principle of law, nonetheless a fact."[2] During the Renaissance, the corollary of this truism dictated that the religion of the ruler was the religion of the ruled. An additional fact: of those rulers who fought for land, wealth, and God, the Pope, though he could no longer exercise the awesome temporal power of an Innocent III, could still count himself a regal potentate to be reckoned with—nor was the Pope ignorant of the Machiavellian wiles necessary for the successful wielding of temporal power.

But the Pope's realm had its own serious problems, problems that were evident in the late Middle Ages, escalated during the Reformation, and began to abate only marginally (if at all) in the centuries that followed. The 1517 Wittenburg declaration of the Augustinian friar Martin Luther had shattered the facade of ecclesiastical unity and escalated the fractionalizing of Christendom; the untutored and unlettered condition of the clergy in general was exceeded only by the massive ignorance of the population at large; and clerical corruption, deceit, and widespread simony at all levels of the institutional church gave credence to Luther's courageous call for reform. John Olin catalogues the decay that had spread into the pre-Reformation church: "the exaggeration of papal power and a concomitant opposition to it both in practice and in theory, the worldliness and secularization of the hierarchy that reached to the papacy itself in the High Renaissance, ignorance and immorality among the lower clergy, laxity in monastic discipline and spiritual decay in the religious life, theological desiccation and confusion, superstition and abuse in religious practice."[3]

The papal court was desperately in need of new directions, new resources, a new Company ready and willing to carry the chastened evangelical message to the four corners of the earth. Ignatius and his companions were determined to shoulder the cross, though that willingness was not then and is not now universally applauded. Then, like now, the Jesuits set out "to help souls"—a recurrent, consistent, and unifying theme that echoes throughout Ignatius's autobiography—that is, to minister to the total well-being of the human individual through the spiritual and corporal works of mercy evident in the life of Christ and in the apostolic tradition.

A rugged visionary with his eyes set faithfully on the next world and his feet set firmly in this one, Ignatius was born in the Basque region of northern Spain in the province of Guipúzcoa, near the town of Azpeitia, and at the paternal castle of Loyola, most likely in the year 1491. Christened Iñigo López de Loyola after an eleventh-century Benedictine abbot, Ignatius had been born into wealth, prestige, and influence; by the fortunate accident of being well born, Iñigo was apparently destined to enjoy the extravagant life of the courtier. W. W. Meissner, a Jesuit psychiatrist and professor of psychoanalysis, recalls a local historian's observation that Guipúzcoa has been interpreted to mean "to terrify the enemy," and Meissner adds that "The Loyolas were one of the great families of Guipúzcoa, and if any family did more to shape the image of the Guipúzcoans as rugged and fiercely independent, history has not recorded it."[4]

The young Ignatius did indeed set out on the path signalled by a domineering, proud, and pugnacious father, Beltrán Yañez de Loyola. Nonetheless, Ignatius's time at the paternal castle was brief and his affection for family no doubt more vicarious than real. Beltrán was more symbol than father, and the women in Ignatius's life more convenient or idealized than maternal. The first of these was María de Garín, a blacksmith's wife who lived in the shadow of the castle of Loyola and who became his wetnurse.

In his mid-teens, Ignatius was sent to Arévalo to live in the castle of a family friend who was in the employ of the Spanish court, Juan Velázquez de Cuéllar, who had volunteered to fashion the young courtier and who had, in effect, taken the place of Ignatius's father after the death of Beltrán when Ignatius was sixteen. For his part, following in the steps of a father who had sired several illegitimate children, and like his brother Pero López (a parish priest at Azpeitia who had fathered four children of his own), Ignatius set out on the libidinous path of the man-about-court and it would seem that he too was very likely the father of a child.[5] Ignatius the courtier seemed destined more to wander the paths of his womanizing and belligerent progenitor than to walk in the footsteps of Jesus of Nazareth; Meissner concludes that Ignatius the courtier suffered from a "phallic narcissism." Indeed, Ignatius's autobiography records that the life of the wayward youth was also marred by a serious felony, perhaps a murder, but certainly a crime sufficiently serious that only the dubious pleading of the tonsured state saved him from receiving the full force of the law.

Velázquez's death in 1517 altered Ignatius's course and sealed his destiny. Having joined the military under the Duke of Nájera and viceroy of Navarre, Ignatius found himself in the Basque town of Pamplona on May 20, 1521, when French troops crossed into Spain and prepared for what was clearly to be a sacking. Thirty years of age, an established courtier fired by the passion and the pride of his Loyola ancestry, Ignatius refused to accept the negotiated surrender that guaranteed the safety of the citizenry; instead, the foolhardy hidalgo took to the citadel where he exhorted his comrades to battle in the face of impossible odds, only to be summarily disabled by cannon fire that shattered his right leg, imposed a lifelong limp on the proud courtier, and significantly altered the march of history.

Ignatius's convalescence was painful and protracted. Luis Gonçalves da Câmara, the chronicler to whom Ignatius recounted his life's story, records that:

> All the doctors and surgeons who were summoned from many places decided that the leg ought to be broken again and the bones reset because they had been badly set the first time or had been broken on the road and were out of place and could not heal. This butchery was done again; during it, as in all the others he suffered before or since, he never spoke a word nor showed any sign of pain other than to clench his fists. . . . As his bones knit together, one bone below the knee remained on top of another, shortening his leg. The bone protruded so much that it was an ugly sight. He was unable to abide it because he was determined to follow the world and he thought that it would deform him; he asked the surgeons if it could be cut away. They said that indeed it could be cut away, but that the pain would be greater than all those he had suffered, because it was already healed and it would take some time to cut it. Yet he was determined to make himself a martyr to his own pleasure.[6]

To speed the passage of time and to urge the healing process, Ignatius looked naturally to the court romances of the day, to exemplary heroes like Tristan and Iseult. But, as fate would have it, the library of his ancestral home no longer contained the chivalric gestes so favoured by Ignatius; in their stead, Ignatius's sister-in-law, the saintly Doña Magdalena de Araoz, provided the wounded warrior with *The Life of Christ* by Ludolph of Saxony (a German Carthusian) and *The Golden Legend* (a collection of saints' lives scribed by Jacopo da Voragine, a thirteenth-century Dominican). In these books, Ignatius found new heroes worthy of imitation. "St. Dominic did this, therefore, I have to do it. St. Francis did this, therefore, I have to do it."[7] The conceit of the court was beginning to be replaced by the humility of the pilgrim, and Ignatius pursued his new pilgrimage with the same passion he had dedicated to his secular shrines; in fact, as Meissner points out, Ignatius's new quest is quite harmonious with the heroic ideals Ignatius was ostensibly setting aside: "The desire to win glory, a major theme in this [the heroic] ideal, is a motif that forms one of the lines of continuity between the swashbuckling Iñigo and the saintly Ignatius."[8]

In March 1522, Ignatius turned his back on his past: his family, his wealth, the courtier's life. Now about 31, he mounted a mule and began his pilgrimage with all the intensity of the newly converted, setting his sights first on Montserrat but with Jerusalem as his ultimate destination—pilgrimage to Jerusalem was not only a Guipúzcoan tradition, it was also the inevitable object of many of Jacopo da Voragine's canonized heroes. On the road, Ignatius encountered a Moor who questioned the church's teaching concerning the continuing virginity of Mary subsequent to the virgin birth. After the Moor's departure, Ignatius was so overcome with guilt for not having defended his lady as he ought, that he was determined to find the Moor and make him pay at the point of his dagger for his blasphemy. However, Ignatius left the life of the Moor to the whim of his mule and the paths the mule would travel, so the two were never reunited. The pilgrim journeyed on to Montserrat where he donned the chaffing garb of the penitent—"the armor of Christ"[9]—and gave what he had left of his fine clothing to an impoverished local beggar before pursuing the road to Manresa.

The initial transformation from the courtier to the Christian was complete: Ignatius had a new lady to serve and a new coat of armour in which to do battle. The simple deliberate life of consecrated poverty coupled with a dedicated commitment to corporal works of mercy, such as clothing the naked, were to become enduring hallmarks of the Society he was to inspire. There are, however, those who do not consider Ignatius's conversion experience with a sympathetic mind. John Donne is among their number. Some ninety years after the event, in his *Ignatius His Conclave* (1611), the accomplished poet and Dean of St. Paul's describes Ignatius as "this worne souldier of *Pampelune*, this *French-spanish* mungrell."[10] Indeed, Donne captures the prejudices of generations of critics when he inveighs against Ignatius, his transformation, and his progeny: "For having consecrated your first age to wars, and growne somewhat unable to follow that course, by reason of a wound; you did presently begin to thinke seriously of a spirituall warre, against the *Church*, and found meanes to open waies, even into Kings chambers, for your executioners."[11] An ex-Roman Catholic during the early days of the Penal Laws, Donne was suspicious of innovation, of all things popish, and of anybody who would question the absolute nature of the divine right of kings.

Ignatius's stay in Manresa lasted almost a year, from March 1522 until early 1523. And the experience of Manresa was to shape both the pilgrim and the companions who have since accompanied him. At Manresa, Ignatius entered an intensive period of meditation and self-denial, subjecting himself to severe fasts, letting his fingernails and hair grow grotesquely, and begging door-to-door for his daily bread. With the same ardor with which he mounted the ramparts of Pamplona he embraced the tribulations of the pilgrim: for Ignatius the companion of Christ, there would be no retreat. At Manresa, therefore, Ignatius began to mortify his body in ways that became so extreme that he suffered the painful effects for the rest of his life; it was an experience that later prompted him to impose strict limits on fasts and physical penances for all members of the Society, to dictate periods of recreation for his Companions, and to emphasize physical well-being. Ignatius learned from his own intemperate experience that the road of moderation, Aristotle's *via media*, was the only reasonable one for the Jesuits to travel.

While at Manresa, Ignatius had a series of apparitions whose origins demanded discernment: were they from God or from Satan? This act of discernment is central to Ignatius's *Spiritual Exercises*, to his invitation to cast off worldly encumbrances and follow Christ. It was at Manresa that Ignatius, though still formally unlettered, composed the bulk of his *Spiritual Exercises*, a handbook on spirituality that quickly became a source of religious controversy and the enduring touchstone of the Jesuit community. Ignatius's Manresa experiences and the lessons of Pamplona are clearly embodied in the Exercises. In them, there is a call for meditative discernment, the challenge to imitate the life of Christ and his saints, the conviction to choose between the two standards: that of Christ and that of Lucifer, of Jerusalem and of Babylon. At Manresa, Ignatius the pilgrim rejected the world with the same passion that Ignatius the courtier had previously embraced it. Ignatius the pilgrim preached poverty instead of the wealth to which he had been born, contempt for the worldly honour he had once so vigorously pursued, humility in place of the pride that had driven the passionate hidalgo. Meissner observes of the Manresa experience:

> Whereas the narcissism of the soldier is connected with the ideals of selfless and loyal service to his king and [that same narcissism] refused to accept defeat even in the face of impossible odds, the narcissism of the saint found its realization in the service of a heavenly king, a service that knew no limits of pain, penance, and sacrifice in the work of advancing the spiritual kingdom. [12]

Early in 1523, having vacillated between extreme ill-health and relative well-being, and having been visited by numerous apparitions of Christ and the Virgin Mary, Ignatius again set his sights on Jerusalem and, accordingly, took to the roads for Barcelona in search of safe passage. Accepting the evangelical directive to concern himself with neither money nor tunic on his journey, Ignatius trusted providence and Christian charity. He went first to Rome where he received the pilgrim's blessing from Pope Adrian VI, then to Venice for final passage, and ultimately to Jerusalem where he trod rapturously in the purported footsteps of Christ. Ignatius was intent on staying in Jerusalem both as a matter of personal devotion and "to help souls," [13] but the Franciscan friar to whom he made his pledge insisted that Ignatius could not be accommodated and that the occupation of the Moors made the plan impossible; in fact, Ignatius needed to be ordered from the Holy Land under the imminent threat of excommunication, so intent was he on staying. He would have to find another way "to help souls."

Ignatius's passion "to help souls" took him back to Spain. In 1524 he reached Barcelona with the apparent assistance of a guiding providence that saved him both from shipwreck and from enemy soldiers, and with the characteristic charity of numerous kind-hearted souls whom he met along the way on his revised pilgrimage. In Barcelona, Agnes Pascual (one of several members of the aristocracy whom Ignatius and his companions were to befriend) took him under her patronage. She provided lodgings for Ignatius and in the evenings helped him to distribute among the poor the alms and food he had begged during the day; she arranged for his education in basic grammar. Then, in 1526, Ignatius left Barcelona to further his education in the liberal arts—logic, Aristotle's *Physics*, and the *Sentences* of Peter Lombard—at Alcalá. There Ignatius and a small group of four disciples had the first of several encounters Ignatius was to endure with the Inquisition (two in Alcalá alone). This first detention was imposed in part because of their still unlettered state, in part because of their peculiar dress (for which they had become known as the Graycoats), and in part because of their teaching of the *Spiritual Exercises*. Indeed, there was much about Ignatius's style and his teaching that raised suspicion about his being a member of the heretical *alumbrados* ("the enlightened ones"), whose approach to spiritual perfection was more illuminative than studied. It was a suspicion that resulted in a brief incarceration and a warning to avoid eccentric behaviour. Suspicion was to dog Ignatius for decades, though his Alcalá encounters did convince him of the need to become better educated if he was to be really helpful to souls: it was a lesson well learned, one that was to be emblazoned in the Jesuit Constitutions, and one that is very much part of the Jesuit mystique even today.

Nonetheless, Ignatius set out for Salamanca where he arrived in July 1527 and where he and his followers began once again their practice of catechetical instruction. They were almost instantly submitted to an Inquisitional inquiry and once more imprisoned.

> After twenty-two days of imprisonment, they were summoned to hear the sentence, which was that no error was found in their life or teaching. Therefore they could do what they had been doing, teaching doctrine and speaking about the things of God, so long as they never defined that "this is a mortal sin or this is a venial sin," until they had studied for four more years. . . . He found great difficulty in remaining in Salamanca, for in the matter of helping souls it seemed to him that the door had been closed by this prohibition not to define mortal and venial sin.[14]

Ignatius had grudgingly come to realize that he had no option but to set out on foot for Paris to complete his education. He arrived there in February 1528, and stayed until March 1535. Now 37, Ignatius enrolled at the notoriously harsh college of Montaigu (alma mater to the likes of Calvin and Erasmus), where he was side by side with mere boys busily engaged in the study of the fundamentals of the humanities. The formerly proud hidalgo had learned a good deal about humility by then, however, and was determined to do whatever was necessary to serve his Lord by working for the good of souls. Such was his state of personal destitution that Ignatius was forced to study by day, beg by evening, and was further compelled to take up quarters in the hospice of St. Jacques, which had been founded to serve the impoverished pilgrims who were making their way to Compostela. Before long, nonetheless, Ignatius had established his characteristic reputation as a protector of the poor.

Many of the students whom Ignatius encountered at the University of Paris fell well short of being sources of edification. Even among the tonsured, gambling, excessive drinking, and womanizing were common forms of recreation; among the professorate, too, laziness, libidinousness, and intellectual arrogance were commonplace. But Ignatius rose above it all and found in the academic structure of the university much to be admired. And so in January 1532 Ignatius completed the arts course at Sainte-Barbe College where for the first time (most likely through linguistic error) the official record refers to him as Ignatius rather than his baptismal Iñigo. In March 1533 Ignatius received his licentiate, followed by his master's degree in philosophy in March 1535; he had earlier begun to study theology with the Dominicans at Saint-Jacques, though he did not receive a theological degree and even as general of the Society of Jesus he made no pretence of being a professional theologian. During his stay in Paris, Ignatius was forced to undertake various trips, one as far as England, in search of the necessary alms to complete his studies; he also continued his practice of assisting the poor and the sick in addition to teaching catechism and debating matters of religion.

Inevitably, Ignatius surrounded himself with like-minded companions who were no doubt united in opposition to the rather decadent social life at the university. The group of them—Ignatius, Peter Faber, Francis Xavier, Diego Laynez, Alfonso Salmerón, Nicólas Bobadilla, and Simón Rodriguez—gathered at the chapel dedicated to St. Denis on Montmartre on August 15, 1534, and took a conditional vow of pilgrimage to Jerusalem:

> they had all decided what they had to do, namely, to go to Venice and then to Jerusalem to spend their lives in the service of souls; and if they were not given permission to remain in

Jerusalem, they would return to Rome and present themselves to the Vicar of Christ, so that he could make use of them wherever he thought it would be to the greater glory of God and the service of souls.[15]

Nineteenth-century French novelist Honoré de Balzac, though an arch critic of the Society of Jesus, saw the Montmartre event as a moment of inspiration:

> Who is there, that would not admire the extraordinary spectacle of this union of seven men animated by a noble purpose who turn towards heaven and under the roof of a chapel lay down their worldly wishes and hopes and consecrate themselves to the happiness of their fellow men? They offer themselves as a sacrifice to the work of charity that shall give them no property nor power nor pleasure; they renounce the present for the future, looking forward only to a hereafter in heaven, and content with no happiness on earth beyond what a pure conscience can bestow.[16]

They were, to use Pedro Arrupe's phrase, "Men for others."

From that moment at Montmartre the Companions had begun to follow a common life: in an informal sense, the Companions of Jesus —the Jesuits—had been born with the vows of Montmartre. In early 1535 they were actively planning their departure for Jerusalem, though for Ignatius a delay was inevitable. Pestered once more by the intestinal ailments that had plagued him since his exuberance of self-denial at Manresa, and badgered once more by the Inquisition over the nature of the Exercises, Ignatius had to postpone the departure. His Companions would remain in Paris to complete their studies and would meet him in Venice in 1537; from there they would all travel to Jerusalem. Late in March 1535, therefore, in the hope that breathing his native air would help restore him to good health, Ignatius set out on what was to be his final journey to the land of his birth. In Guipúzcoa province, Ignatius associated himself with the hospital at Azpeitia, and continued to preach and to minister to the church: he led an assault on gambling; he convinced the governor to legislate against the frequent violation of the local custom whereby the married women of the area covered their heads as a sign of fidelity to their husbands, a custom that had degenerated to the point where the numerous concubines of priests and married men had begun to cover their heads as a sign of fidelity to their illicit lovers; he arranged for the ringing of bells in the morning, noon, and evening for the praying of the *Ave Maria*; and, since the care of souls involved a concern for the complete individual, he lobbied successfully for local ordinances to provide for the requirements of the poor, insisting "that there should be no poor who have to go about begging but that they should all receive the help they need."[17] At the same time, "He persisted in his penitential practices. Witnesses recalled his fasting, the hairshirt he wore at all times, the metal chain with the sharp points with which he girded himself, the lacerations and festering wounds on his shoulders from the self-inflicted scourgings."[18] Finally, late in 1535, Ignatius—the Apostle of Azpeitia—took to the roads on foot for his torturous journey to rendezvous with his companions in Venice.

In January 1537, Ignatius was reunited in Venice with the original group, whose numbers had been augmented by Claude Le Jay, Paschase Broët, and Jean Codure. Here Ignatius set about giving the Exercises once again and the group engaged themselves in the corporal works of mercy, especially doing volunteer work in hospitals where they cared for the sick, scrubbed floors, and buried the dead.

Finally, on March 16, the band begged their way to Rome to seek a papal blessing for their pilgrimage to Jerusalem. They were well received at the court by Pope Paul III who not only granted their wish but, so impressed was he by their erudition, also provided financial support for their pilgrimage. Ignatius, however, did not make the trip to Rome, thinking his presence would be ill advised. For one thing, Dr. Pedro Ortiz, who had denounced Ignatius to the Inquisition in Paris, was present in Rome serving as a special counsel with respect to the marriage of Catherine of Aragon. As events transpired, however, Ortiz served as a useful ally to the group by supporting their request. Ignatius's second concern was more to the point: the newly elevated cardinal, Gian Pietro Carafa, the future Pope Paul IV, was also at the papal court, and Ignatius had fostered a lifelong enemy in Carafa. By refusing to enfold his Companions into the Theatine community that Carafa had established, by criticizing Carafa for living too extravagantly, and by admonishing his community for not being sufficiently involved in the corporal works of mercy, Ignatius had effectively burned his bridges with a future papacy. He had hardly been the soul of diplomacy; in a letter to Carafa he ironically outlined his disapproval both of his future nemesis and of the community he had founded:

> I am not scandalized or disedified when a person in such a position as yours makes his noble origin or the dignity of his station in life a reason for indulging greater elegance in dress or the furnishings of his apartment, especially if he does so with a thought of those externs who may come to deal with him. . . . I think it would be part of wisdom to call to mind saints like the blessed Francis and Dominic and others of long ago, and consider especially their manner of life in dealing with their associates and the example they gave at the time they were forming their orders.[19]

Of Carafa's Theatines, Ignatius observed rather bluntly but with the same ironic tone: "I have no doubt, indeed I firmly believe, that even though they do not preach or engage in any of the corporal works of mercy, they are justified in expecting food and clothing according to the order of divine charity."[20] Cardinal Carafa was predisposed to disliking Spaniards; Ignatius had crossed a line with a lack of discretion that was to haunt him for the rest of his days. It was an indiscretion, however, that clearly signed the intensity of Ignatius's convictions and affirmed the uniqueness of the vision shared by Ignatius and the Companions who had elected to walk with him. The Society of Jesus would set out in bold new directions.

Paul III also gave his blessing to the ordination of all of the companions who were not yet priests, but for Salmerón who was still less than the required 23 years of age. The Sacrament of Orders was administered by the Bishop of Arbe, Vincent Negusanti, in Venice on the feast of St. John the Baptist, June 24, 1537. But still the long-planned pilgrimage to Jerusalem was not to be: the wars with the Turks rendered the expedition too perilous. Instead of initiating their pilgrimage, the Companions, by necessity, remained in Venice for a time and then dispersed in groups of two or three, busying themselves with preaching, teaching, working in hospitals, and giving the Exercises. Lamenting the constant badgering by the Inquisition and reacting to those inveterately suspicious of the urbane and ambitious band, in a December 19, 1538, letter to his longtime patron Isabel Roser, Ignatius reflected on events and explained that he had turned to influential allies to testify on the Companions' behalf. In so doing Ignatius provided a graphic illustration not only of the nature and breadth of their support but also of the energetic diversity of their activities:

> The cities of Siena, Bologna, and Ferrara also sent their authentic testimonies here, and the duke of Ferrara, besides sending testimony, took the affair very much to heart because he had seen the good fruit brought forth in his city and also in the other cities where we had labored (though we had not known quite how to sustain ourselves and to persevere there). For this we gave thanks to God our Lord because from the time we began until the present moment we have never failed to give two or three sermons on every feast day and also two lectures every day; some were occupied with confessions and others with the spiritual exercises. Now that the sentence has been given [and we have been exonerated once again], we hope to increase the sermons and also our classes for boys.[21]

In November 1537 the group decided to disperse once more, with Ignatius, Faber, and Laynez making their way to Rome in potential fulfilment of their Montmartre vow to put themselves at the disposal of the Pope. On this journey Ignatius, who had previously advised the band that if asked they should identify themselves as "the Company of Jesus," had a vision that was to have a lasting impact on the companions. Just fifteen miles outside Rome, at the crossing of the Claudian and Cassian Ways, at a place called La Storta, Ignatius entered a small chapel. There he had an illumination of Jesus and his Father in conversation, and the Father said to Jesus, "I wish that Thou take him for Thy servant," adding the now famous promise: "*Ego ero vobis Romae propitius*" (I will be propitious to you in Rome). Rome was to become Ignatius's Jerusalem.

Thomas Lucas, the cultural historian who restored Ignatius's private quarters in Rome, explains the novelty, importance, and impact of this small group of idealists:

> The Pope saw trump cards in his hand. Here were ten of the best-educated priests in Europe who were ready to go anywhere and do anything that was necessary. They gathered together, they did simple pastoral work, they set the city on fire by preaching in churches that hadn't had a preacher for fifty years. They preached in the squares and on street corners. In their house, the masters of Paris set up a soup kitchen for the poor while at the same time they were being consultants to cardinals. With their broad background, with their readiness to do anything, in effect they put into the hands of the papacy a very strong and flexible tool.

While Laynez and Faber lectured on the scriptures at the Sapienzia in Rome, Ignatius provided the Spiritual Exercises; all three were also engaged in caring for the sick, the starving, and the homeless. At first they worked from a small house at 11 Via San Sebastianello, where the motherhouse of the Congregation of the Resurrection is now located, and eventually moved near Via dell' Aracoeli where the Gesù is now situated and where Ignatius lived out his earthly days. The agreed-upon final date for their departure for Jerusalem, January 8, 1538, had come and gone—given the political turbulence of the moment, the times were not propitious for a journey to the Holy Land. By the end of the Easter season of that year Ignatius had assembled all the companions in Rome; then, in late November, keeping their Montmartre vow, the Companions formally placed themselves at the disposal of the Pope, a gesture he fully accepted, providing informal sanction for the emergent Society of Jesus.

When, acting on the authority offered to him, Paul III began assigning members of the group to various postings, the Companions realized that there was a pressing need for a more formal union. As a result, between Easter and June 24 of 1539, the Company met to debate their future, and to fashion the document that would serve as the basis for their Constitutions as a religious community. Apparently written by Ignatius himself at the request of the Company, the Formula consists of Five Chapters that, in essence, confirmed past decisions made by the group, recognized its customary activities (its *modus procedendi*) as they understood it in 1539, and reinforced the fact that the Society of Jesus was sometimes modelled on but essentially different from any ecclesiastical organization that had preceded it.

Drawing on their "way of proceeding," the Companions agreed that their objectives should centre on service to the Lord, "spiritual comfort," and the works of mercy—all for the greater glory of God; they also saw their mission distinctively directed towards catechetical teaching, especially the teaching of basic Christian doctrine to children. Consistent with their vow taken at Montmartre, the Companions of Jesus agreed to incorporate into their Formula a special obedience to the Pope "to offer to go to any region whatever." It was a decision that caused immediate concern about their own sense of community—was community a matter of physical location or was it a more existential union?—and that was to create its own organizational problems with respect to papal authority. These problems reach directly and obtrusively into the early 1980s when Pope John Paul II saw fit to impose his will on the internal running of the Order. The Formula also put particular emphases on the vows of obedience and poverty, values in which Ignatius had a personal interest both as a result of his life as a courtier and of his conversion experiences at Manresa. More problematic with respect to external assessments of the Jesuits and of their Formula were the signs of their distinctive nature: the Formula specified that the monastic choir, the singing of the divine office and of mass, were not appropriate for so mobile a company, nor were penitential austerities that could sap the energy needed in the practical service of souls. Ignatius's vision was to fashion an order dedicated to "contemplation in action"; indeed, the very title of the unifying principle of the Society, "Spiritual Exercises," embodies this sense of the contemplative and the active. "Contemplation in action" put a premium on good deeds and free will,[22] a premium that would position the Jesuits strategically at odds with the Protestant Reformation as well as with the Dominican Order (which was to become an enduring and sometimes openly hostile critic of the Society), and a premium that would ultimately lead the Jesuits into a losing confrontation with the French Enlightenment. Nonetheless, the Company would consist of men of God engaged in the world, men for others, men whose prayer life would be enfleshed in the spiritual and corporal works of mercy. To be true Jesuits, the companions were to be modern-day exemplars, men distinguished both for their learning and for their integrity, men prepared to go wherever asked and to be of service to others in the name of the church.

When the final document was presented to Pope Paul III he was reportedly pleased with what he heard (though his opinion was not a universally shared one):

> In a letter written on Wednesday, 3 September [1539], and delivered to St. Ignatius by [Antonio] Araoz, [Cardinal Gásparo] Contarini tells us: "Today I was with His Lordship, and in addition to my request by word of mouth I read out to His Holiness all the Five Chapters, which gave him great satisfaction so that with the greatest good will he approved and confirmed them. On Friday we shall come to Rome with His Holiness and orders will be given to the most Reverend [Cardinal Giralomo] Ghinucci to have the Brief, that is the Bull, drawn up."[23]

Although the Farnese Pope Paul III, who found himself embroiled in political and religious ferment, was quick to give his *viva voce* approval to the Formula, its passage into written form was not as smooth. Ignatius had several times fallen under suspicion with respect to his religious orthodoxy; he had made enemies at the papal court; and a curial conviction held that there were already too many religious orders about. Writing to his nephew Bertram Loyola and discussing Paul III's oral approval, Ignatius comments with gratitude that in sanctioning the Formula the Pope had acted "in the face of so much opposition, misadventure, and conflicting opinions"[24] But papal approval did not end the matter. When Cardinal Bartolomeo Guidiccioni, an avid advocate of institutional retrenchment, was asked to function as arbiter in the drafting of the papal bull that would legitimize the new religious order, he did so with natural reluctance and only after negotiated compromises, perhaps the most significant of which would limit the number of professed members (that is, members under full vows) to sixty. Nonetheless, in the Palazzo Venezia on September 27, 1540, Paul III gave formal approval to the papal bull *Regimini militantis ecclesiae* and with the promulgation of this document the Society of Jesus drew its first legal breath.[25]

Cardinal Guidiccioni's victory was more apparent than real. Interest in the Society of Jesus was instant and widespread. The original limit of sixty professed members was quickly met, and in 1544 Paul III rescinded the numerical restriction in a bull entitled *Iniunctum nobis*. When Ignatius died in 1556 the Order had swollen to more than 1,000 members, though fewer than fifty were fully professed. Thomas Lucas reports that "When Ignatius died in his house on Via Aracoeli in 1556, his company that had numbered ten companions in one house in 1538 had about 1,000 members in 74 houses on three continents. In 1579 there were 5,165 members in 200 houses; in 1600, 8,500 in 350 houses. When the Society celebrated its centennial in 1640, the Order had grown to 15,683 members in 868 houses."[26] When Vatican II held its opening session in 1962, the Society numbered nearly 36,000. Guidiccioni's limit of sixty professed members failed to anticipate both the novelty and the enduring attractiveness of the Company envisioned in the Formula.

In the opening paragraph of *Exposit debitum*, a 1550 update of the Formula, the Vatican repeats many of Ignatius's earlier words and succinctly summarizes both the purpose and the vision of the Society of Jesus:

> Whoever desires to serve as a soldier of God beneath the banner of the cross in our Society, which we desire to be designated by the name of Jesus, and to serve the Lord alone and the Church, His spouse, under the Roman pontiff, the vicar of Christ on earth, should, after a solemn vow of perpetual chastity, poverty, and obedience, keep what follows in mind. He is a member of a Society founded chiefly for this purpose: to strive especially for the defense and propagation of the faith and for the progress of souls in Christian life and doctrine, by means of public preaching, lectures, and any other ministration whatsoever of the word of God, and further by means of the Spiritual Exercises, the education of children and unlettered persons in Christianity, and the spiritual consolation of Christ's faithful through the hearing of confessions and administering the other sacraments. Moreover, this Society should show itself no less useful in reconciling the estranged, in holily assisting and serving those who are found in prisons

> or hospitals, and indeed in performing any other works of charity, according to what will seem expedient for the glory of God and the common good.[27]

Ignatius's sense of ministering to the good of souls is encapsulated in this introductory paragraph, just as his practical sense of the application of the theory, the practical implication of putting contemplation into action, is epitomized in a letter he wrote to Father John Nunez Barreto, Patriarch of Ethiopia, in which Ignatius offers concrete advice on Jesuit service:

> Although you are ever intent on bringing them to conformity with the Catholic Church, do everything gently, without any violence to souls long accustomed to another way of life. . . . You might think over and suggest to his highness in Portugal whether it would be a good idea to send along with you some men of practical genius to give the natives instructions on the making of bridges, when they have to cross rivers, on building, cultivating the land, and fishing. And other officials too, even a physician or surgeon, so that it may appear to the Abyssinians that their total good, even bodily good, is coming to them with their religion.[28]

Constitutionally, therefore, the Jesuits are an order of men who have "dedicated their lives to the perpetual service of our Lord Jesus Christ"—so state the opening lines of *Regimini militantis ecclesiae*. Hence, "Jesuit": the "-ite" suffix designates connectedness, community, belonging, and fellowship, as in the words Jansenite, Wycliffite, Israelite, Brooklynite, et cetera. Walking in communion with Christ, the Jesuit is committed to "working in the vineyard of God": reaching out to the leper, ministering to the prostitute, preaching in the synagogues, providing a visible contact between the human and the divine—"fulfilling with an ardor worthy of the highest praise, in all parts of the world where they have travelled, all the offices of charity and the ministries needful for the consolation of souls."

With the Jesuit vision officially recognized by Rome, the first item of business was to elect the superior general (prepositus or prelate: one who is placed over all), who would lead the Companions to the realization of their dream within a "well-regulated community."

Regimini militantis ecclesiae records the names of the ten founding Jesuits: Ignatius of Loyola, Peter Faber, James (Diego) Laynez, Claude Jay, Paschase Broët, Francis Xavier, Alfonso Salmerón, Simón Rodriguez, Jean Codure, and Nichólas Bobadilla. In the minds of all but Ignatius, it was Ignatius who should assume the office of general. As Francis Xavier testified in casting his ballot by letter:

> I, Francis, also say and affirm, being in no way persuaded by anyone, that in my judgement the one who is to be elected as the leader of our Society, whom we must all obey, should be, it seems to me, speaking in accordance with my own conscience, our old and true father, Don Ignatius, who with no little effort brought us all together, and who, not without effort, will be able to preserve, govern, and cause us to advance from good to better, since he has a greater knowledge of each one of us than anyone else.[29]

On April 19, 1541, Ignatius, now 50, accepted with reluctance. Rome had indeed become Ignatius's Jerusalem, and henceforth he was seldom to breathe the air outside her walls.

Advancing from Good to Better: 1541–1556

For the Society of Jesus and for Ignatius of Loyola, advancing from good to better quickly became a much more complicated undertaking than the Montmartre group could ever have imagined. The number of Jesuits dedicated to fulfilling the mission virtually exploded, but so did that mission itself.

Thomas Lucas concludes that Ignatius, as general of the Order, was:

> something of an organizational genius. We tend to focus on him as a man of mystical prayer and a man of great holiness, which he was without a doubt. At the same time, the structure which he created, which pulled the best elements from other religious traditions and put them together in a radically new form provided the Jesuits with a very, very flexible model of a very institutionalized organization. It sounds contradictory,

> and I suppose that to a certain extent it is. His genius was to be able to legislate in a creative way and put his dream not into cement but into flexible steel so that in the generations that followed there was room for adaptation.

As Ignatius's admonition to Cardinal Gian Pietro Carafa and as the opening lines of the papal bull *Exposit debitum* had clearly established, the Order over which Ignatius had been given the administrative responsibility was inspired by the "apostolic" tradition. As a result, anyone wishing to become a member of the Society of Jesus—"This least congregation,"[30] as Ignatius called it in apparent imitation of Francis of Assisi's humble designation of his Friars Minor—would have to be prepared to carry the evangelical message in imitation of the apostles, going forth to teach all nations. The Formula, therefore, was amended by Cardinal Bartolomeo Guidiccioni specifically to highlight the humility embedded in the Jesuits' fourth vow, in which they profess their primary obedience to the Bishop of Rome:

> for the sake of our greater devotion in obedience to the Apostolic See, of greater abnegation of our own wills . . . we are to be obliged by a special vow to carry out whatever the present and future Roman pontiffs may order which pertains to the progress of souls and the propagation of the faith; and to go without subterfuge or excuse, as far as in us lies, to whatsoever provinces they may choose to send us—whether they are pleased to send us among the Turks or any other infidels, even those who live in the region called the Indies, or among any heretics whatever, or schismatics, or any of the infidels.[31]

The life envisioned for the Jesuit was a demanding one, one that required not only the commitment to be useful to the pope and the church, but also the humility to act in total obedience to legitimate authority. Humility, obedience, exceptional learning: a rare combination of human characteristics. Contrary to the accusations of its detractors, the Order was necessarily selective in its recruits. According to the Constitutions that Ignatius shaped as a concrete expression of the Formula of the Society, only those are to be accepted as fully professed members who "have achieved the diligent and careful formation of the intellect by learning," after which "they will find it helpful during the period of the last probation to apply themselves in the school of the heart, by exercising themselves in spiritual and corporal pursuits which can engender in them greater humility, abnegation of all sensual love and will and judgment of their own, and also greater knowledge and love of God our Lord; that when they themselves have made progress they can better help others to progress for glory to God our Lord."[32] Indeed, both Ignatius and Francis Xavier culled large numbers of recruits—and even some of the professed—who ultimately proved themselves unsuitable for the Society. Several of Xavier's letters explain the dismissals of those he deemed inappropriate. He was particularly impatient with disobedience to a lawful superior. His advice: "If anyone is disobedient, since he is opposed to obedience and refuses to obey you, you must expel him from the Society."[33] Expel them Xavier himself did, always with the subsequent approval of the superior general.

When the founders of the Society designed its political structure, they had in mind the natural rhythms of a hierarchically ordered world. The Jesuits were to be ruled by a superior general in charge of the overall Society, provincial superiors in charge of geographical units, local superiors in charge of houses within the provinces; there were to be the professed (full-fledged members under permanent vows), scholastics (students under temporary vows), clerical coadjutors (priest assistants who would not be full members under the four vows—poverty, chastity, obedience, obedience to the pope with respect to availability for mission), and lay coadjutors (nonclerical members who would perform supportive tasks). For the system to work, there needed to be a respect for the order of things, an absolute respect for authority: total obedience. As a result, Ignatius wrote frequently about the need for obedience. In the Constitutions, for example, he provided a section on the virtue in which he noted that "We ought to be firmly convinced that everyone of those who live under obedience ought to allow himself to be carried and directed by Divine Providence through the agency of the superior as if he were a lifeless body which allows itself to be carried to any place and to be treated in any manner desired, or as if he were an old man's staff which serves in any place and in any manner whatsoever in which the holder wishes to use it."[34]

The rationale for this absolute obedience, as Ignatius notes in an often-quoted letter to the Society in Portugal, lies in the fact that at the top of the societal hierarchy is the general whose authority derives directly from God, the apex of the hierarchy: the general is "His vicar on earth."[35] Even among the angels, Ignatius continues, such a hierarchy is to be found. Moreover, "we see the same on earth in well-governed states, and in the hierarchy of the Church, the members of which render their obedience to the one universal vicar of Christ our Lord. And the better this subordination is kept, the better the government." Indeed, Ignatius explains, this is the highest form of obedience: to see the will of the superior as the will of God and, as a result, to offer joyful (but not irrational) compliance. It was an orderly, medieval, and wholly theocentric world view whose application to the social realm was to cause the Society boundless grief in the eighteenth century.

The harkening to the apostolic tradition, the papal vow, the emphasis on obedience and even the new-found concern about a well-educated clergy were intimately connected—and all were essential in moving the Society "from good to better." As integral as the vow of obedience was, it was not as easy to live as it was to state. Although the records do show a consistent (and even humble) adherence to the vow of papal obedience both in Ignatius's days and in our own, obedience to the religious superior has not always been viewed as conscientiously as obedience to the will of God. Even today it is difficult to find a Jesuit willing to proffer serious criticism of the pope, but not so difficult to find one willing to question his religious superiors—remarkable, given the generally gifted nature of the members of the Society, the constitutional emphasis on formal intellectual development, and the exhortations with which the Spiritual Exercises begin concerning the unambiguous necessity for personal choice, personal enlightenment, and personal discernment.

During Ignatius's tenure as general, the most celebrated confrontations with religious disobedience centre on two of the original companions, Simón Rodriguez and Nicólas Bobadilla, especially on the former whose intransigence resulted in Ignatius's much-quoted disquisition on the nature of religious obedience, which was developed in a March 26, 1553, letter addressed to the members of the Society in Portugal.[36]

Portugal was essential to the emerging and expanding Society for several reasons: the number of vocations it provided, its serving as a base for missionary expeditions both to the Far East and the Far West, and especially for the energetic support of its monarch, John III, whose enthusiasm for the Jesuits accounted in part for the Community's thriving in Portugal: *cujus regio, ejus religio*.

Rodriguez, a native of Portugal and a close friend of the king, had been stationed in his homeland as early as 1540 and was appointed provincial in 1546 coincident with the formal designation of the Portuguese province. Rodriguez quickly established himself as his own man, generally ignoring Ignatius's repeated directive (ultimately formalized in the Constitutions) that all religious provinces of the Society communicate directly with the Roman motherhouse and through the motherhouse with one another on a regular basis; in addition, Rodriguez both favoured and permitted the long hours of prayer as well as the rigorous fasts and penances that Ignatius and ultimately the Constitutions reasoned to be incompatible with the demanding life of a scholastic or the practical life of an apostolic order. Portugal was rife with excessive penitential practices and Ignatius's own conversion experiences had taught him to be cautious of excess. From the outset, however, Ignatius's efforts to right the situation in Portugal not only engaged him with an intractable Rodriguez, but also with a king sympathetic to Rodriguez and in whose court Rodriguez had taken up residence, and with whom he had been able to mediate effectively on behalf of the Society, the pope, and the church.

Disturbed by stories of the scholastics' nocturnal cries of penance, their preaching half-naked on the streets, and their taking corpses to their rooms as an aid to effective contemplation on the transience of human existence, Ignatius wrote a long letter on May 27, 1547, to the fathers and students at Coimbra where the Society was flourishing to such an extent that there were some eighty scholastics in formation. In this letter, Ignatius prescribed the Philosopher's antidote, "Nothing in excess"; he warned of the temptation to vainglory inherent in penitential and devotional excess; and he advised: "If you have a great desire of mortification, use it rather in breaking your wills and bringing your judgments under the yoke of obedience rather than in weakening your bodies and afflicting them beyond due measure. . . ."[37]

But Ignatius's interventions had little effect, and he repeated his exhortation to obedience in a subsequent letter dated January 14, 1548; then, on December 27, 1551, his patience at an end, the superior general wrote once more to Rodriguez bringing the three-year ordeal to an end and tactfully but firmly relieving Rodriguez of his duties in Portugal. Diego Miró was named as Rodriguez's replacement and, as an ill-advised face-saving measure, Rodriguez was appointed provincial superior in the proximate province of Aragon. Rodriguez balked at the order to leave Portugal and his removal was greeted with general insubordination within the province; the Portuguese even contemplated schism with the Roman generalate, ultimately prompting Ignatius's landmark letter on obedience, dated March 26, 1553. In the meantime, Miguel de Torres was appointed an official visitor to deal with the Portuguese problem, in which capacity he dismissed scores of the Society's members while many others decided to leave voluntarily. John O'Malley notes that modern estimates of those who lost their societal status range from 33 to over 100;[38] Hollis puts the number as high as 137.[39]

Rodriguez, however, was not content to remain in Aragon, returning instead to Portugal and thus forcing Ignatius to write to him, first on July 12, 1553, politely inviting him to come to Rome so that they could confer "on other matters of universal import" that concerned the whole Society, and that could not be "satisfactorily dealt with unless [Rodriguez were] actually present." Again, however, Ignatius was firm: "As it is a matter of great importance, I bid you in virtue of holy obedience and in the name of Christ our Lord to come, taking a land or sea route as you shall judge best. And this must be with the least possible delay. You must begin your journey, which is not to be interrupted, not later than eight days after you have received this letter."[40] Still not sure how Rodriguez had reacted to this correspondence, Ignatius wrote two follow-up letters to Diego Miró dated July 26, 1553, and July 24/August 3, 1553, in which he provided Miró with detailed instructions on how to deal with Rodriguez's dismissal from the Order should he fail to comply with the written obedience to return to Rome. Rodriguez dallied for several more months but ultimately complied, returning to Rome and at first repenting for his disobedience but then growing resentful of the punishments imposed upon him. After a stormy period in Rome, Ignatius exiled his longtime companion from his native Portugal and Rodriguez retreated in discontent but relative comfort to Bassano in northern Italy.

Though it was highly regarded and usually observed, the vow of obedience demanded not only an unshakeable religious faith but unflagging humility as well. Being overlooked for administrative advancement in the Order drove Nicólas Bobadilla, another of the Montmartre companions, to numerous entanglements with Ignatius, and in the aftermath of the July 31, 1556 death of Ignatius, Bobadilla fanned the flames of discontent that Ignatius's ill-advised letter to Cardinal Gian Petro Carafa, now Pope Paul IV, had ignited. When the First General Congregation of the Society of Jesus (1556–1558) was convoked to elect Ignatius's successor, the Pope was not reluctant to intervene directly in the proceedings. For his part, arguing that the Constitutions had not yet been validated and that Ignatius had exercised his authority as superior general in an autocratic fashion, Bobadilla prodded Paul IV to interfere in the process that was destined to elect Diego Laynez as Ignatius's successor. Although Bobadilla had found early allies in the fray, including Simón Rodriguez and Paul IV, they quickly saw the error of their way: Bobadilla, finding himself isolated, grew increasingly disgruntled, and Paul IV, distracted by his own political skirmishes, lost interest in the matter.

As Ignatius had commented in his letter to the Society in Portugal, "the better this subordination is kept, the better the government." And on the whole it has been well kept, even in the face of late twentieth-century efforts to democratize a Society grappling with a modern world not so sold on the concept of divinely ordained hierarchies or on the natural obedience owed to properly appointed superiors.

As for the constitutional stress on the Jesuits as men of learning, Ignatius had learned firsthand the importance of formal instruction and understood the wisdom of making it one of the pillars on which to construct the new Order. The original Companions were, as *Regimini militantis ecclesiae* recalls, all Paris-trained masters, but the Jesuits' emphasis on an educated clergy was a significant departure in its day, a departure that was later to be embraced by the Council of Trent (1545–63) in its determination to counter the Reformation with a reforming of its own. As a result, the Society's constitutional emphasis on the nature and training of the scholastic planted the seed for what was to become the formal tridentine system of seminary training, though the training required of Jesuits continued to be more demanding, more thorough, more rationalized than that expected of their diocesan counterparts. In addition, the Society's determination to provide formal education for its Jesuits in training, its scholastics, caused the Order to found centres of learning specifically for this purpose; these centres of learning, in turn, formed the eventual basis for the first system of free universal education.

Regimini militantis ecclesiae recalled the fundamental importance of education as a cornerstone for the Christian life and formalized the Jesuit as teacher, especially of the young and the disadvantaged. The Formula exhorts:

> Above all things let them have at heart the instruction of boys and ignorant persons in the knowledge of Christian doctrine, of the Ten Commandments, and other such rudiments as shall be suitable, having regard to the circumstances of persons, places, and times. For it is very necessary that the Prepositus and his council watch over this business with the greatest diligence, both because without foundations the edifice of faith in our neighbours cannot be raised to a fitting height, and also because there is danger for our own members, lest the more learned they become, the more they may be tempted to belittle this field of work, as at first sight less attractive, although there is none more useful, whether for the edification of our neighbour, or for our own training in love and humility.

The practical advice to remain sensitive to persons, places, and times is characteristically Ignatius and characteristically Jesuit in all its areas of activities, and it is advice that reflects the traditionally Christian approach to homiletic instruction. In the field of education it is advice that spread quickly through the mission fields, resulting in dictionaries, geographical and cartographical studies, linguistic disquisitions, dramatic productions, and the use of song and poetry. In the modern world it has caused the traditional Jesuit emphasis on a classical academic education to evolve into areas more practical, as books like Peter McDonough's *Men Astutely Trained: A Study of the Jesuits in the American Century*, the professional programmes offered through the Lincoln Centre and Harlem campuses of Fordham

University, and the St. Louis Institute of Jesuit Source's exploratory journal *Conversations* make amply clear.

In Ignatius's day, the admonition to teach catechism to the young and the unlettered was pursued conscientiously. Each novice was expected to be formally engaged in the catechetical exercise. Hence, Ignatius's directive to Peter Canisius concerning students of theology that: "Not only in the places where we have a residence, but even in the neighbourhood, the better among our students could be sent to teach the Christian doctrine on Sundays and feast days. Even the extern students, should there be suitable material among them, could be sent by the rector for the same service. Thus, besides the correct doctrine, they would be giving the example of a good life, and by removing every appearance of greed they will be able to refute the strongest argument of the heretics—a bad life, namely, and the ignorance of the Catholic clergy."[41] Ignatius himself taught the Christian catechism to the Jews who were his neighbours in Rome.

Understandably, therefore, fully professed members of the Order such as Peter Canisius became internationally recognized for their expertise in teaching the basic principles of their Christian faith. As the Apostle to Germany, Peter Canisius was confronted with the need to counter Martin Luther's *Kleiner Katechismus*, which he did with his *Summa doctrinae christianae* (1554), *Catechismus minimus* (1556–57), and his *Catechismus minor* (1558), the second two of which were to prove particularly influential, with Canisius's question-and-answer format establishing the Roman Catholic methodological standard for centuries. Other Jesuits in other countries produced their own catechetical texts. For example, Francis Xavier's short catechism, *Doctrina christiana*, was composed in 1542 in Portuguese and was printed in Goa in 1557, a few years after the missionary's death.[42] In addition, before his death in 1552 Xavier oversaw the preparation of catechisms in the native tongues of the converted both in India and in Japan. The famous Jesuit preacher Émond Auger, dubbed the "Chrysostom of France," earned the designation "Canisius of France" for his work on catechesis in that country, and Diego Ledesma's *Doctrina christiana* appeared in Spanish, Polish, and Lithuanian towards the end of the sixteenth century. Soon Jesuit catechisms began to appear in numerous countries and flowed from many pens, often from those of early martyrs.

Although the educational apostolate had been expressly excluded from the Society's original self-definition, in November 1546 Nicolò Lancilotto wrote to Ignatius from the College of St. Thomas in Goa, asking for the assistance of additional men "who are good and learned, especially since the main purpose of our order is to teach Christian doctrine."[43] The teaching of Christian doctrine required an educated cohort; an educated cohort required a system of education. Even in their formative days, the Jesuits' acknowledged reputation as masters in the educational field attracted the attention of the temporal powers who urged them to establish schools in their regions. King John III of Portugal had made such a request of his good friend Francis Xavier as early as 1540, and Xavier wrote from Goa in September 1542 asking Ignatius about the progress of the university at Coimbra. The founding of the Jesuit university at Messina in 1548 pointed the Order in a direction that in some ways began to consume it, in that its successes posed major problems of staffing and institutional definition. Requests came from all over Europe and eight more colleges were added in 1551; manpower was strained. In 1553, the Society decided to accept future requests only if they were accompanied by donations of land, buildings, and sufficient financial support. The manpower problem inherent in the Jesuits' flourishing educational system is an acute one also in post-conciliar Canada, the United States, Great Britain, and indeed throughout the Western world.

Ignatius's model for the Jesuit university was understandably the one he found at the University of Paris. Spanish universities were not sufficiently structured academically for him. At Paris, however, Ignatius discovered

> small classes, carefully regulated progress through increasingly difficult subjects, and meticulously expurgated classical readings. . . . Jesuit education proved attractive: a heavy emphasis on writing and staging plays, normally in Latin, sometimes six hours long, and often visually spiced with collapsing idols and flying saints, gave their schools a special flair. It also proved flexible. When the Jesuits saw that young aristocrats needed practical as well as classical instruction to make their way as professional soldiers, they added fencing, drill, and artillery practice to their literary offerings.[44]

Because the Jesuits had quickly established a reputation for being an educated elite, they were both held up for admiration and placed under the microscope of suspicion. Wishing to take advantage of a reformed voice at the Council of Trent, Pope Paul III asked the Society to provide a Jesuit presence and Ignatius responded by sending Diego Laynez and Alfonso Salmerón. As their participation expanded, so did the Jesuits who quickly became the "pope's theologians." (John Donne charged that the Jesuits used their influential role at the Council of Trent to entrench their own theological liberalism.[45]) Claude Jay soon joined his Companions, but when the unpopular Bobadilla tried to manoeuvre a similar appointment he found little enthusiasm for the idea among his colleagues. As sought after as the Jesuits became for their learning, however, they also became the targets of ridicule. Perhaps the most damaging of these assaults was the 1554 attack launched by the University of Paris, the alma mater of the founding fathers and, certainly in Ignatius's mind, the unchallenged academic exemplar of an effectively structured academic environment. The faculty of theology charged that "This Society appears to be a danger to the Faith, a disturber of the peace of the church, destructive of monastic life, and destined to cause havoc rather than edification."[46] Though Ignatius was able to marshal a convincing defence, the attack was not without its effect, nor was it to be the last serious blow the Jesuits were to receive from Paris: Paris's next thrust was intended to be fatal.

As flattering and as important to the Society as this recognition was, a major component of the Companions' original vision as a community was to be actively engaged apostolically; indeed, apostolic engagement was a key element in the Society's progress "from good to better." From their earliest encounters with one another and with the world, the group had been energetically involved in teaching catechism to children and the disadvantaged, to visiting the sick, feeding the hungry, and working with the urban disadvantaged. The early Jesuits were revered for their commitment to the performance of the corporal works of mercy as enunciated in Francis Xavier's Short Catechism: "The corporal works of mercy are seven: The first is to visit the sick. The second, to give food to one who is hungry. The third is to give drink to one who is thirsty. The fourth is to redeem captives. The fifth is to clothe the naked. The sixth is to give shelter to pilgrims. The seventh is to bury the dead."[47] Contemplation in action.

In this respect, Ignatius's June 15, 1551 letter to Father John Pelletier provides an excellent summary of the Society's ideals as well as poignant insight into the practical mind of a spiritual man of action. Among the many recommendations Ignatius made with respect to active urban ministry, the following are to the point:

9. You should be careful to help the prisoners and visit the jails if you can, and preach occasionally, and exhort the inmates to confession and a return to God. Hear their confessions if opportunity offers.
10. Do not forget the hospitals. Try to console and give spiritual help to the poor as far as you can. Even in these places some exhortation may be profitable, unless circumstances seem to advise otherwise.
11. In general you should try to keep informed about the pious works in the city where you reside, and do all you possibly can to help them.
12. Although many means of helping the neighbour and pious works are proposed, discretion will be your guide in the choice you must make, it being taken for granted that you cannot do all. But you should never lose sight of the greater service of God, the common good, and the good name of the society.[48]

Like Jesus's exercise of the corporal works of mercy, Ignatius's went beyond the healing of the sick to the inclusion of a sympathetic ministry to prostitutes. This is so despite Ignatius's stated concerns that the Companions "not have any dealing with young women of the common people, except in an open place . . . [since] they are lightheaded, and whether there be foundation for it or not, it frequently happens that such dealings give rise to evil talk. . . . After their devotions are over, they not infrequently turn, sometimes to the flesh, sometimes to fatigue."[49] It is a suspicion about women reinforced by an unhappy experiment pressed on him by an insistent Isabel Roser, an experiment with women as religious associates that caused Ignatius to connive with Pope Paul III to have women formally excluded from membership in the Society. Nonetheless, perhaps because of his own experience as a member of the court, or because of this acculturated suspicion of woman's inconstancy, or perhaps because of the example of Jesus, Ignatius and the early Jesuits also took a special interest in assisting the women of the streets.

Prostitution had been a prevalent and socially accepted way of life in late medieval Rome, though the growing menace of venereal disease had made the prostitute a less desirable member of the state. Converted prostitutes frequently took up the veil and moved into nunneries; others who had amassed a dowry were married into respectability. When Ignatius founded his home for reformed prostitutes, therefore, he was reacting both to a gospel imperative and a social need. His Casa Sancta Marta provided lodging and assistance for prostitutes being rehabilitated into mainstream society and could accommodate up to sixty residents. Nonetheless, despite Ignatius's clear intention and the careful carrying out of his ministry, his efforts inevitably fell victim to wagging tongues. Undaunted, the Jesuits expanded their ministry. In his doctoral dissertation, "The Vineyard at the Crossroads," Thomas Lucas catalogues their achievements: Sancta Catarina (a house for the daughters of prostitutes as a means of saving them from a fate similar to their mothers'), Sancta Maria in Aquiro (a home for orphaned boys), Sancti Quattro Coronti (a home for orphaned girls), Dodici Apostili (a home for the elderly poor), Sanctus Giovanni della Pigna (a home for prisoners), and several other similar centres catering to the corporal and spiritual needs of Roman society.

As Lucas observes, "No work of charity was beyond the imagination of the nascent Society of Jesus."[50] Their enthusiasm for the care of souls had carried the concept of the Society unambiguously from "good" beginnings to "better" service for a suffering humankind.

Expansion and Suppression: 1556–1773

When Ignatius died in 1556, his Society was well established, and its future directions were being ambitiously charted. The embrace of the Society of Jesus was wide enough to include theologians, philosophers, scientists, poets, dramatists, explorers, and cartographers—men bent on the social betterment of people as a Christian obligation and salvific mission. Seventeenth-century Jesuit Baltasar Gracián later captured the tenor of the man and of his dream in an unusual collection of oracular observations entitled *The Art of Worldly Wisdom*,[51] which has become a modern-day best seller in the United States. These Jesuitical aphorisms illustrate the dynamic combination of discernment and action as well as the Jesuit's time-honoured sensitivity towards realpolitik and his willingness to adapt: "Not everything should be speculation; you must also act" (p. 131); "Using novelty, wise people have found room in the roster of heroes" (p. 35); and "It often happens that two people meet head-on, and each presumes he is right. But reason is true, and never has two faces. In such encounters, proceed with wisdom and caution. Sometimes take the other side, and cautiously revise your own opinion" (p. 165). The Jesuit has always understood the art of worldly wisdom; his practical cunning is both admired and denounced. It has always been part of the Jesuit mystique.

No individual better embodies the pragmatic missionary zeal of the Society of Jesus than Ignatius's longtime friend and Sainte-Barbe roommate Francis Xavier. True to his vows, Xavier was willing to minister wherever and whenever he was asked. Nobly born to a Basque family of Navarre on April 7, 1506, Xavier became a close friend of Ignatius, and though he had set out for Portugal and from there was to have gone to India before the promulgation of *Regimini militantis ecclesiae*, upon receiving word of the Society's legal formation he immediately vowed his dedication to an Order of which he later declared: "if I should ever forget the Society of the Name of Jesus, may my right arm be forgotten."[52] To this day, Xavier's right forearm is enshrined for public viewing in the church of the Gesù on the Via dell' Aracoeli in Rome.

Driven by the selfless ideals of his Jesuit companions and charged by the prevailing triumphal assurance that there can be no salvation outside the Roman Catholic Church—*Extra ecclesiam nulla salus*—on April 7, 1541, Xavier and two Jesuit companions set out on a long and torturous passage to India. On January 1, 1542, he wrote to Ignatius, recounting the difficulties of the journey and issuing the first of an endless series of requests for additional Jesuit missionaries. Within months Xavier had established an expanding mission in Goa, and was actively engaged in preaching, baptizing, and teaching his basic catechism to the inhabitants. By September of the same year he had complied with the governor's enthusiastic entreaties and established the College of St. Paul on Goa's east side, a college he claimed was already capable of sustaining 100 students and would soon be able to accommodate 300; in addition, the college housed a church that Xavier assured Ignatius was "twice as large as the church of the college of the Sorbonne."[53] The letter included the first of a chorus of pleas for Jesuit instructors to staff what he claimed quite accurately was sure to be a thriving academic enterprise. There were other practical requests but these were of a religious nature: plenary indulgences for the sick and permission to move Lent from the climatically punishing months of February and March to the more propitious ones of June and July, when India was in the midst of its winter.

Not content with establishing the necessary ecclesiastical and educational structures at Goa, Xavier set out to teach, to preach, to convert, and to baptize along the Fishery Coast; he instructed the villagers on the error of idol worship and translated the Creed, the Lord's Prayer, the Hail Mary, the *Salve Regina*, and the Sign of the Cross into Malabar—before long he would also compose a catechism in Malay. Xavier pushed on indefatigably; so energetic was he in baptizing the pagan inhabitants that he reported that his outstretched arms grew weary: "There are days when I baptize an entire village, and on the coast where I now am there are thirty Christian villages."[54] The fields were rich but the times were troubled. Unfriendly tribes attacked the newly Christianized villages; wayward Portuguese merchants were dismayed by the Jesuits' inculcation of Christian morals into the previously compliant population; and the confusing collision of Christian, Jewish, and Moslem doctrines ultimately prompted Xavier to write to his good friend and benefactor, King John III of Portugal, to suggest the imposition of the Inquisition on the Indian colonies as a means of controlling the European menace and protecting the Indian converts, a request that was granted in 1560.[55]

Xavier's zeal for the care of souls carried him farther and farther from the home base of Goa, to Ceylon, the Malay peninsula, and the Molucca islands; it was a zest that would arguably leave those Jesuit missionaries at work in the original Christian colonies underregulated and eventually drive Xavier himself to an early grave. In

November 1546, Nicolò Lancilotto wrote from Goa to Ignatius complaining of his superior that "he [Xavier] knows little about this college, having never been able to stay here. I think that he is driven by the spirit of the Lord to those regions. India is so large that a hundred thousand very learned men would not be sufficient to convert it. . . ."[56]

For his part, on January 20, 1548, Xavier wrote to Rome about the wondrous rumours of Japan: he reflected that either he would go or he would send others. On the same day, he wrote to King John III suggesting that because of the lack of true assistance he had received in India, he would likely turn his missionary ken towards Japan. And so, in January 1549 Xavier wrote to Ignatius to explain his disenchantment with India, its vocational infertility, the ill-treatment the Portuguese Christians accorded the native converts, and the theological confusion created by the presence of the Jews and Muslims; Japan, on the other hand, was ripe for conversion and it was his intention to accept the challenge. Two days later, on January 14, Xavier had pen in hand once more, rehearsing for Ignatius in two additional letters the difficulties of converting the Indians and ruminating about the plentiful harvest to be reaped in Japan and China. On June 24, Xavier set sail for and on August 15 arrived in Japan. On November 5, 1549, he wrote a long letter from Kagoshima to inform the Companions in Goa both of the nature of his voyage and of the culture of the Japanese as well as to lament their moral laxity.

In Japan Xavier set to work with his characteristic passion for catechesis and conversion, translating prayers and instructional materials into Japanese, and baptizing huge numbers of the inhabitants. Indeed, Xavier complained that "almost all the people of the land would have been converted if it had not been for the priests of the land."[57] As was the Jesuit custom, and as Xavier himself had done in India, he set out at once to ingratiate himself with the politically influential and did so with no little success, though the local priests remained persistently problematic. Still, spurred by his Christian and Jesuit enthusiasm for the care of souls, and supported by the unstinting generosity of the King of Portugal, Xavier established colleges and religious houses while generally engaging himself in the spiritual and corporal works of mercy. But by January of 1552 Xavier had concluded that if he was to be really successful in Japan he had first to Christianize China. He reasoned that China was a peaceful land populated by cultured citizens ripe for conversion, as well as being the source of Japan's religious sects: to Christianize China was, therefore, to lay the exemplary groundwork that would culminate in the Christianizing of Japan.

Predictably, early in 1552 Xavier was back in Goa busily finalizing his plans for China, and, characteristically, on October 22 he records his arrival in Sancian, which he notes in a letter is thirty leagues from Canton. He goes on to explain that he is waiting for a merchant who had been hired to transport him secretly to Canton, a necessarily clandestine operation since China was then closed to foreigners. In Sancian, however, Xavier took ill, and on November 13, 1552, he penned his final correspondence. The Chinese merchant never did honour the appointed rendezvous, and on December 3, 1552, Francis Xavier's pilgrimage ended. Unaware of the death of his good friend and religious companion, Ignatius wrote to Xavier on June 23, 1553, lamenting with unintended irony that "God our Lord would have been better served by your person if you had remained in India. . . ."[58] Two months after his death, when Fancis Xavier's body was exhumed for final transport to Goa, it was discovered to be still intact, and so it remains.

In 1622 Francis Xavier was canonized a saint in the same ceremony that similarly elevated his longtime friend and religious companion, Ignatius of Loyola—a fitting conclusion to what Philip Caraman terms "one of the closest friendships that's ever been recorded in secular or religious history."

Francis Xavier's aborted excursion into China did not mark the end of the Jesuits' ambitions for her conversion, though the history of the Catholic Church in China is far from a happy one. Twenty-five years after the death of Francis Xavier, the most distinguished of the Jesuits' apostles to India, Matteo Ricci, set foot in Goa and found a population neither to his liking nor, as he saw it, inclined towards intellectual conversion. At the same time, Xavier's rather romantic views of Japan had begun to evaporate within the Society, even though Pope Gregory XIII's *Ex pastorali officio* of 1585 had designated the island exclusive Jesuit mission territory and there were still some 116 Jesuits in Japan when they all but deserted the mission in 1614 under a cloud of interfaith bickering and mercantile greed;

Jesuit eyes had begun to turn towards China and in 1581 the Jesuits were poised for an evangelical incursion into the mainland. China, in the mind of the General of the Order, Claudio Aquaviva, was composed of a cultivated, civilized, urbane, and intellectual population: an ideal Jesuit mission field. To an extent that the societies of India and Japan could not, China provided the Jesuits with a clear intellectual challenge, with a culture older and more refined than the European Christian one that the Jesuits were intent on introducing. The Jesuits' missionary approach needed to be tailored to their task. Whereas Xavier had ultimately concluded that what was needed in India were not Jesuit intellectuals ("the people of these regions being very barbarous and ignorant"),[59] but Jesuits of sound moral example, the conversion of China demanded Jesuits who were not only exemplary for their manner of living but also for their manner of reasoning. As a result, when Alessandro Valignano planned the evangelization of China he envisioned a team of well-trained and talented Jesuits—Jesuits with scientific and astronomical expertise who would impress the influential cultured classes. Matteo Ricci, an accomplished scientist, mathematician, and linguist, was one member of that elite team that entered the ancient empire in 1583.

Ricci, for his part, was attracted by the innate pacifism of the Chinese, the inventiveness and ambiguities of their language, and their refined social order. Like Valignano, Ricci quickly came to respect the Chinese and their customs, and to see in Confucianism no threat to the Christian message; like Valignano, Ricci was determined to meet the Chinese on their own ground. He worked towards the establishment of an indigenous clergy and towards the use of cultured Chinese in the celebration of the Roman mass. The Chinese, in turn, were much impressed by Ricci's scholarship and his established interest in their language, literature, and culture. He was quickly accepted by the mandarin class and the door simultaneously swung open for other of his companions. Conversions mushroomed and when Ricci died in 1610 a foothold had been established, but established on the basis of Ricci's tolerant perception of the compatibility of Chinese custom and Christian practice.

Ricci's vision was reinforced by a flood of Jesuit missionaries; one estimate suggests that some 600 Jesuits had been commissioned to China during the century following Ricci's death, though only some scant hundred of them arrived safely on China's mainland.[60] Nonetheless, among rival evangelizing groups there was much suspicion of Ricci's tolerance, especially his acceptance of the compatibility of Confucian ancestor worship with the Christian faith. In 1704 Pope Clement XI backed the Holy Office of the Inquisition's prohibiting Catholics from participating in Confucian ancestral rites. Bangert argues that "As an issue which affected so closely in a practical way the approach of the Church toward an Oriental civilization, it was one of the most difficult and delicate ever considered by the Holy See."[61] In the aftermath, the Jesuits were accused of diminishing the Roman religion in favour of Chinese superstition. Suspicion of the Jesuits' motives coupled with outright contempt for the Society soon saw the dispatch of a papal legate to review the Chinese situation. The pope appointed Carlo Tomasso Maillard de Tournon to act in this capacity. In short order, the collaborative trust that had been established with the emperor K'ang-hsi had been shattered, and the fifty-nine Jesuits who had had the ear of the emperor quickly fell under imperial suspicion. De Tournon declared the Jesuits the villains of the peace, and the conversion of China ground to a halt. Then, in 1742, Pope Benedict XIV issued his *Ex quo singulari*, a document that provided Rome's final constitutional statement on the evangelization of China; *Ex quo singulari* was an absolute rejection of the Chinese rites and an explicit repudiation of the Jesuits' missiology. Although a select number of Jesuits had earlier remained in the imperial court as scholars and advisers, Ricci's tolerant vision of a fusion of Confucian and Christian ritual was at an end, at least until 1939 when Pope Pius XII repealed his predecessor's decree.

The early history of the Society of Jesus is populated by other Francis Xaviers and other Matteo Riccis; it is shaped by other efforts to incorporate indigenous civilizations into the Roman Catholic culture of western Europe; and it is characterized by other partial successes and other failures. Driven by the example of the apostles to go forth and teach all nations and certain in the conviction that there could be no salvation outside the Roman Catholic Church, thousands of Jesuits faithful to their vows to the pope and to their Order set out for mysterious lands, both charted and uncharted, to preach a gospel of charity and human concern. If their methods were not always appreciated—and they were not—they were certainly consistent not just with the thought of Ignatius of Loyola but also with the directives issued by a much-celebrated earlier pope of the missions, Pope Saint Gregory, whose seventh-century advice to his missionaries to England sounds very much like Ignatius's. In a letter written at the close of the sixth century, for example, Gregory advised Augustine of Canterbury, whom he had sent to Christianize the Angles, that "in these days the Church has to correct some things strictly, and allow others already established by custom; others have to be tolerated for a while, in the hope that forbearance may sometimes eradicate an evil of which she disapproves."[62] Consistent with his own advice, in a letter written to Abbot Mellitus on his departure for Britain in 601, Gregory directed: "we wish you to inform him [Augustine of Kent] that we have been giving careful thought to the affairs of the English, and have come to the conclusion that the temples of the idols in that country should on no account be destroyed. He is to destroy the idols, but the temples themselves are to be aspersed with holy water, altars set up, and relics enclosed in them. For if these temples are well built, they are to be purified from devil-worship, and dedicated to the service of the true God. In this way, we hope that the people, seeing that its temples are not destroyed, may abandon idolatry and resort to these places as before, and may come to know and adore the true God."[63] These are directions that Ricci would have rejoiced to hear and they are the same sentiments that prompted Gregory's successor, Pope Boniface IV, to dedicate Marcus Agrippa's Roman pantheon to the Virgin Mary on November 1, 1609, thereby initiating the Christian feast of All Saints on the doorstep of the pagan home of all the gods. It is a pragmatic approach to missionary work that Baltasar Gracián would have applauded as worldly wisdom, the kind of practical wisdom that also produced Canada's Huron Carol, reportedly composed by Jesuit missionary Jean de Brébeuf. Its opening lines make the pedagogical method clear: " 'Twas in the moon of wintertime when all the birds had fled, / That mighty Gitchi Manitou sent angel choirs instead. . . . " Such is the art of Christianizing pagan shrines, what Augustine of Hippo would have called plundering Egyptian gold. In a similar vein, the countless medieval handbooks on preaching, the *artes praedicandi* with which Ignatius and his companions would have been intimately familiar, instruct the preacher to be effective by employing forms, means, and images that are part of the audience's natural environment. It is a practical matter of putting contemplation into effective action.

The Jesuits sent hundreds of missionaries into Latin America—William Bangert records that by 1626 their numbers had reached 1300 in the Spanish colonies and that 258 were commissioned to Portuguese Brazil in the seventeenth century. Early Jesuit history in the Americas is a litany of savagery on both parts, the natives' and the Europeans'. The progress of colonization in the Americas is a scarred tale of the clash of cultures, of exploitation and self-defence, of charitable intentions sometimes misunderstood. In this sordid tale, Portuguese Jesuit Antônio Vieira emerges as the Bartolomé de Las Casas of Brazil. Bangert cautions that the record is overstated but symptomatic: "With burning words [Vieira] exposed and denounced the terrible injustice of the European slave traders. He proclaimed that in the region of the Amazon alone, Portuguese mistreatment of the Amerindians caused the death of two millions."[64] For such interference in the mercantile ambitions of the colonial agents, the Jesuits were often maligned, sometimes martyred, and on several occasions simply sent packing. Still other Jesuit heroes grasped the spiritual imperative of the Christian message and gave their lives to the persecuted. Peter Claver, for example, dedicated his life to the service of negro slaves, performing both spiritual and corporal acts of mercy even in the holds of the slave ships and baptizing literally hundreds of thousands of otherwise hapless souls during the first half of the seventeenth century.

Perhaps the Jesuit reduction is the best-known of the Society's initiatives designed to Christianize, educate, and defend the indigenous peoples of the Americas; although there are several examples of the experiment, the best-known and most successful of these were in Paraguay, an area that extended well beyond the present borders of that modern state. The Paraguayan reduction spread out from a central courtyard and included all of the educational, agricultural, industrial, and religious necessities of life that seventeenth-century European culture could conceivably transplant into the New World. Throughout the Americas, experience had driven the Jesuits to conclude that "stability of residence was a necessary condition of thorough christianization."[65] In Paraguay, this stability of residence, the reduction, had the unfortunate result of centralizing the native population, making them easy prey for ruthless slave traders. As a result, tens of thousands of the native peoples were either murdered or spirited away.

The 1750 treaty between Spain and Portugal dealt a final blow both to the reduction and to the natives. According to the terms of the agreement, Spain transferred her reductions to Portuguese authority in exchange for the wealthy colony of San Sacramento, a transfer that resulted in the immediate dislocation of some thirty thousand native people. Hollywood has captured the ruthlessness that brought about the demise of this noble experiment in *The Mission* (1986), an award-winning and cinematographically gorgeous depiction of dedication, corruption, and unbridled greed (a film for which New York Jesuit Daniel Berrigan served as advisory consultant and in which he played a bit part). This slaughter of the innocent was a calculated blow directed not against the hapless natives, but against the Society of Jesus. Because of Jesuit interference in the otherwise unchecked quest for gold, rumours about sinister motives and suggestions of Jesuit self-interest, the possession of lucrative mines laden with precious metals, began inevitably to circulate—today's story of Jesuit service in Mexico, and in Central and South America resonates eerily with echoes from the past: it is a persistent and pejorative element of the Jesuit mystique. As *The Mission* so graphically illustrates, through their care for souls the Jesuits had unwittingly sown the seeds of their own suppression.

In North America the bravery of the Jesuits is recorded in the Jesuit *Relations*. The *Relations* consists of an invaluable collection of graphic descriptions of the dedication, the successes, and the martyrdom of North American Jesuits as drafted by the religious superiors of the French Jesuits of Quebec between 1632 and 1673, when Pope Clement X embargoed all writings on the missions in an effort to defuse the rising rancour over the situation in China. An extension of the epistolary reports demanded by Ignatius, the *Relations* served not only as a means of informing the Jesuit mother house of the activities of the missions, but, like Francis Xavier's prolific flow of letters from the Far East, satisfied a ravenous European hunger for information on exotic exploits and as a result served as an important vehicle in raising financial support for Jesuit missionary activities. Indeed, the exploits of Isaac Jogues, Jean de Brébeuf, and their companions have become a part of the popular imagination. They are stirringly captured in E. J. Pratt's Canadian epic poem *Brébeuf and His Brethren* and are more generically reproduced in the movie of Brian Moore's 1985 novel *Black Robe* for which Montreal-based Jesuit Marc Gervais served in a consultative capacity.

E. J. Pratt outlines the mission in the Americas in these enthusiastic lines:

> On the prayers,
> The meditations, points and colloquies,
> Was built the soldier and the martyr programme.
> This is the end of man—Deum laudet,
> To seek and find the will of God, to act
> Upon it for the ordering of life,
> And for the soul's beatitude.[66]

It is a thesis wholly consonant with Ignatius's view of the Companions' mission. Indeed, the brief readings for Matins in the Divine Office for the feast day of the North American martyrs, September 26, record the exemplary dedication of Isaac Jogues, Jean de Brébeuf, and their companions, noting that "Their life was like a martyrdom because of the character and the wretched conditions of the Huron Indians of that time. . . . Some of them endured almost unbelievable tortures with such invincible courage as to arouse the admiration of the savage executioners themselves."[67]

The first Jesuits to set foot in the New World were Pierre Biard and Ennémond Massé, who entered America through Port Royal on May 22, 1611. Other Jesuits streamed into North America, especially into Maryland where the Jesuit mission was led in 1634 by the English priest, Andrew White, the author of the celebrated *An Account of the Journey to Maryland*. Some Jesuits, like Jacques Marquette, set out to explore the vastness of their new world, while hundreds of others established schools; taught, baptized, and ministered to the English and French colonizers; and sought to insulate the natives from the consuming ravages of greed. Eventually, as colonial powers undertook to negotiate treaties with the aboriginal inhabitants during the eighteenth and nineteenth centuries, Jesuits began to act as counsellors and legal advisers in an effort to protect the natives' interests.

Reflecting on all of this and speaking as a witness to our late-twentieth-century perspective, the present general of the Jesuit Order, Peter-Hans Kolvenbach, stood on an Idaho reservation in May 1993 in a town named after the famous Jesuit missionary explorer Peter De Smet and offered the Society's apologies for "the mistakes it has made in the past" since, he lamented, "the church was insensitive toward your tribal customs, language, and spirituality."[68]

By the time Ignatius died on July 31, 1556, his Companions had spread to virtually every part of the globe, though the area of the known world that most eluded the Society's missionary outreach lay close by—to the south of Italy, in Africa, and especially Ethiopia, which Ignatius was keen to Christianize. By any reasonable measure, however, the Society was eminently successful. Perhaps it was too successful. In Ignatius's day and during the whole of the following century the Society grew at a staggering rate. It was precisely the enviable achievements of the Jesuits that led inevitably to their suppression in the eighteenth century. The Society had become the darling of kings, queens, and the upper classes; and as it grew in influence and prestige it also became one of the most hated organizations within the Roman Catholic Church. Scores of books and pamphlets were spewed forth, denouncing the power and intentions of the Society. During the seventeenth and eighteenth centuries, scientists such as Blaise Pascal, poets such as John Donne, philosophers such as Voltaire, monastic reformers such as Armand de Rancé, and scores of well-known, little-known, and unknown intellectuals, churchmen, and politicians denounced the Society. Because the Jesuits had become masters of both rhetoric and the niceties of scholastic logic, by 1613 the word "jesuitic" connoted mental equivocation and by 1640 "jesuit" was a synonym for dissembler. The Jesuit was not to be trusted. Accordingly, John Donne caps his short history of the "liberty of dissembling, and lying" by noting that the Jesuits had given it a rational and theological respectability through the doctrines of Mental Reservation and Mixed Proposition.[69]

From the rational and scientific point of view of the Enlightenment of the eighteenth century, religion was an authoritarian evil to be repulsed and the Jesuits were the preeminent embodiment of that evil. Ultimately, it was the political influence of three countries in particular, and of one politically dominant family (the Bourbons), that manufactured the near-universal suppression of the Society in 1773. France, Portugal, and Spain stood united in open hostility towards the Society of Jesus; in addition, Henry VIII's rebuffing of the papacy in 1533 and James I's subsequent Oath of Allegiance provided ominous examples of a national church wholly independent of Rome, while the relative prosperity of the renegade English reinforced the growing perception that non-Catholic countries flourished while Roman Catholic ones languished.

France's Jesuits found themselves under intense pressure to prove themselves loyal sons both of the motherland and the mother church. Italian Jesuit Robert Bellarmine's thesis of indirect papal authority in the temporal realm proved particularly problematic for France's Jesuits as did the 1625 spirited defence of Bellarmine published by another Italian Jesuit, Antonio Santarelli. (Such accusations were in the air. John Donne's *Ignatius His Conclave* makes frequent reference to the Jesuits as advocates of regicide, and notes, too, the constant friction between French Gallicanism and Roman Ultramontanism.) In an effort to bring the Jesuits into check, the French Parlement presented them with a series of directives the intent of which was an enforced Gallicanism formally signed in 1626, implicitly affirming the absolute temporal power of the French king while simultaneously recognizing the spiritual power of the pope. Louis XIV brought the simmering question of legitimate proper authority to a boil again in 1673, 1681, and 1682; indeed, his passion to consolidate power, even ecclesiastical power, within the jurisdiction of France prompted him to recall all French Jesuits from Rome in 1689 as a means of applying pressure on Jesuit general Tirso González. Louis XIV also directed his aim at a stubborn Pope Innocent XI.

But the Jesuits' problems in France were not just political: the Society also found itself at odds with one of France's favourite sons, Cornelius Jansen, to whose *Augustinus* the Jesuits took serious exception, especially for its pessimistic view of fallen humankind and its Calvinistic theory of divine grace; the Jesuits, for their part, came under attack for preaching a supposed moral laxity through an excessive dependence on casuistry and an unhealthy affection for rhetorical subtlety. Unfortunately, the Jansenist debate also spread into the influential parlours of the intelligentsia and inevitably into

Parlement itself. In the end, the Jesuits' lifeblood in France was sapped both by mounting antagonism towards institutional religion as such and a blossoming nationalism that forced the Jesuits into a dilemma of impossible loyalties.

In 1761 the French Parlement ordered the burning of the books of twenty-three Jesuits and, given its purportedly corrupting influence on the young, forbade the Society from accepting further novices. In addition, all Jesuit schools in France were to be closed by April 1, 1762.

> . . . on August 6, 1762, this same Parlement announced that the so-called Society of Jesus, obnoxious to civic order, violator of the natural law, destroyer of religion and morality, perpetrator of corruption, was barred from France. Several particular directives implemented this general decree: each Jesuit had to withdraw from his community and sever connections with the Society elsewhere; further, each Jesuit had to refrain from university studies, abstain from positions of teaching and civic responsibility unless he first took an oath by which he repudiated the Society's rules, disavowed its moral teaching as expressed in the *Extracts*, and accepted the Gallican Articles of 1682. All the Society's buildings and estates were declared confiscated.[70]

Jesuit fortunes in the Iberian peninsula and the colonies that relied directly on Spain and Portugal fared no better. It was Portugal, in fact, that led the attack against the Jesuits. Although the heady days of King John III's enthusiastic support of the Society both at home and abroad had long since passed—even though their numbers had reached 861 in Portugal by 1749 and the Society itself was enjoying an intellectual feast—the banquet was about to end. Spurred by confidant of the court and avid advocate of the ideals of the Enlightenment Sebastiño José de Carvalho, King Joseph I oversaw the destruction of the reductions in the Americas and the demise of the Jesuits at home. Carvalho led the charge against the Jesuits, negotiating the treaty with Spain that gave him direct control over the once-Spanish reductions. He plotted and intrigued, imprisoning the saintly and aging Jesuit Gabriele Malagrida for what was argued to be the treasonous act of delivering a homily with the formulaic warning that the 1755 Lisbon earthquake was a sign of divine displeasure. Carvalho also crafted a hate-mongering pamphlet, designed to expose the jesuitical threat: *A Brief Account of the Republic which the Jesuits have established in the Spanish and Portuguese Dominions of the New World and the War which they carried on against the armies of the two Crowns, all extracted from the Register of the Commissaries and Plenipotentiaries and from other Documents.*

A man driven by his cause, Carvalho successfully convinced both the king and Cardinal Francisco Saldanha, a papal visitor dispatched by Pope Benedict XIV in 1758 to investigate the Portuguese situation, that longstanding rumours of Jesuit wealth and corruption were well founded. Rome was unimpressed by the intelligence it was receiving, since neither Carvalho nor Saldanha had produced any proper evidence to substantiate their allegations. Joseph I, however, needed no proof—the Jesuit mystique was sufficient; on April 29, 1759, he expelled the Jesuits from Portuguese territory. On September 17 of that year 153 Portuguese Jesuits, the first of approximately 1100 to be so treated, were herded aboard a ship in Lisbon harbour, refugees of the Enlightenment under order of deportation and destined for a life of exile in the Papal States. On June 15, 1760, the papal nuncio joined their ranks. One hundred and eighty Jesuits from the missions and from abroad were cramped into Portuguese dungeons, and one of their number, the previously mentioned Gabriele Malagrida, was publicly executed after a cruel imprisonment and a mock trial. Deprived of so significant a core of her intellectual leadership, Portugal suffered a severe blow to her educational system, her colonies, and her commonweal.

Spain, too, was about to join the fray. By the mid-point of the seventeenth century, Spain's golden age had passed and the Jesuits' fortunes in the home of their birth began to flag, along with those of the motherland. Racked by plague and poverty, Spain began to turn an envious eye on the successes of the Society. Burdened by Spain's problems, the Jesuits began to lose recruits and with them the intellectual mantle they once wore. With the coronation of the Bourbon king, Philip V, in 1700, and his Italian wife Elizabètta Farnese, however, Spain began to experience the flush of a renaissance, especially among the influential noble class to whom the Jesuits now turned their educational talents in a determined effort to play a directive role in the new society. Guillaume Daubenton, Philip V's personal confessor, even involved himself in advising his penitent on affairs of the realm.

The winds of the Enlightenment with their rationality, nationalism, and rejection of authority, and particularly of religious authority, however, soon stirred Spanish resentment against Jesuit political theory and especially the political theory of Jesuits like Francisco Suárez, which held that while the authority of the monarch derived immediately from the people it was rooted ultimately in God. As was the temper of the times, incidental monetary and political events combined with rumour and suspicion to conspire against the Jesuits. Anti-Jesuit feelings soared to such a height that on February 27, 1767, King Charles III signed an expulsion decree that emptied the Spanish colonies of some 2300 missionaries and crippled the Jesuits' educational system under Spanish aegis: some 188 colleges and 31 seminaries. Spain's Inquisition had taken a dramatic turn: today it was the Jesuits under interdict; shortly it would take another with the church itself under attack.

Not content with the local suppressions that had been successfully executed in their own countries, the Bourbon courts were determined to receive papal ratification for their actions. Pope Clement XIII came under severe pressure to issue a papal edict of dissolution, pressure he successfully resisted until his death in 1769. His successor, Clement XIV, who had previously expressed an apparent willingness to comply with the Bourbon intention to suppress the Order faced the same determination from Portugal, Spain, and France. Clement was bluntly reminded of the English example of a state religion independent of Rome. Maria Theresa, who had been trained by the Jesuits and who nursed a clear admiration for them, was reluctant to deliver Austria to the Bourbons, thus providing the pope with an excuse to prevaricate. But Maria Theresa, too, was ultimately, if hesitantly, brought into line: the Bourbons were, after all, her sons-in-law. With no allies at hand and the enemy at every door, on June 8, 1773, Pope Clement XIV reluctantly signed the papal brief *Dominus ac redemptor*, enacting Rome's official suppression of the Society of Jesus. On August 16, 1773, 239 years and one day from that historical gathering at Montmartre from which the Society drew its inspirational origins, Pope Clement IV enacted a papal decree designed to eradicate the vision of 1534 and to deal a death blow to the Company. Of that Company, which had grown to 23,000, many were now imprisoned, some had turned to the secular priesthood, and a few had renounced their vocation. Lorenzo Ricci, their unfortunate Superior General, drew his last breath a prisoner in the Castel Sant'Angelo just outside the walls of the Vatican. For him, Pope Pius VI's determination to set the captives free would come unmercifully too late. And for a Society that had progressed with relative rapidity "from good to better," things were now going very badly indeed.

From Suppression to Restoration to Renewal: 1773–1983

Though the Superior General died an unhappy captive and though the Society he led had suffered a severe blow, the stroke was far from fatal. Decimated by the unchecked ambition of the Bourbon monarchs and the antireligious tide of the Enlightenment, the Society was, however, sustained by the immense success of its educational apostolate and the practicalities of international politics. Unwilling to sacrifice an unparalleled educational system freely provided and amused at the prospect of spurning the ambitions of their more westerly counterparts, Frederick the Great of Prussia and Catherine II of Russia were eager to offer the Jesuits a safe refuge. Elsewhere, determined members of the Order went underground, and others, stubbornly refusing to accept what appeared to be the inevitable, adopted names like "The Society of the Faith of Jesus" and "Brothers of the Faith of Jesus." Some, on the other hand, left the Order to become diocesan priests, and others, though surprisingly few, accepted the tenor of the times and turned their backs on the Society.

In 1801 the political face of western Europe had once again taken on a new complexion. The Bourbon dynasty was in the process of disintegration (by 1830 the theory of divine right would be reduced to an historical recollection) and Napoleon Bonaparte's political star was about to flash meteor-like through the troubled pages of European history. Equally important, there was a new pope in Rome who was determined to reclaim so supportive a pool of talent as the Jesuits, especially in light of the tide of atheism, doubt, and rationality sweeping western society. In 1801 Pope Pius VII recognized the continuing existence of the Society in Russia, formally restoring its name, and recognizing Franciszek Kareu as the superior general in Russia. Not content with this initial and limited success, Kareu immediately set out to restore the Society beyond the Russian border. Then, in August 1814, Pope Pius VII promulgated the papal bull *Sollicitudo omnium ecclesiarum* formally reinstating the Society of Jesus. Jesuit provinces were quickly established in France, Spain, and England; the Emancipation Act of 1829 returned to Roman Catholics those political, legal, and educational rights suspended by the Penal Laws of the late sixteenth century. A new, more tolerant era had risen from the smouldering aftermath of the Enlightenment—and the Society of Jesus, too, had found a new life.

Predictably, the reemergence of the Society was not a cause for universal celebration, however, and its history continued to be a contentious one. René Fülöp-Miller records the reaction in the United States:

> "I do not like the reappearance of the Jesuits," wrote ex-President John Adams, as early as 1816, to his successor Thomas Jefferson. "Shall we not have regular swarms of them here, in as many disguises as only a king of the gipsies can assume, dressed as printers, publishers, writers and schoolmasters? If ever there was a body of men who merited eternal damnation on earth and in hell, it is this Society of Loyola's. Nevertheless, we are compelled by our system of religious toleration to offer them an asylum. . . . " Jefferson replied to his predecessor: "Like you, I disapprove of the restoration of the Jesuits, for it means a step backwards from light into darkness. . . . "[71]

Indeed, from a Modernist's perspective, the Jesuits' institutional commitment to the philosophical teachings of Thomas Aquinas did represent a "step backwards" from the individualistic and liberal dogmas that formed a major part of the inheritance of the Enlightenment. Aquinas's theses of the common good and of the role of the state in assuring that good, of the social use of private property and the role of the state in assuring its proper disposition were essentially at odds with a liberal Enlightenment theory of the individual good, the amoral and hence objective nature of the state, the legitimacy of the quest for material well-being and personal pleasure, and the functional divinization of the individual.

Enlightenment distrust of institutions, of authority, and of institutional religion leads logically to the separation of church and state, to a reversal of the medieval/renaissance conviction of *cujus regio, ejus religio*. The divinely appointed sovereign gives way to the self-anointed sovereign individual and state religion gives way to the religion of the individual. The Enlightenment gospel separates church and state in a way that is wholly antithetical to traditional Roman Catholic philosophical and social thought as well as to the medieval Thomism to which the Jesuit and his church were wedded. To tolerate religion, all religion, would seem ultimately to render the moral and the sacred commonplace and to undermine the character of the inherently sacred; it would celebrate instead the sanctity of the self and discard all pretence at objective moral underpinning by preaching an ultimately subjective and individualistic morality.

As a representative of what Pius IX would call a Modernist perspective, John Stuart Mill worried about the state interfering with individual rights and about the morality of the ruling class establishing the binding morality for all. He explores the nature of the problem when he explains in his essay *On Liberty*:

> In the part which merely concerns himself, his independence is, of right, absolute. Over himself, over his own body and mind, the individual is sovereign. . . . [T]he principle requires liberty of tastes and pursuits, of framing the plan of our life to suit our own character, of doing as we like, subject to such consequences as may follow, without impediment from our fellow creatures, so long as what we do does not harm them, even though they should think our conduct foolish, perverse or wrong. . . . Mankind are greater gainers by suffering each other to live as it seems good to themselves, than by compelling each to live as seems good to the rest.[72]

Cardinal Newman had argued that Roman Catholicism thrives best where genuine religious liberty exists; others have noted that state religion breeds state control of religion. Ironically, it is precisely for this reason (constitutional separation of church and state) that the Society of Jesus has flourished in the United States.

Fearful of the new liberalism and determined to retain a sense of traditionally objective and universal truth, the Roman Catholic Church staked out what was on balance an aggressively preservative territory in the late nineteenth and early twentieth centuries. Pius IX, who had been initiated into Ignatius's Exercises as a young man and who had even entertained the possibility of a vocation to the Society, led the attack with his Syllabus of Errors (December 8, 1864) and shortly after convoked Vatican I during which he formalized the contentious doctrine of papal infallibility (1870). Then, early in the twentieth century, Pius X continued the papal assault on the newly developing liberal approach to social and religious reconstruction with a series of pronouncements, culminating in his famous condemnation of the "doctrines of modernists," *Pascendi dominici gregis* (1907). The imposition of this anti-intellectual document was reinforced by Pius X's subsequent introduction of a controversial Oath Against Modernism in 1910, inspired in part by the English pastoral against modernism penned by two Jesuits and edited by the General of the Society, Luis Martín.[73]

Despite the accusations of being troublesome innovators that had been levelled against Society members during the preceding four hundred years, the newly restored Society contributed its own influential and conservative voice to the Vatican-centred debate raging around them. No doubt a significant element within the Society thought it best to tread discreetly until the yoke of suppression was finally removed; but there can also be no doubt that individual Jesuits were motivated by a sincere Thomistic concurrence with the dangers of a world modelled on the anti-institutional, antiauthoritarian, and pro-individualistic principles of the Enlightenment. And, as for the *Syllabus of Errors*, it did proclaim at its heart the ancient principle that was part of Pius IV's profession of faith in 1564 and the spirit of which Ignatius and his Companions had embraced uncritically: *Extra ecclesiam nulla salus*.

Jacques Monet, a distinguished historian of the Society and president of the University of Sudbury in Ontario, Canada, notes that there is much more to the matter than a group of postsuppressionist priests "concerned about minding their p's and q's." Those Jesuits who survived the forty years of suppression were by the nature of things quite elderly members of the Order whose sense of the difference between the letter and the spirit of the presuppression Society had been clouded by time and circumstance. In addition, when the Order emerged from its forced exile it was inundated with new members who had to be trained by people without any real sense of the Society as it had been. According to Monet,

> They tended to take the text literally. They didn't know the difference between the text and human behaviour. So, for example, they understood the fourth vow and the Jesuits' ultramontane character differently from the way these things were understood before the suppression. It is a matter of the letter of the law instead of its spirit. It took a long time to develop a balanced sense of the Constitution and the rules of the Society. I think that's the main consideration with the suppression and restoration. But there was also the problem of supply and demand: there was so much to do and so few to do it. As a result, the formation of the first post-suppression Jesuits was very brief and very spotty as compared to the formation of their pre-suppression counterparts.

To elaborate on his point, Monet points to two recent books: Alain Woodrow's *Les Jésuites: Histoire de Pouvoirs* and David G. Schultenover's *A View From Rome: On the Eve of the Modernist Crisis*. Woodrow argues that the Jesuits had always been able to identify with the secular powerbrokers within the Society's areas of influence, but in the case of the Enlightenment the Companions made a tactical blunder. Schultenover documents the conservative nature of the Jesuit curia at this time, exposing its penchant for making sacrificial lambs of the more liberal members of the Order during so tempestuous an era of ecclesial retrenchment. Indeed, according to the primary evidence convincingly paraded by Schultenover, the Jesuit Curia was so intent on pleasing Rome and defeating the interrelated evils of Lutheranism, Protestantism, individualism, Modernism, and Americanism that it was willing to falsify information and engage in covertly political subterfuge.

To stem the tide of liberal political and theological theory, it was the Vatican's determined intention to turn all eyes (and minds) to Rome. Reflecting on the passion for centralization and retrenchment characteristic of the pontificate of Pius IX, Jacques Monet explains that the Society was eager to offer its active support to Rome's wishes:

> The Catholic world of the nineteenth century was ultramontane or it was nothing. Were the Jesuits leaders of that growing movement, as they had been, for instance, in the promotion of the humanities in the education of the sixteenth and seventeenth centuries? Hardly. But, in lieu of leading it, they clearly reflected the spirit of the age, and its undoubted devotion to the promotion not only of the pope's special spiritual mission in the universal church, but also of the new Roman policy of centralizing the church's administration and government there.
>
> In the promotion of papal power, two specific popular devotions played a critical role. One was the Apostleship of Prayer; the other was the devotion to Our Lady's Immaculate Conception.
>
> The first, founded by the French Jesuit François Xavier Gautrelet in 1844, was linked to the Society's traditional devotion to the Sacred Heart. It became an important ultramontane vehicle through its emphasis on the "morning offering"—recited every day by hundreds in France during the 1840s and hundreds of thousands world-wide by the late 1860s—in which a "general intention" was personally proposed by the pope every month. It was not the only thing that made Pius IX the most "popular" pope in the history of the church, but it certainly was the most influential.
>
> The promotion of the Immaculate Conception [the dogma that Mary was herself conceived without sin] as a dogma of Faith to be held by all Catholics predated by far the founding of the Jesuit Order. But it had been a favourite cause of many Jesuits in the Old Society. After 1814, the restored Society made this proclamation one of its main missions. Theological scholars such as Giovanni Perrone, Dean of the Jesuits' Gregorian University, and Carlo Passiglia, one of its more eminent professors, enthusiastically endorsed both the devotion and its wide promotion. In this, they were stoutly supported by *La Civiltà Cattolica*, founded in 1850 by Pius IX himself and

entrusted (over Jesuit General Jan Roothaan's objections) to the Jesuits. Its editor, Carlo Curci, a Jesuit priest, was indefatigable in promoting the proclamation of the dogma. This would be, arguably, the first time a pope made an infallible declaration outside the work of an ecumenical council. Once done—in fact, the text of the decree proclaimed by Pius IX on December 8, 1854, was prepared mainly by Jesuit father Giovanni Perrone—the proclamation would become a proof of the pope's personal infallibility and an incentive towards its definition.

The proclamation of the dogma was followed by the apparitions at Lourdes in 1858, and their sequel of increasingly large popular pilgrimages, that most often also continued to Rome on the new railway recently extended to the eternal city by Pius IX. Again, the Jesuits were not the principal organizers of these travels—the Assumptionists outdid them in energy and zeal—but the contribution of their preaching and writing became vital to the promotion of the pilgrimage.

Nor were the Jesuits the initiators of the *Syllabus of Errors*. These were Bishop Olympe Philippe Gerbet of Perpignan [author of an influential pastoral instruction *sur diverses erreurs du temps present* disseminated in 1860] and several of his conservative theologians in southern France who proposed the idea to Pius IX in 1861. But Jesuits linked it to infallibility by arranging to have it published on December 8, 1864, ten years to the day after the proclamation of the Immaculate Conception. Father Giovanni Perrone and other professors at the Gregorian, including the future Cardinal Johann Franzelin, ghost-wrote the encyclical *Quanta cura* that presented it.

Fathers Perrone and Franzelin were also leading architects of the scholarship leading to the solemn definition of the pope's infallibility at Vatican I. In this area, as well, others had led the way—Redemptorist theologians especially, and those of the School of Mainz as well as very influential archbishops such as Manning of Westminster and Deschamps of Malines. Still, as a group, Jesuit theologians, especially those from the Gregorian University, played leading roles at the Council. Fr. Perrone, who helped with formulating *Pastor aeternus*, the

> decree on infallibility, may, indeed, be the only person, other than Pius IX, who actually co-authored two infallible definitions.
>
> By the 1870s, the Jesuits were often referred to as "the Grenadiers of Pius IX." In fact, many Jesuits often "balanced," with a liberal critique, the strong ultramontanism of their brethren. Such were the Italian philosopher, Luigi d'Azeglio, who first used the term "social justice," or the French writers of *Études* who, in the years leading up to Vatican I, often took a moderate and modern stand. Still, the description is an accurate one. For, as Lord Acton has suggested, Pius IX was undoubtedly successful in channelling the Jesuits' absolute loyalty to the church into the promotion of his ultramontane ideals and policies.

Echoing Monet's observations, Bangert suggests that Pius IX did not much like the Jesuits, but found in them a useful ally in the war against liberalism. In its Decree 12, for example, the 23rd General Congregation of 1883 expressly renounced liberalism, worried that "there are grounds for fear that some of Ours might be touched by this pestilence,"[74] and, as an act of papal solidarity, wholeheartedly embraced both *Quanta cura* and the *Syllabus of Errors*. In addition, German Jesuits not only rejoiced in the appearance of the *Syllabus* and produced articles in its defence, but even sought extreme interpretations of its condemnatory articles. And *La Civiltà Cattolica* added its voice to mainstream Jesuit compliance in a published article in which French Catholics were divided into two groups, Catholics and Liberal Catholics, the former consisting of those who longed for a positive definition of papal infallibility and the latter those who opposed the idea altogether. Three years earlier, the Jesuits' *Études* had been censored by the Jesuit provincial in France for printing anti-*Syllabus* materials. The editor of *Études*, Henri Brémond, a liberal at heart, had grown so disenchanted with the direction the church had been charting in its route to retrenchment that he ultimately decided to leave the Order and to seek laicization.

Meanwhile, other Jesuits publicly defended the modernist message and in the unhappy case of Dublin-born, English Jesuit George Tyrrell the outcome would be even more traumatic than that endured by Brêmond. A one-time thoroughgoing ultramontane, Tyrrell was the object of outright student rebellion at Stonyhurst because of his rigid neo-Thomism; removed from his teaching position, and reflecting on his fate while exiled to Farm Street in the heart of London, Tyrrell underwent a complete intellectual conversion. His Modernist views were soon brought to the attention of Pope Pius X who demanded that the Society act. Under intense pressure from Rome, the Jesuit general, Luis Martín, ordered Tyrrell to issue a public repudiation of his published reformist ideas. When Tyrrell refused, he was dismissed from the Society, eventually excommunicated, and ultimately buried in unconsecrated ground. In addition, Martín removed the English provincial, John Gerard, from office for his spirited defence of Tyrrell and his expressly stated sympathy both for Tyrrell and for his defence of Americanism.

On the political front, Christopher Hollis points out that in nineteenth-century Portugal and Spain, "It was the custom of the militant Catholics—Jesuits and others—to talk of themselves as the defenders of righteousness against the forces of unbridled evil. . . . [T]he upshot was that the Jesuits in those countries in the nineteenth century allowed themselves to become the mere creatures of the conservative party and monotonously went in and out with the success or failure of that party."[75] This sense of conservatism continued into the twentieth century so that during Spain's civil war (1936–39) the Jesuits for the most part sided with the right-wing dictatorship of General Francisco Franco, with only the Basque Jesuits providing a unified dissident voice. Even in Latin America, where Jesuits had been the unflinching champions of the suppressed, the Order became identified with the ruling factions and jettisoned its liberal colours.

North of the Rio Grande, the constitutional separation of church and state rendered the loyalties of the Jesuits more a moot than a practical point, and though old antipapist and anti-Jesuit sentiments lingered, the constitutional climate for religious tolerance worked to the benefit of the Society. Forced to minister as a diocesan priest under the terms of the suppression, one-time Jesuit John Carroll, for example, established Georgetown College in 1789 and in so doing planted the seeds of postsecondary education in the United States. Georgetown was immediately deeded to the Jesuits, and its graduates helped to allay old anxieties and instill new admiration both for the Society and for Roman Catholicism by distinguishing themselves on the national scene. Moreover, as the Society in the United States began to ordain its own native clergy, the Jesuits were increasingly viewed as part of the national landscape, no longer as a band of foreign missionaries. Non-natives like Belgium-born Peter de Smet were quickly Americanized, and de Smet became something of a national hero for his effective mediation of Native hostilities, quelling Sitting Bull and other combatants.

In Canada, the obituary for the Society had been prematurely written in 1759 when the English defeated the French on the Plains of Abraham and set out to eradicate all vestiges of Roman Catholicism. The Jesuits, who were an essential part of the French hegemony in North America, were refused permission to accept new recruits and their properties were confiscated by the Crown. When in 1800 Joseph Casot, the last of the early Jesuits in Canada, finally died, there was no Jesuit presence until 1842 when a French mission was established. Administratively, the newly arrived Jesuits in Canada became part of the New York–Canada mission until 1879, and their foreign associations quickly garnered for them the reputation of annexationists as the tensions between the Canadian colonies and the ever-expanding United States of America continued.

In Italy, mid-nineteenth-century nationalistic aspirations ultimately viewed both Pope Pius IX and the Jesuits as the enemy of unification. Many prominent clerics lost their lives in the wake of the pro-Italian wave then coursing through the Italian states: the pope and the Jesuits fled Rome in search of safer quarters. As modern Italy began to take shape, the antinationalist cloak in which the Jesuits had at least perceptually wrapped themselves left them isolated and unwelcome except in the papal states. Suspicion of the Jesuit position was confirmed in part by their support of Metternich when they were allowed to return to Austria and accepted an invitation to establish themselves in Austria's disputed Italian provinces of Lombardy and Venetia.

In France, the traditional charge that the Jesuits were aligned with a foreign power in their support of the papacy was resurrected, and the Society was alternately in and out of favour and influence depending on whether the centre of power lay with the left or the right; the

Jesuits' accustomed allegiance with the monarchist government proved once more to be misplaced, as the Society put its influence behind a losing cause. Initial French vocations after the lifting of the suppression tended to be from the aristocracy who supported the *ancien régime* and the monarchical principle. But the French harkening to a hierarchical past was short-lived. Belgian Jesuit Philippe Delvaux publicly argued (and with no little courage) the ideals of liberalism and the value of the American democratic revolution. *Études* echoed his sentiments. For its part, the Vatican was determined to pursue a policy of concordat, a policy that culminated in the 1929 Lateran Treaty with Benito Mussolini. The impetus for a close working relationship between church and state lay firmly rooted in the pages of Roman Catholic political history, and it was a policy that had the solid backing of the ultramontane Jesuit Curia. Indeed, Jesuit priest Pietro Tacchi-Venturi played a major role in negotiating Rome's capitulation with Mussolini. Absorbed by the tenor of the times, many Jesuits actively supported right-wing totalitarian regimes.

In a very real way, therefore, nineteenth-century Jesuits had difficulty throwing off their ultramontane past as they understood it and embracing the new world order. In the twentieth century, however, they began to reassert their ancient self-understanding as men for others and as apostolic innovators.

The Society of Jesus in the early twentieth century retained strong semblances of its nineteenth-century ultramontane conservatism, but also prepared the way for the church's and the Society's own reformation as unleashed by Vatican II. True to the letter of Decree 15 of the 23rd General Congregation, in which the Society reaffirmed Thomas Aquinas as its "own teacher" (this as an explicit means of demonstrating "by solemn and public testimony the fullest extent of its filial obedience and assent" to Leo XIII),[76] the Jesuit Curia accepted Pope Leo XIII's invitation to establish a reactionary beachhead for the transmission of traditional Thomism at the Gregorian University. Indeed, it was two professors from the Gregorian who drafted Pope Pius XI's 1930 tough-minded and objectively philosophical encyclical *Casti connubii*, which preaches an outright ban on all forms of contraception (and which formed an important basis for Paul VI's divisively controversial 1968 encyclical on the same topic and reinforcing the same theme, *Humanae vitae*). At the same time, it was a team of German and Austrian Jesuits appointed by General Wlodmir Ledochowski who were responsible for *Quadragesimo anno*, a 1931 update of Leo XIII's landmark statement on the new social order, *Rerum novarum*, the theoretical bedrock for the development of the church's teaching on justice in the marketplace locally, nationally, and internationally. Ledochowski would himself fall under suspicion as being sympathetic to modernists. Aveling observes of the time:

> The Jesuit presence in Rome was impressive but much thinner on the ground and less influential than it appeared at first sight. The teams of experts were small and contained few of the Society's best minds; its real talent was suspect of liberalism or retained at home in France and Germany to man the new enterprises. The main command structure of the Roman Curia was firmly in the hands of a cabal of conservative Italian Cardinals, "Ignatian" to a man, but disposed to hold Jesuits at arm's length.[77]

Although the Jesuit Curia at the turn of the century had made it abundantly clear that it was unwilling to defend its own when their Modernist statements attracted the attention of Rome, and although Ledochowski would tolerate no scholarship that might ruffle Rome's feathers, nonetheless the Society did produce some of the most influential theological, philosophical, social, and even scientific thinkers of the twentieth century. Pierre Teilhard de Chardin was one of the first to test the troubled waters, choosing as he did to work in the intellectually dangerous area of palaeontology. Even though Teilhard has become the darling of the late twentieth century, Rome began to denounce him and his writings in 1923 amidst stories of stolen manuscripts, a Vatican inquisition, and clandestine detective work. Teilhard was ordered not to publish his research. His optimistic view of cosmic evolution and human anthropology seemed to contradict traditional church teachings on the nature of Original Sin, and, just as bad, Teilhard was a charismatic individual and a fine lecturer who attracted widespread acclaim. Rome managed to have him silenced and banished to a Chinese safe haven where he remained until 1946, when he was transferred to France and finally to New York where he worked the final nine years of his life.

Jesuit intellectuals in the preconciliar church began to write under assumed names and to circulate the findings of their research clandestinely, to form secret groups of like-minded men, to publish in non-Catholic sources, and even to disguise the innovative in apparently traditional forms. It was in this way that leading Jesuit intellectuals—Henri de Lubac, Karl Rahner, Jean Daniélou, and others—helped to shape the intellectual world for Pope John XXIII's *aggiornamento*, the Second Vatican Council (1962–65). John XXIII indeed provided a "new tomorrow" both for the church and for the Society of Jesus as well as for the world in which they are firmly rooted and which they serve. Vatican II not only reshaped the time-honoured thesis *Extra ecclesiam nulla salus* and offered a welcome embrace to other religions, but also opened its arms to the world and extended U.S. Jesuit John Courtney Murray's thesis of democracy and individual conscience into its landmark expression in the Council's *Dignitatis humanae*. Even before the Council, there had been inklings of an openness to more traditionally Jesuit concerns for social justice, but John XXIII's vision of the modern church clearly provided for the rebirth of the Society.

Michael Campbell-Johnston, an English Jesuit with vast experience of Third World poverty and the church's response to it after Vatican II, traces the early developments of the Council and the Jesuits' involvement therein. Noting that the Jesuits had at least begun to prepare the way for Vatican II, Campbell-Johnston explains:

> Obviously, it's a continuum. You can't draw lines and say one is B.C. and one is A.D. It was a continuum of thought. I don't think the Jesuits were particularly ahead of their time. I'm thinking for example of the influence some of the leading Jesuit intellectuals had on Vatican II. Particularly, I think of de Lubac. De Lubac, of course, in his old age, became somewhat different, but I believe one of the most influential books before Vatican II was de Lubac's *Catholicism*. It is a book which was looking at the social dimensions of dogma, that's the subtitle, in fact, and if you just call it *Catholicism* you get no idea of what's inside it; but in the subtitle there are the social aspects of dogma. He's showing how the principal dogmas of the Catholic faith, including the Trinity, especially the Trinity—all

the other dogmas and the sacraments—are fundamentally social in their very essence and of course this is a reaction against the extraordinary individualism which was present in so much religion and religious practice in the nineteenth century and the early years of this century. I would see that as one of the principal changes. It almost explains the whole of Vatican II because the new concept of the sacraments takes place in a community, the parish is a community. . . . De Lubac played a significant role in that, as did other Jesuits, and others who were not Jesuits, well before Vatican II.

So, I would say Vatican II didn't come out of a vacuum. There was a lot of process behind it and I am thinking in particular of the sort of social dimension of our work. One of the first of our Fathers General who really spoke strongly on that was Father Jean-Baptiste Janssens, the predecessor of Father Pedro Arrupe. In 1949 Father Janssens wrote the first-ever letter of a Jesuit general to the whole Society. I remember the date very well because I had just joined the Jesuits that same year. He wrote it on the social apostolate and he was probably way ahead of his time—it's quite a remarkable letter. He was calling for Jesuits, as an ordinary part of their training, to be sent to work, for example, in factories to experience the sort of ordinary working conditions of the poor. That letter, I remember, had a big influence on me personally.

Another point I will make is that Ignatius himself was deeply concerned with poor people and from the very first moment of his conversion he started giving a lot of time and attention to working with the poor. It is very well known how when he got to Rome and when he was trying to write the constitutions for the Jesuits, dealing with cardinals and popes and bishops, and all the rest of it, he nevertheless actually opened his own house which he was living in, to the poor who were living out in the streets in Rome at that time. There was a plague and he had over 400 people at one moment living in his house. So, from the very beginning of the Society, there was that concern for the poor. Another very well-known example is when he instructed the two papal legates who were going to the Council of Trent, who were two top theologians, Diego

Laynez and Alfonso Salmerón—he instructed them to go to the Council of Trent, to do their work as theologians, but every day to go into the hospitals and look after the sick and the poor. Of course, the hospitals in those days were not what we would understand by hospital today. They were dreadful places where those who were sleeping out would get a bed for the night and so on.

That existed right from the start of the Jesuits. What changed, I suppose, was a new understanding of what a real social apostolate was and that really began 100 years ago with the publication of *Rerum novarum*. Bit by bit that had an effect on the Society as well and we started setting up these social institutes. The first one to be set up was in 1903 in France, Action Populaire, and that was only a few years after *Rerum novarum*. That was to give a new prominence to this sort of social teaching and to try to get Christians, Roman Catholics, to look not just at charitable works of mercy—feeding the poor, clothing the naked, giving housing to the homeless, and so on—but to try to start examining the causes of these problems. And that is what the real social apostolate is. So, from the very beginning the Jesuits were involved in this work as were other religious congregations. But bit by bit we came to see much more clearly, and as the problem grew, it had to be an essential part of everything we were doing, not just a sort of specialized apostolate for a few people, the social few.

Janssens's letter, therefore, implies a rediscovery of our original charism. He's not much spoken about these days because the Society had this big change immediately after him. But he was a man who certainly had a great vision and he himself has one wonderful letter that he wrote, not the one I just mentioned, another one, where he says that the charitable works of mercy are what Christ in the Gospels commands every Christian to do, and he insists that these are the ones we will be judged upon at the last judgement when we are asked, "Did you feed the hungry? Did you et cetera, et cetera?" But, he said, there is a second type of charity which is much deeper and better than that first type and that is to try to get at the causes of these problems. That's where the social apostolate comes in. Janssens saw that very clearly. But of course Vatican II came at the same time and gave that an extra push.

Indeed, Jean-Yves Calvez notes that it was Janssens's burning desire to promote social justice causes by establishing centres for social research and social action in every province of the Society and that at the time of his death there were twenty such centres in existence.[78] The consequences of Vatican II and the implementation of its directives, however, lay with the new General (the Society's twenty-eighth) appointed in the final days of the Council, Basque-born Pedro Arrupe. In fact, Arrupe was perfectly fitted to implement the social dimension of the Council. A year before his appointment as General of the Order, Pedro Arrupe had linked atheism with matters of social justice. In an interview with *El Correo Espagnol* he explained that "The battle against atheism is identical in part with the battle against poverty which was one of the causes of the mass exodus of the working classes from the Church."[79]

The cause of justice and faith quite naturally became a characteristic of Arrupe's public profile. In a presentation to the Secretary General of the United Nations, for example, he linked the Jesuits' cause with that of the U.N.:

> May I, as head of the Society of Jesus, identify myself with that same faith and hope in you and in what your organization is doing. For we Jesuits, relatively few [their numbers peaked at 36,038 in 1965] but active in five continents, are pledged to work with right-minded men of all creeds and none, for a more truly human society. World justice and peace, a sense of family and of joint effort among the nations: these are United Nations ideals to which many good men today devote the best of their lives. And these ideals take top priority among Jesuit aims and objectives.[80]

From Vatican II to the New Society

Arrupe's concept of the role of the postconciliar Society was to reach its fulfilment in the 32nd General Congregation of the Society that met in Rome from December 2, 1974 to March 7, 1975.

The most controversial and the most definitive elements of the

32nd General Congregation relate to Decree Four, which was edited by and large by Jesuits from Canada and northern Europe. Decree Four states in part:

> 2. The mission of the Society of Jesus today is the service of faith, of which the promotion of justice is an absolute requirement. For reconciliation with God demands the reconciliation of people with one another.
> 3. In one form or another, this has always been the mission of the Society; but it gains new meaning and urgency in the light of the needs and aspirations of the men and women of our time, and it is in that light that we examine it anew. . . .
> 11. In short, our mission today is to preach Jesus Christ and to make Him known in such a way that all men and women are able to recognize Him whose delight, from the beginning, has been to be with the sons of men and to take an active part in their history.

Christ's active role in the history of humankind is the theoretical basis for the application of the Gospel to modern social problems, it is the basis for liberation theology, and it is the principle that has caused the spilling of Jesuit blood in numerous countries around the globe. It is also the basis for the care of souls so central to Ignatius's view of the Society, which was and is a pressing issue both for the defenders and the critics of today's Jesuits since the Second Vatican Council decree on religious life, *Perfectae caritatis,* defined the renewal of religious orders and congregations in terms of their founding intention, their founding charisms. The Council fathers prescribed the procedure: "The appropriate renewal of religious life involves two simultaneous processes: (1) a continuous return to the sources of all Christian life and to the original inspiration behind a given community and (2) an adjustment of the community to the changed conditions of the times."[81] The implementation of the service of faith and the promotion of justice was shaped in these lights and has had a profound effect on every aspect of the Society's life. It is at heart an Ignatian vision of contemplation in action, a vision that was not always welcome in his day and has not always been welcome historically, either within the Society or without. Peter Rawlinson's

The Jesuit Factor and Malachi Martin's *Jesuits: The Society of Jesus and the Betrayal of the Roman Catholic Church* record the disapproval of a distinguished commentator and an ex-Jesuit, respectively. Jesuit priest Joseph Fessio is also clear where he stands on the question—and Pedro Arrupe is no hero of Joseph Fessio.

> I think that there had to be changes in the Society. I don't think the Society of the 1950s and 1960s was entirely where it should have been. However, I think it is significant that every single change that you can document in the Society since 1965 has been a change for greater ease or greater comfort. At least that fact should raise a little suspicion. I don't necessarily believe that if it's hard it's holy, but still there was a sense of discipline, there was a sense of community, there was a sense of order in one's life that I think has very much diversity and I think it's a mistake to forget all that. A lot of the criticism that you find of Jesuits you will find in places like James Hitchcock's work, for he knows the Society and he did his work entirely on the evidence from published sources on the Society's position, especially on social issues. Basically, he showed that the positions taken by Jesuits were almost always positions that represented the liberal wing of the U.S. Democratic Party. He mentioned situations where I think Jesuits opposed papal teaching and the papal magisterium. I think that we have really seriously diluted the sense of a corporate, communitarian prayer life in the Society of Jesus—in the West for sure and maybe elsewhere as well. I don't think those changes are good. Community life is at the root of Jesuit life. If you strike at the root of that you are really striking at the lifeblood of the Society. Especially the formation process—novitiate, philosophy, theologate—the Society has been consciously trying to form a different kind of Jesuit for the past twenty years.

The Vatican, too, was concerned about the direction the modern Society was taking, but those concerns extend right back to the conclusion of the 31st General Congregation in November 1966. On November 16, Pope Paul VI joined with members of the General Congregation in a closing mass in the Sistine Chapel and presented an address partly in praise of the Society, urging its members to be faithful to the mind of Ignatius. In his address the Pope also worried obliquely about "certain reports and rumours [which have] come to our attention about your Society just as about other religious families as well—and We cannot remain silent on this—have caused us amazement and in some cases, sorrow. What strange and evil suggestions have caused a doubt to arise in certain parts of your widespread Society whether it should continue to be the Society conceived and founded by that holy man, and built on very wise and firm norms?"[82] Although the Pope does not get specific about the reports and rumours that have come to his attention, he does refer to a purported renunciation of spiritual and ascetical customs, a relaxation of discipline and obedience, a slackening of the "intense practice of prayer, a humble and fervent discipline in the interior life, examination of conscience, intimate conversation with Christ, as though the exterior action were enough to keep the soul wise, strong and pure, and as though such activity could achieve by itself a union of the mind with God." Such practices, the Pope assures his audience, are not the preoccupation only of monks; contemplation in action involves both action and contemplation.

For Pope Paul, the matter was a pressing one, especially in light of the theme of his opening address to the assembly on May 7, 1965, in which he outlined the Society's special role in combatting contemporary secular society's most pressing problem, widespread atheism. Having raised his concerns, however, Paul VI is content to set the matter aside, assuring the General Congregation that these apprehensions "were clouds on the horizon, but they have been dispersed in large measure by the conclusions of your Congregation!" For Father General Pedro Arrupe, "The battle against atheism is identical in part with the battle against poverty which was one of the causes of the mass exodus of the working classes from the Church"; article 30 of Decree Four of the 32nd General Congregation would conclude: "The Promotion of Justice is, therefore, an integral part of evangelization." For the Society of Jesus, the clear skies were destined to be purely temporary.

In an unprecedented step so early after the 1966 sessions, Pedro Arrupe felt it necessary to convene another General Congregation, the Society's 32nd, in an effort to chart more certainly the future direction of the Society. For his part, lest the meeting get off to a false start, Paul VI inaugurated the 32nd General Congregation on December 3, 1974, in a lengthy address, which was both an assurance of trust and a word of warning. Faithful to the directives of *Perfectae caritatis*, the Pope reminded the members of the assembly of their charism, as it was embodied in the life of their founder and in their founding documents. But before providing his vision of the Jesuit charism at work in the modern world, he reiterated the concerns with which he had concluded the previous General Congregation:

> Have not the "clouds on the horizon" which we saw in 1966, although "in a great measure dispersed" by the Thirty-first General Congregation, unfortunately continued to cast a certain shadow on the Society? Certain regrettable actions, which would make one doubt whether the man were still a member of the Society, have happened much too frequently and are pointed out to us from many sides, especially from bishops of dioceses; and they exercise a sad influence on the clergy, on other religious, and on the Catholic laity. These facts require from us and from you an expression of sorrow, certainly not for the sake of dwelling on them, but for seeking together the remedies, so that the Society will remain, or return to being, what is needed, what it must be in order to respond to the intention of the Founder and to the expectations of the Church today.[83]

Paul VI kept an eye on the proceedings. On December 3, 1974, he sent a letter through his secretary of state, represented by Jean Cardinal Villot, informing the members of the congregation that there would be no change to the fourth vow of special obedience to the pope "with regard to missions." On February 15, 1975, the Pope sent his own letter assuring the delegates of his resolve in this matter: only those appropriately professed and appropriately prepared would be permitted to profess the fourth vow. There would be no creeping egalitarianism under the banner of *aggiornamento*. Paul VI also had some concerns about "certain orientations and dispositions which are emerging from the work of the General Congregation. Is the Church able to have faith in you here and now, the kind of faith it has always had?"[84] The Pope followed his question with one he had asked two months earlier, "Where are you going?"; and then, to make it clear he was overseeing the meetings, he asked to receive, in advance of any publication, copies of decisions taken or to be taken. In addition, as the 32nd General Congregation ended, the Pope provided a brief statement, both acknowledging and defending his need to intervene in the proceedings, and providing an exhortation to each member of the Society: "Be loyal!"[85]

On May 2, 1975, some two months after the conclusion of the General Congregation, Paul VI responded to the proposed decrees as accepted by the delegates, doing so in order to express his concerns and provide a basis by which the decrees were to be interpreted (lest their import be misunderstood). In the Pope's correspondence, again delivered through the office of Jean Cardinal Villot, he worried that the connection between the promotion of justice and the process of evangelization be understood in accord with the spiritual and supernatural end of the Society; that is, the Society of Jesus must not confuse its priestly and spiritual role with the secular and mundane one more appropriate to the laity. And in the formation of seminarians, theological studies are to be deepened "with the help of speculative reason exercised under the tutelage of St. Thomas. . . ."[86]

The Society was on notice. Nor were its problems to end with the death of Pope Paul VI in August 1978. When Albino Cardinal Luciani of Venice was elected to succeed Paul VI on August 26, 1978, and assumed the name John Paul I, he prepared his own letter of caution, which he intended to deliver to the Society on September 30, 1978, when Jesuit delegates were scheduled to gather in assembly. John Paul I's unexpected death the evening before his anticipated presentation to the Society did not silence his message. Indeed, Karol Wojtyla, who became John Paul II, the new bishop of Rome, on October 16, 1978, proved an even more aggressive critic of the Society than either of his two immediate predecessors. Chastened by his experiences of communist Poland, John Paul II was suspicious of any accommodation with Marxism and, consequently, was chary of liberation theology and its Jesuit advocates in Latin America.

Advancing in years and no doubt wearied by the fray, Arrupe began to contemplate retirement. In 1980 he made his wishes known. John Paul II asked for time to consider the matter, but within days he fell wounded in the Vatican, victim of a would-be assassin's bullet; then, on August 7, 1981, Arrupe suffered a stroke at Leonardo da Vinci airport on his return from a trip to the Orient. Weakened by his stroke, Arrupe was too ill to shoulder the burdens of office, and on October 6, 1981, the Pope intervened personally to appoint long-time Jesuit confessor to popes Paolo Dezza as his personal delegate to administer the affairs of the Society, and Jesuit priest Giuseppe Pittau as Dezza's deputy. This formal interregnum pertained until September 13, 1983, when the 33rd General Congregation elected a 54-year-old Dutchman, Peter-Hans Kolvenbach, as the Society's 29th Father General.

John Paul II's direct intervention into the administrative affairs of the Society was unprecedented. Some of its members thought of resigning, others urged calm and recalled the Society's traditional obedience to the pope. Not surprisingly, various Jesuits remember the events in their own private ways.

Ted Hyland, a member of the Jesuit team at the Centre for Social Faith and Justice in Toronto, equates the papal intervention with church politics and human differences.

> It's clear that there was a breakdown in trust and communication between our curia, Father Arrupe, and the Vatican. I see part of it as just the political situation and that kind of internal politics within the church. To be quite honest, I don't know what the basis was for this distrust. I've heard one member of the Society—an elderly Jesuit who knew Father Arrupe—who would say that one of the reasons why the Vatican was unhappy with Father Arrupe is that they felt he didn't exercise enough control over Jesuits and they felt that Jesuits were getting out of hand and that he was either unable or unwilling to come in and lay down the law. My own reading is that Father Arrupe—and I think that's why he evokes such affection —is that he trusted the Jesuits. There was his trust and his belief. I don't think it was naive but there was this sense about him. . . . I met him once when he was in the infirmary. We didn't have a conversation or anything like that, but what came through then as it does also in his writings is this man of tremendous joy and conviction and belief in people. How could you not respond to that? That's infectious. I don't know why the Vatican didn't trust him to be quite honest.

Giuseppe Pittau looks back on the early '80s and, having been close to the eye of the storm, recalls that as events unfolded in Rome the Society responded with characteristic dedication:

> It was not a problem only of the Society of Jesus; it was, let's say, after the moment of general crisis. After a general council, an ecumenical council, new orientations, new visions, new theologies, interpretations of ecclesiology, and so on, had arisen and that is natural. There was really a moment of great discussion, of great vitality, of great creativity, and people who are asked to work in research, to work in all parts of the world, that they may have different ideas I think is natural and is very good for the church. The only thing, and this I feel was the reason why the Holy Father wanted to intervene in the government of the Society, was that there should be a moment of reflection. Sixteen years after the Council, he wanted a moment of reflection, and before electing the new general, he was saying, "Please reflect on these past experiences." He did not want to stop the creativity, the research, and so on, but probably by talking to the Society of Jesus he wanted to talk also to all the other religious orders and congregations. He probably wanted to say: "Experimentation is very good, but also, please, do reflect whether all those experimentations are according to your charism and are according to the general orientations of the church." And Pope John Paul II saw that really he had a body of obedient people, because when he intervened and many people were doubting whether the Jesuits would obey him or not, then he saw that everybody did obey. So, after only a few months, he gave us practically a clean sign, the green light to start the preparations for the General Congregation at which Father Kolvenbach was elected.
>
> It was a moment of reflection. The Holy Father wanted us to stop a little bit—not stop the apostolic work, but reflect. I think it was a positive experience. Many people felt it with great pain, but after all we came out of this experience stronger, and I think more ready to serve the church.

As for Peter-Hans Kolvenbach, he has walked masterfully through the Vatican minefields. There was, for example, the sensitive matter of Fernando Cardenal, the Jesuit priest and member of Nicaragua's Sandinista government, brother of Ernesto Cardenal (the Sandinista Minister of Culture whom John Paul II publicly chastised with a waving magisterial finger), and the individual responsible for the celebrated literacy programme central to the Sandinistas' social policy. Rome wanted him removed. Kolvenbach complied, but at the same time he wrote a letter of explanation and exoneration to Fernando's mother. Fernando understood. The Society understood. John Paul II was satisfied.

In the same vein, Kolvenbach's published interviews with Renzo Giacomelli reflect the social faith and justice perspectives both of Pedro Arrupe and the 32nd General Congregation. He approaches issues optimistically ("From Ignatius, I've learned to take a positive view of whatever goes on in the Church"),[87] diplomatically but with candour, and with philosophical precision: liberation theology, yes; but a theology based on committing oneself to changing conditions of abject poverty "for the Gospel's sake."[88] Kolvenbach seems to have brought the Society into line in a way that is satisfying most of the Companions of Jesus and Pope John Paul II. No small achievement. Reflecting on the 33rd General Congregation that elected him and reaffirmed the general principles of General Congregation 32, but whose delegates also confessed, "We are not unaware that recently our fidelity under certain circumstances has not been perfect and has caused concern to those who exercise pastoral office,"[89] Kolvenbach observed:

> I am in a position to declare that the first result of the General Congregation, that is to say, the return to normal government, thanks to the fundamental unity of the delegates (which some people deemed problematic, if not impossible) has been received favourably by the whole Society. This result put an end to a period of doubts and anxieties; it restored faith in the Society as an apostolic body, constantly able to rediscover its Ignatian charism and respond to the appeals of the Holy See and of our times; capable too of absorbing in all its vastness

> the spiritual heritage of the most recent General Congregations and of Father Arrupe.[90]

This is no small accomplishment for a Society that embraces such divergent individuals as Jon Sobrino, Dean Brackley, Daniel Berrigan, Robert Drinan, Joe Fessio, Joseph O'Hare, Walter Ong, Jim Webb, and some 24,000 other voices, 24,000 other personalities. For, ultimately, the Society is the lived expression of the people who embody its charism in their service of others—their "care of souls," as Ignatius called it.

11

Jesuit as Spiritual Director

Law professor and author Robert Drinan knows what it means to be a Jesuit. He has been one for most of his life. And he knows, like every other Jesuit, that the defining mark, the true signature of the Companion of Jesus, can be found in that enchiridion—spiritual handbook, if you like—written by the founder of the Order himself: *The Spiritual Exercises of St. Ignatius Loyola.*

> It is remarkable that they have the power to guide you, almost like the *Imitation of Christ*. You pick it up at any point and you find out what you need to know at that very moment. The *Spiritual Exercises* gives you the foundation, but I think that, like St. Ignatius himself, we need to move beyond the basics. He was a mystic for most of his life, his spirituality deepened as he matured, and I think that you can say that for most Jesuits. They deepen their own spiritual lives by going back to the things of Ignatius, to the first thirty-day retreat, and then to the second thirty-day retreat that we do during our tertianship. The concepts of the *Spiritual Exercises* have a way of getting into your soul in such a manner that you may not be able to articulate them, but they are there—real, pervasive and determinative.

The guide, initially conceived by Ignatius as a record of his own spiritual transformation, abounds with spiritual, mystical, psychological, and pastoral insights. They are the key to Ignatius:

> The exercises can be called the school of prayer created for, and taught by, the Society of Jesus. Ignatius composed them as a manual for the person giving them. They are to be experienced, not read or studied, by the one making them.[1]

To understand something of the Jesuit mystique one must appreciate the role the *Exercises* has played, not only in the life of its originator, but in the life of the Society itself. As Jack Costello, President of Regis College, Toronto School of Theology, observes:

> The *Spiritual Exercises* is at the heart of Jesuit spirituality because it deals with life as a journey, as a journey of transformation in relation to the movement of history. It's not simply an internal conversion, but an internal conversion in relation to what God is doing in the world. Essentially, it raises the question: "Can you dig it"? Can you put yourself on the side of this great thing that is happening in the world despite the horrors, despite the obvious sign that there is as much shadow as there is light? Can you be on the side of light and yet share in the experience of the shadow?
>
> There is a big difference between the Enlightenment maxim that says that if we don't do it it won't get done—and there is a great deal of Jesuit energy that goes into that kind of endeavour—and the more radical view of God, the view one finds in the *Exercises*, which argues that God is already doing it, that our first job is to be at God's side helping to realize the divine intention with everything we have by way of tools, intelligence, and human spirit.

The God of the *Exercises* is a God to be experienced, not conceptualized, a God to be touched not etherealized. In a characteristically Jesuit-like approach to finding God in all things, spiritual father Gerard W. Hughes delineates three competing spiritualities that he whimsically identifies as aerosol can spirituality, goretex anorak spirituality, and golf course spirituality. Having dispensed with the first two as inadequate, escapist, and self-occupied, he advances the case for golf course spirituality on the grounds that it is firmly rooted in the principle of "keeping your head down," of playing from your heart, your centre point. Acting on the advice of his golf-expert nephew, Hughes comes to appreciate the spiritually sound counsel that your hands must be aligned with your heart, your swing with the still point of your body. He concludes that

> as the golf course is a reality check on our golf theories and fantasies, so life is the reality check on our spirituality. Aerosol spirituality avoids reality checks and goretex spirituality concentrates on playing out of bunkers, neglecting other aspects of the game. Golf spirituality finds God in every event.[2]

Finding God in every event, in all things, requires the operating conviction that God is wilfully inserted into human history, that this vital, energetic, engaging God is not indifferent to struggling humanity. The God of Ignatius, the God who can be found in all things

> is at once the God of our hearts and our intimacies as well as the God of our history and the histories of other peoples. . . finding God in all things means caring for justice, and acting on behalf of those who are not being permitted to flourish as personal images and likenesses of God. . . finding God in all things sees that every effort to behave truly is cutting a new path: it is a walking on water, a giving over of ourselves in faith and a discovering of the implications only much later.[3]

The spirituality of Ignatius of Loyola, then, is a pragmatic and apostolic spirituality. It is, in the words of the renowned Jesuit spiritual master John English,

> a spirituality of choice at the level of faith, at the same time as it is a spirituality of response, and it can be distinguished between its particularly Jesuit face and its more universal Ignatian face. Jesuit spirituality has a more communal and institutional dimension to it with a specific emphasis on obedience and decision making whereas Ignatian spirituality applies to everybody.

It is not just Jesuits who can lay claim to the wisdom of the *Exercises*. This spiritual handbook is universal in its appeal and accessible to all.

And the *Exercises* bears the unmistakeable sign of the courtier-cum-pilgrim, of the man who was crippled at the Battle of Pamplona in

1521 and who subsequently endured a long and utterly levelling convalescence; it bears the unmistakeable sign of a man who remade himself in the image of the trinitarian God. While his body healed with his enforced rest in the ancestral home at Loyola, his restless spirit was fired by his reading of the lives of the saints, heroic figures who lived with an intensity the young hidalgo could scarcely imagine.

Ignatius emerged from his convalescence in February 1522, nine months after his incapacitation. He was 30 years of age. He had decided to switch loyalties from serving his temporal lord, the Duke of Navarre, to serving his Eternal Lord, Jesus of Nazareth. He felt a deep sense of his own unworthiness and of the emptiness of his life. He resolved to adopt a strict vegetarian diet, to fast rigorously, to do penance, and to flagellate himself in order to subdue the stirrings of the flesh. Years later, as we have seen, he lamented the folly of weakening the body to serve the soul and regretted the lasting damage he had done to himself with his youthful fanaticism. He did everything he could to counsel his fellow Companions against his own zealous severities regarding the flesh.

Ignatius set out on pilgrimage to the famous Benedictine monastery of Montserrat, home of the Black Madonna (a dark brown statue of the Virgin Mary considered by the faithful to be miraculous). At this reformist monastery, known for its austerities and the purity of its rule, he sought the protection of Our Lady of Montserrat and turned his face towards Jerusalem. But before he could commence such a journey, he knew that he would have to strip away the old man in order to put on the new. He divested himself of the rich clothes of the gentleman and donned the rough sackcloth of the palmer. He kept vigil in the Chapel of Our Lady and confessed the sins of his life. But now he lay down his sword not for his Lady Love but for the Virgin. The knight had irrevocably shifted his allegiance.

Four days after his arrival at Montserrat, he departed for Manresa. He put up in the little hospital of Santa Lucia just outside the town, begging for food and earning his bed by assisting in the hospital. In time he moved into a solitary cell attached to the Dominican priory and divided his time between living there and in a cave overlooking the valley of the Cardoner River. The time he spent in Manresa—March 1522 until February 1523—were the most important months in his life. The knight had become a hermit. And it was here on the banks of the Cardoner that he had a rare and overwhelming illumination:

> He was once on his way, out of devotion, to a church a little more than a mile from Manresa, which I think was called Saint Paul. The road followed the path of the river and he was taken up with his devotions; he sat down for a while facing the river flowing far below him. As he sat there the eyes of his understanding were opened and though he saw no vision he understood and perceived many things, numerous spiritual things as well as matters touching on faith and learning, and this was with an elucidation so bright that all these things seemed new to him. He cannot expound in detail what he then understood, for they were many things, but he can state that he received such a lucidity in understanding that during the course of his entire life—now having passed his sixty-second year—if he were to gather all the helps he received from God and everything he knew, and add them together, he does not think they would add up to all that he received on that one occasion.[4]

Out of what Ignatius received by the Cardoner River would come his classic contribution to the spiritual life, his *Spiritual Exercises.* Although he wrote the rudiments of the *Exercises* during his Manresa months, he continued to add to and refine it until it was first published in 1548. What is critical in the Manresa experience—the absolute uprooting of identity and the subsequent reconstitution of the self—was to prove fundamental in shaping Ignatius's perception of the radical nature of authentic conversion and the reorientation or new life commitment necessitated by such a conversion. Jesuit psychiatrist and biographer of Ignatius W. W. Meissner writes of this core experience:

> The reshaping of identity that the pilgrim sought in the cave of Manresa was distilled into the practices of the *Spiritual Exercises.* He proposed to his followers and to those whom he directed in the *Exercises* the same end—a restructuring of the self, of one's sense of self, one's identity, in terms of total commitment to God's will and to unstinting enlisting in His service. The entire

> corpus of the *Exercises* is organized and directed to this end. It proposes nothing less than a restructuring of one's life, one's ideals and values, one's goals and hopes, and the commitment of that life to the service of the King of Kings.[5]

The *Spiritual Exercises* define Jesuit identity. They bear the distinct stamp of Ignatius's own personality: his acute introspectiveness; his preference for an orderly and programmed way of experiencing and understanding God (in that order); his creative and unrestricted use of all that is material, of all that is human, in his relentless pursuit of the Divine Majesty.

Ignatius gave the *Exercises* on numerous occasions to countless women and men; all future Companions were to make the Exercises, and they in turn were obliged to direct others in making them; all Jesuit novices were required to make the full thirty-day retreat, and since 1616 all Jesuit priests have repeated the *Exercises* during the period known as their tertianship, the third year of probation, the *tertius alius annus* following their studies and ordination. In short, *The Spiritual Exercises* is the common and essential component to be found in Jesuit training and identity.

Original though it is, *The Spiritual Exercises* draws upon what precedes it; it did not pop up in Ignatius's mind fully conceived *in vacuo*. His own nascent spirituality was greatly shaped by what was known as the *devotio moderna*, a school of spirituality that emphasized the practical over the abstract. In addition, some scholars argue, Ignatius was influenced by the Franciscan appeal to evangelical simplicity and radical Gospel witness. His genius was to combine, in a unique way, the method of the *devotio moderna* with the content of the Franciscan tradition.[6]

If the pristine mystical insights of *The Spiritual Exercises*—in its unpublished and ad hoc retreat format—caused not a little consternation to the learned divines and Fathers Inquisitor during Ignatius's post-Manresa and pre-Paris phase, by the time Pope Paul III approved the book in 1548, Ignatius had managed to meld the new with the old, to incorporate the idiosyncratic and original with the conventional and orthodox:

> Dr. Bartolomeo Torres, a most able defender of the Spiritual Exercises, observed in 1544 that St. Ignatius "speaks the same

> language as the philosophers, the saints, and the Scriptures"; that the content of the Spiritual Exercises is as old as Christianity itself.[7]

Ignatius would not have been unhappy with such a judgement. He was not interested, in spite of the suspicions of the Inquisition, in the novel or the heterodox. He was satisfied to be a part of the Catholic tradition; not for him the discontinuity generated by a radical eruption or revolutionary innovation. Whether during his years as an itinerant preacher, as a theology student, or later as the General of the Society, Ignatius grounded his mystical insights and spiritual doctrine firmly in the soil of his Christology:

> The Ignatius who so loved to speak of "all things on the circumference of the earth" was the same Ignatius who wrote in one of his letters: "One must love Christ in place of all things." Ignatius loved the world in Christ because it had been lifted "above" by Christ the Mediator. . . [As Ignatius notes] "The more taste a man finds for Jesus Christ, the more distaste he will find for all which is not Christ."[8]

And the Christ of Ignatius is the healing Christ, the saving Christ, the suffering Christ, the Christ who is that Divine Majesty the Basque courtier and his companions vowed to serve. Christ is at heart of Ignatius's spirituality; Christ is the centrepiece of the *Exercises*. And yet, as the British Jesuit and lecturer in spirituality David Lonsdale notes, one need not be a Christian to benefit from the *Exercises*.

> This slim book, with its hobbling syntax and almost total absence of literary grace, has been influential for more than 400 years among a small group of mainly Roman Catholic Christians. At present, however, the *Spiritual Exercises* are enjoying an unprecedented revival of interest both within Roman Catholicism and well beyond its boundaries. Anglicans, Methodists, Presbyterians, members of the United Reformed Church, Quakers, Mennonites, honest God-seekers who belong to no church and agnostics are all taking part in growing numbers in courses, retreats and workshops inspired by this book.[9]

Its appeal is wide and universal. But why is this so?

The *Exercises* is not a spiritual treatise nor a major theological tome. There is nothing in it of the controversies of the day, no factual or philosophical rebuttals of the learned opinions of the Reformers, and unlike Ignatius's other writings—*The Spiritual Diary*, the *Constitutions*, the letters, or the *Autobiography*—there is very little in the way of personal disclosure in its pages. It is terse, undecorative, skeletal, and compact. Compendium, program, and teaching aid, the *Exercises* is greater than the sum of its parts. And it is, primarily, to be experienced.

The first section consists of "introductory explanations," which outline the nature and structure of the *Exercises*. Ignatius declares at the very beginning, in the first of these twenty explanations, the meaning and import of the term "spiritual exercises," by which

> we mean every method of examination of conscience, meditation, contemplation, vocal or mental prayer, and other spiritual activities, such as will be mentioned later. For, just as taking a walk, travelling on foot, and running are physical exercises, so is the name of spiritual exercises given to any means of preparing and disposing our soul to rid itself of all its disordered affections and then, after their removal, of seeking and finding God's will in the ordering of our life for the salvation of our soul. [10]

The Exercises are flexible and versatile. They are intended as a dialogue between the one directing and the one making the Exercises (the exercitant), and they are designed as a structured yet malleable framework for nothing less than the very ordering of one's life. After the "introductory explanations" comes the first of four "weeks," designations that are not chronological in nature but rather correspond to the traditional division of the mystical path into the purgative, illuminative, and unitive way. But, before we get to the exercises proper of the First Week, Ignatius presents both the particular and general examination of conscience and, most important of all, the Principle and Foundation.

This section consists of five short paragraphs and yet contains within its startling brevity the essence of the *Exercises*: "to desire and choose only that which is more conducive to the end for which we are created." To attain this goal, the exercitant must cultivate an attitude of "indifference" to all created things in order to pursue without hindrance the trifold purpose of created humanity: "to praise, reverence, and serve God our Lord, and by means of doing this to save their souls."

The exercises or meditations of the First Week—and each meditation conforms, with some variation, to a standard structure (preparatory prayer; two preludes; three main points; a colloquy)—focus on the theme of sin, damnation, and hell. The Ignatian meditation is designed to be experienced and as such works through its use of the "application of the senses" and the "composition of place" to taste, smell, touch, hear, and see the subject matter of the meditation, that is, the sin of Adam and Eve. The meditation affords little in the way of that detachment that defines the purely speculative exercise. The exercitant is inserted into the muck, mire, and misery of sin and its consequences: the murder of love and the crucifixion of divinity. Ignatius grants no respite.

The Second Week has two key meditations that emphasize the *call* to serve Christ: the "Contemplation of the Kingdom of Jesus Christ" and a "Meditation on Two Standards, the One of Christ, Our Supreme Commander and Lord, the Other of Lucifer, the Mortal Enemy of Our Human Nature." These exercises specifically highlight the central question of the "election," by which Ignatius means to focus on one's choice of a particular state of life or on the reformation of one's current state of life. Ignatius outlines at some length several considerations and methods that should be employed in making a right election and reminds all exercitants that "everyone ought to reflect that in all spiritual matters, the more one divests oneself of self-love, self-will, and self-interests, the more progress one will make."

The Third and Fourth Weeks involve the exercitant more fully in the paschal mystery of Jesus's life: his passion, death, and resurrection. The last Week concludes with the "Contemplation to Attain Love," in which Ignatius reminds the exercitant that "love ought to manifest itself more by deeds than words [and that] love consists in a mutual communication between the two persons." Harvey Egan observes that this contemplation

> is a summary of Ignatian spirituality: transforming awareness of God's many gifts that evokes gratitude, reverential love, service, and total self-oblation to God's will. It is the key to finding God in all things, to finding all things in God, and to being with the Trinitarian Christ to serve.[11]

But to authentically serve one must as authentically discern, judge, and choose. In his "Rules for the Discernment of Spirits"—one of several Supplementary Matters following the Fourth Week—Ignatius reveals how astute a psychologist he is. Building on his own mystical experiences, Ignatius urges the exercitant to discern—to recognize and distinguish between the good spirits and the bad—so that through mature self-knowledge one can genuinely grow in wholeness/holiness. Unless one can judge one's own motivations with honesty and clarity, and unless one can penetrate through the carapace of egoism, the capacity to enter deeply into the divine life is seriously curtailed. The exercitant must strip away the consoling veil of self-deception because it is a false consolation.

The Spiritual Exercises is not an arcane collection of unworldly maxims, nor a manual for the gnostic or spiritually elite. It is the product, argues John English, of "a simple lay person with very little education who had this great experience at Manresa." In a sense, it is for simple folk.

> I think that *The Spiritual Exercises* still works because it is a classic work of literature. Like a Shakespearean play it is always being interpreted and then reinterpreted, changing and adjusting to different cultures and times. The key to the *Exercises*, it seems to me, can be found in its internal dynamic of experience, reflection, articulation, and interpretation. For example, when a person gets in touch with her experience, she then reflects on it and tries to discern what it means in terms of her relationship with God. And then she comes and talks to her spiritual director and articulates her understanding of what is happening. The director works with the person to try to understand or interpret that experience. After all, experience is central to the *Exercises*. For a number of years, of course, the *Exercises* was just a book of doctrine to which you went to preach on sin, hell, the mercy of God, and the call of

Christ. You preached it to people, but you didn't really use it as an instrument of experience.

Today, we follow more closely the dynamic of the *Exercises*. In some cases we give the actual text for people to work with and in other instances we select scriptural passages, basic historical experience, whatever. Their own stories sometimes. The way I tend to go is to follow Ignatius's own dynamic. I start with our creaturehood, like he does with the Principle and Foundation, and talk about how I am sustained by God and need to become free of everything that is not God. That helps me to get a sense of a benevolent God who brought me into being and sustains me, a creature, in love. Then, and only then, I move to sin and discover something else about myself and the world. I look at myself, my own disorder, and I reflect on the destructive forces in humanity, in which I participate. And then I discover what forgiveness is, and I get a whole new awareness of God.

Now, this is all by working with a dynamic that brings me from my foundational experience of creaturehood, to that of my brokenness or sinfulness, to my transforming experience of forgiveness, of being forgiven unconditionally. Out of this triadic experience comes a sense of call: "I have to do something."

Now Ignatius leads me as I direct the exercitant to discover Christ. It is all quite experiential and eventually leads to the central question of the Election, or decision-making moment. Every retreatant, exercitant, or client comes with a decision to be made and the director has to help them discover what that decision is.

The spirituality of Ignatius—as crystallized in the *Exercises*—is a spirituality for everyone. It is egalitarian, accessible, and non-esoteric. It is there for the taking, or perhaps more precisely, for the doing. But the doing was really only done for Jesuits and by Jesuits for centuries. Ignatian spirituality was almost exclusively identified with Jesuit spirituality: it was their property. And then a revolution occurred.

Many North American Jesuits did their tertianship in the '50s and '60s under the celebrated retreat master Paul Kennedy at St. Beuno's in Wales. Kennedy was a strong advocate of handling the Exercises on a one-on-one basis. A French Jesuit was doing likewise. And then a Canadian Jesuit began giving one-on-one retreats to Jesuit scholastics at Regis College in Toronto. By the late '60s Jesuit scholastics were getting one-on-one retreats instead of the conventional preached retreats. And it wasn't only Jesuits who were benefiting from the new style. John English was one of those who

> gathered a team together in May 1969 and took about forty religious women through the Exercises and directed each of them individually at the same time. We would have about a half-hour interview with them and each one of the team took about six to eight people, so it was really a full day's work for each of us. This was the first time anywhere where you had a large group doing a personally directed retreat.

The face of Jesuit spirituality had changed. The time for the florescence of Ignatian spirituality had arrived. And still the *Exercises* was at the heart of it. Historian John Padberg notes:

> In text they make up a rather small book; in style they would hardly win any literary prizes. But in the substance of what they hope to do they, more than anything else, have shaped the Society of Jesus and the choice of its works. In the last generation the elements of imagination, discernment in personal prayer and communitarian relevance of the Exercises have again come to the fore after long being in eclipse. In addition, as the Exercises have been recovered in their authenticity in the Society, they have become more widespread within the Catholic Church and have also moved out ecumenically into the larger Christian world. It is today in no way unusual for members of the other Christian Churches to engage in the Exercises, both "making" them and serving as directors for them. In all instances they are meant to lead a man or woman to a deeply personal knowledge of God and God's gifts and to an utterly free choice of how best to love and serve the Lord in return.[12]

Jose M. Fernandes Machado s.j.

In this mural panel, The Principle and Foundation, drawn from his impressive mural on the Spiritual Exercises at the Inazio de Azevedo Novitiate Chapel in Sao Paulo, Brazil, Jose M. Fernandes Machado s.j. provides a stunning visualization of the intense experiences associated with making the Exercises. The Principle and Foundation is the starting point of the *Spiritual Exercises* of Ignatius Loyola. According to Luis de la Palma as quoted in the Ganss edition of *The Spiritual Exercises of Saint Ignatius:* "It is called a **principle** because in it are contained all the conclusions which are later explained and specifically expounded; and it is called a **foundation** because it is the support of the whole edifice of the spiritual life."

D.R. Letson

Father General of the Society of Jesus, Peter-Hans Kolvenbach s.j. with a saintly Companion peering over his shoulder.

Two Jesuits on a camel.

D.R. Letson

The Jesuits' principal church, the Gesù, in the heart of ancient Rome. Ignatius's rooms as reconstructed by Thomas Lucas and the Jesuits' International College stand adjacent to the Gesù and just off to the right of the picture.

A Jesuit missionary baptises an infant in a simple rural ceremony in the parish of Tierralta in Colombia.

D.R. Letson

Margaret Hebblethwaite is an Ignatian spiritual director, author, mother and assistant editor of *The Tablet* of England.

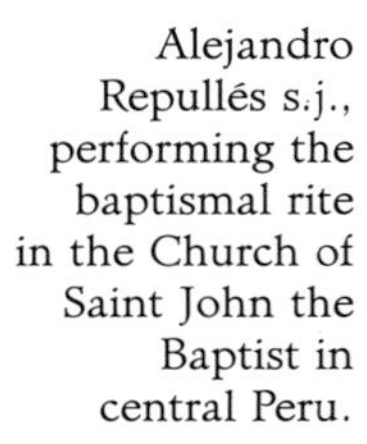

Alejandro Repullés s.j., performing the baptismal rite in the Church of Saint John the Baptist in central Peru.

Robert Allen

(l to r)
President Mary Robinson of Ireland with European provincials Salvat and Harnett.

D.R. Letson

John English s.j., internationally respected retreat master and specialist in Ignatius' Spiritual Exercises.

D.R. Letson

Irish Jesuit and spiritual director Michael Gallagher at the Manresa Centre for Spirituality, Dollymount, Dublin.

D.R. Letson

Michael Campbell-Johnson s.j., with his grandfather's skull at Farm Street in London, England.

A Canadian Jesuit missionary prepares a class for baptism in the sea at Annotto Bay, Jamaica.

D.R. Letson

The authors' translator in El Salvador and Nicaragua, Laetitia Bordes s.h., framed by political graffiti at Despertar in San Salvador.

D.R. Letson

Obdulio Lopez, husband to the murdered housekeeper, Elba Ramos, stands by the roses he planted where the blood of the UCA martyrs ran into the soil.

Margaret Hebblethwaite—writer, lay theologian, mother, editor, and Ignatian spiritual director—is one of those contemporary women who have made "an utterly free choice of how best to love and serve the Lord" and in doing so has brought the relevance of the Spiritual Exercises of Ignatius Loyola into full public prominence.

> I give the Spiritual Exercises of St. Ignatius in what is called the Nineteenth Annotation version, which means that my retreatants or clients make the Exercises in daily life: praying usually for a half-hour or hour each day and seeing me once a week. For the rest of the time, life is normal, being a mother and going to work, etc.

Hebblethwaite had done her first Nineteenth Annotation retreat with onetime Jesuit editor and writer the late Peter Hebblethwaite, the man who would later be her husband. She followed this experience two years later in Rome with a different Nineteenth Annotation retreat under an Indian Jesuit while taking a course on spiritual direction at the Gregorian University. When she and her family returned to Britain she continued her practical training under the general supervision of one Jesuit and one former Jesuit, both of whom provided wisdom and counsel of markedly different but congruent orientations.

So armed, Hebblethwaite began her ministry, steeped in the Exercises:

> One of things that I value most in the Spiritual Exercises is its individual emphasis, because it is not a program that is the same for everyone. It does not force you to fit into a predetermined, univocal mould. I feel that the whole point of spiritual direction in the Ignatian pattern is based on noticing what is happening in the prayer life of the person you are directing and then helping them pay attention to what is going on and responding appropriately.
>
> Another aspect of Ignatian spirituality is its emphasis on bringing a broad range of human qualities to our prayer experience, excluding nothing that can be constructively used. For instance, the imaginative element in the Ignatian tradition is

very important. What a tremendously rich resource there is in this alone.

Almost any kind of prayer can be included in some way or another within Ignatius's scheme. For example, a lot of people today are very keen on breathing awareness, reflecting the current interest in modes of eastern spirituality. You can find this very same awareness in Ignatius's Three Methods of Praying. Or, a lot of people continue to value set prayers, which Ignatius also uses and encourages when helpful. He also encourages a more reasoned way of praying through his use of "points"—meditating on different aspects in relation to an imaginatively reconstructed scene. As for the body, he talks about actually inching—physically—your place of prayer. You may not be in a church but you can still have a few inches of your carpet in which you are consciously entering the presence of God. Ignatius talks quite explicitly about the freedom we can use in our different bodily postures.

I find the Ignatian approach very inclusive, for it is not so much a program or method of prayer as it is a whole approach to helping people learn to pray. In that, it is quite different from any of the other traditions.

It is not her ex-Jesuit spouse, however influential he may have been, who first and formatively instructed her in the ways of Jesuit spirituality. Nor was it the influence of the Jesuits resident at Campion Hall when she was doing her theology degree at Oxford. Her primordial encounter preceded all of these.

My first brush with Jesuits was when I was at school as a teenager and when I had just decided to become an agnostic, which I think in itself is an excellent phase in any adolescent's life. I found my new freedom intellectually challenging, but I also felt the very real insecurity that comes from not having a faith and not knowing if there is any meaning to life. Into this rather desolate period, quite suddenly, three Jesuits walked.

We had a school retreat and my class teacher was none too keen on my making the retreat because she was fearful that I might be a disruptive influence, and not without reason given that I had informed her that I was interested in the retreat

> from the point of view of one engaged in a detached study of the phenomenon of religion, and not as a practitioner. I was allowed to attend the retreat, but only on the condition that I not disturb the others.
>
> It was not the others, however, who were ruffled or disturbed. It was me. I was bowled over by the Holy Spirit within the first couple of hours and it was those three Jesuits who mediated that profound and personally determinative spiritual experience.

As critical as this adolescent experience was, it did not stamp her with the seal of Ignatian spirituality per se. That would come later, much later in fact, after Oxford and after the arrival of the second of her three children. It was all uncharted turf: there was very little in the way of seminars and courses for lay people interested in Ignatian spiritual direction; the nonclerics who were being trained as Ignatian directors included laymen and laywomen in consecrated life and not unprofessed, uncloistered laywomen; and the whole enterprise of Ignatian direction itself was still seen as Jesuit property and fiercely guarded as such. But Hebblethwaite persisted, finding her own way and convinced that in that she was completely faithful to Ignatius. She began where she was, or in other words she discovered that the locus of her spirituality was to be found in the very context of her day-to-day life as mother, fledgling writer, and wife. And in that, too, she was faithful to Ignatius.

> My spiritual life can be found in the thick of family life. Not only have I been prevented by the sheer responsibility of raising a family from taking the thirty-day retreat ("long retreat"), for many years I couldn't even make the eight-day version ("short retreat"), because when you are breast feeding you simply can't. But I have since taken the eight-day retreat several times, and because they are so precious a school of spiritual nourishment and self-discovery I have thrown myself into them with tremendous enthusiasm.

But, as Hebblethwaite is at pains to point out, it isn't the retreat experiences, as valuable and enlightening as they may be, that constitute the primary focus of Ignatian spirituality.

> As a layperson, proud of the freedom and variety of the lay life, I have always maintained Ignatian spirituality is the ideal approach for us, because everything is individually tailored, and there is no fitting square pegs into round holes. . . . The Ignatian school of prayer is rich and comprehensive because it teaches not so much by providing a method as by helping people notice what the Spirit is doing in them, because the ways by which the Spirit works are as manifold as creation itself. There is nothing God has made that cannot be used to speak to us of God and lead us to God; if we want to explore the length and the breadth, the depth and height of God's love, then we must look all around us, for creation is full of it. . . . Instead of propounding sublime ideals of what prayer is, so that you feel inadequate and do not know where to begin, Ignatian spirituality very practically tells you what to do. And when you have done it, it tells you what to do next. And if the suggestion does not feel right, but something else does, then it tells you to follow the something else, because it is not Ignatius who is running your prayer life but God.[13]

God is to be found in the practical and the mundane—the geography of ordinary life—and is not confined to sublime locales, elitist manuals, and extraordinary feats of self-discipline or ascesis.

> The idea of finding God in all things runs through all my work as mother, writer, and spouse. It is the principle that undergirds my early book *Motherhood and God* in which I took my experience of being a mother stage by stage—pregnancy, birthing, child at the breast, toddlers, etc.—and at each stage tried to show how one can find God. Such a strategy, which is a very Ignatian thing to do, upset my publisher at the time because he argued that you *either* write a book on prayer *or* write a book about washing nappies. But I insisted that the 50/50 split—personal experience and religious reflection—was authentically Ignatian. I won.

To hear God speak to us through experience—our common and often banal experience of daily living—requires attention, a concentrated and prayerful focus that is immeasurably helped by Ignatius's use of the imaginative faculty. For instance, when meditating on a biblical text Ignatius invites us to create a visual portrait—an imaginative scenario that he calls the *compositio loci* or composition of place—that allows us to enter more concretely into the meaning of the text. In this way, Ignatius bypasses the restricting consequences of abstract reasoning and allows ordinary folk to touch the truth.

> I think that we do touch truth through our imagination. I always explain to people that it's rather like a painting. We can have a dozen different paintings of the Last Supper or of the Nativity of Jesus with all kinds of caves, stables, rooms, and dining tables, and on one level they all appear to be contradicting each other, but on another level it's only when we have all these concrete details that we can reach out and touch the fundamental truth that runs through them all. That is why we learn far more from a novel about love than from a speculative philosophical paper. The same is true about the imaginative approach of Ignatius. By having us actually become present at a scene, say the Last Supper, in a way in which perhaps all the details may be completely wrong doesn't matter because the very fact that we have some details—sitting on a chair, touching a table, eating and drinking the food, feeling and hearing the quality of air in the room—allows us to become present to Christ, and that presence is far deeper than all the details which we have employed and which have helped to focus our attention.

Whatever the context—catechist in a youth custody centre, mother of three children, assistant editor of an international weekly, or Ignatian spiritual director—Hebblethwaite seeks God in all things and, in conformity with the Contemplation to Attain Love,

> will consider how God dwells in creatures; in the elements, giving them existence; in the plants, giving them life; in the animals, giving them sensation; in human beings, giving them intelligence; and finally, how in this way he dwells also in myself, giving me existence, life, sensation, and intelligence; and even further, making me his temple, since I am created as a likeness and image of the Divine Majesty.[14]

It is unlikely that Ignatius conceived of women as major consumers, if you like, of the *Exercises*. And yet, following the explosion of interest in Ignatian spirituality after the Second Vatican Council, women like Margaret Hebblethwaite have become recognized interpreters and commentators on the universal applicability of the Spiritual Exercises.

This does not mean, however, that the more traditional Jesuit-directed retreat has become an antediluvian lizard. There are still Jesuits engaged in retreat-giving, although they too have adjusted to the new, or better yet rediscovered, emphasis on the one-to-one retreat. Jesuits like Michael Gallagher of Ireland celebrate the restored one-to-one retreat experience as a recovery of the authentic emphasis Ignatius himself intended.

> The one-to-one dimension of the Spiritual Exercises is a very high point in recent retreat developments because we now take a person where he is and not where he should be and bring him along on his own spiritual journey at his own pace and on his own level. This new/old emphasis has simply transformed people's lives and is very dissimilar to the old-fashioned priest-centered retreat which had the net result of rendering the retreatants as passive recipients of the retreat master's spiritual wisdom.

The Jesuit retreat has such a special meaning for Gallagher because it was by means of a retreat at the now-designated Manresa Centre for Spirituality in Dublin that he first encountered, at a meaningful level, the invitation to live his life as a Jesuit. Twenty-six years of age, increasingly restive in his occupation as a bookkeeper, and eager to find some direction in his life, Gallagher went on retreat at Manresa. The experience unsettled him. He found himself attracted to the *idea* of being a Jesuit, but not to the *fact*. He tried to put the thought out of his head by raising the prospect of his becoming a Jesuit with one of the resident Fathers, confident that the priest would tell him that his age was an insuperable barrier. The average entry age for a Jesuit seminarian at the time—pre-Vatican Council—was 17 or 18. Gallagher calculated that the Jesuit would give him an unequivocal "no." On the contrary, the priest told him that he was not too old and that he should think about it. And so he did, with the greatest reluctance. But a year later he returned and has remained in the Society since.

Throughout most of his priestly life Gallagher has been involved in retreat work and student chaplaincy; he understands something of how to read the human heart. He knows from his long and varied retreat experiences that one has to measure oneself, find discipline in the many hours of careful listening, devise periods of rest to alternate with periods of intense counselling, intersperse physical with mental activity, the pedestrian with the heroic. Gallagher has stretched the human capability to attend in prayer and sympathy to the struggles and turmoil of others and he entertains no illusions about the costs such intensity can exact. The retreat-giver needs also to go on retreat, to replenish his emotional and spiritual resources. And to that end, Jesuits engaged in retreat work need to experiment.

> Jesuit retreat directors here at Manresa have experimented in recent years with retreats that have a clear social justice component. This is in keeping with the efforts of Father General Pedro Arrupe to link justice with faith in all Jesuit enterprises. We have even had such justice-focused retreats for the Jesuit directors at Manresa. For instance, we were each given a small amount of money, something like two pounds, and told to go to a poor area of Dublin, walk around it, find lunch with our pittance, and then come back at night and share our experiences. Ignatius himself was full of such inventive experimentation. The thirty-day retreat in the novitiate is an experiment, going on a pilgrimage (a conventionally Ignatian thing to do) is an experiment, and choosing to live with the poor as a preferential option is an experiment—noble, a little mad, and redemptive.

Having directed scores of people on thirty-day, eight-day, and weekend retreats, Gallagher is now involved in the training of future spiritual directors in the Ignatian tradition. He takes this task very seriously.

> Spiritual directors, like psychoanalysts, need to taste the goods they proffer for sale. Just as a good psychoanalyst needs to be psychoanalyzed, a good spiritual director must undertake an

intense immersion in the Exercises, must at some point have been directed herself. The director must have a certain reflective self-knowledge, a deep capacity for empathy, a working knowledge of the scriptures and human psychology, and very importantly, an ability to discern when a client or retreatant needs psychological as opposed to spiritual counselling.

Although for centuries retreat-giving has been an almost exclusively clerical preserve, Gallagher knows that Ignatius gave the Exercises as a layman—in spite of his difficulties with the Inquisition—and that non-Jesuits properly schooled in the Ignatian tradition can continue, and indeed generously expand, the work of individually centred retreats, even in the face of a decline in Jesuit ranks if not because of such a decline. Ignatius and his Exercises have become common property.

They are clearly not, however, to everyone's taste. In spite of the central place of the Spiritual Exercises in the history of Christian spirituality, the unparalleled influence of Jesuit confessors, directors, and confidants on the elites of society, and the critical role of Jesuit spirituality on scores of male and female religious congregations, alternative spiritualities have proven variously attractive or antagonistic. Jesuit spirituality is sometimes seen as too militaristic, too regimented, too this-worldly, and too masculine.

Margaret Brennan is professor emerita of pastoral theology at Regis College in Toronto and former vice president of this Jesuit graduate institution. She has worked with Jesuits for years and has a deep respect for their charism and history. Her years at Regis have been "among the most meaningful of my life. I have been deeply challenged and influenced personally by Ignatian spirituality."

However, I find it ironic that at the same time that there is a debate about the *Exercises* being too geared toward a male type of discipleship, too oriented toward a male perception of governance and leadership, that there are more women doing the Spiritual Exercises and more women directing the Exercises than there are men. The attraction many women feel toward Ignatian spirituality, however, does not vitiate the need for a severe and on-going feminist critique of Jesuit structures and mentalities.

> Jesuits know who they are. They have worked out the best way, for them, to operate and to those of us who assist them in their various apostolates their notion of consensus, of collaboration, can be quite exclusivist, if not in intention certainly in effect. When you work with them you have to go in their door. And this is surprising in some ways because in spite of their being the great teachers of discernment, of collegial and corporate decision-making, they can often opt more for *Roberts Rules of Order* than the *Exercises*.
>
> They are more inclined to act out of the head than the heart, and as a consequence they often read the *Exercises* in a cerebral way carefully keeping their feelings at bay.

Sister Laetitia Bordes is a U.S. member of the international congregation of religious women known as the Society of Helpers. Like Margaret Brennan, Bordes has a long association with the Jesuits, but unlike Brennan it is not so much through their educational enterprises—although she has studied theology at two Jesuit institutions, Boston College and the University of San Francisco—but rather through her social involvement with Salvadoran and Nicaraguan Jesuits. She serves as a translator and as the coordinator of the El Salvador Peace Education seminars struggling to bring justice to the poor, monitoring human rights abuses, and conscientizing (consciousness-raising) the illiterate. For Bordes there are Jesuits and then there are Jesuits.

> The Jesuits had a very great influence on the founding of our congregation because our foundress had a Jesuit spiritual director. She decided on the Ignatian rules and constitutions because she felt that her apostolic community would be engaged in the same thing as the Jesuits: to be free to be at the service of other people and to help in all manner of good, and not semi-cloistered like monks or friars bound to sing the Divine Office on a daily and regular basis.
>
> Some of the traditions that we adopted from the Jesuits—holding the napkin a certain way during the *benedicite* or blessing in refectory—had nothing to do with being a woman religious, but the bigger legacy that we received was the Spiritual Exercises, although I prefer Franciscan humility to Jesuit

> rigidity. Still, Jesuit spirituality, properly interpreted, produces a level of commitment which is both admirable and very beautiful. Although I find many U.S. Jesuits arrogant and lacking the *joie de vivre* of the Franciscans, the Jesuits I have come to know in El Salvador are very intelligent and capable men who happen also to be genuinely humble. With and in them I touch Ignatius.

For Hebblethwaite, Brennan, and Bordes, Ignatian spirituality, either within or outside an explicit Jesuit context, can be liberative, transformative, and inclusive. The *Exercises*, sensitively interpreted, is more visceral than cerebral, and more inclined to consensus than hierarchical dictat.

As the supreme embodiment of Ignatian spiritual understanding, the *Exercises* can be adapted to any culture, and inserted with flexible imagination into any social context when stripped of its eurocentric accretions. The inculturation of the Spiritual Exercises harkens back not only to Renaissance missionaries such as Ricci and De Nobili in China and India, respectively, and to the Iberian Jesuits experimenting with their brilliant but ill-fated "reductions" in the New World in the eighteenth century, but also to the work of the North American Martyrs, as they are called, the Jesuit priests, brothers, and companions slain in 1649: Jean de Brébeuf, Isaac Jogues, Gabriel Lalement, Antoine Daniel, Charles Garnier, Noël Chabanel, René Goupil, and Jean de la Lande.

On May 22, 1611, fifty-five years after the death of Ignatius, the first Jesuits, Pierre Biard and Ennemond Massé, set foot at Port Royal on what is now the north shore of Nova Scotia's Annapolis Basin. Known to the natives as the Mukedekuniek, or the Blackrobes, because of their black cassock or soutane, they had their work cut out for them. They went first to the Micmacs, then to the Montagnais, and then to the Algonquins, bringing with them the faith of Catholic Europe.

In 1639 they built their "house of prayer and home of peace" at Ste. Marie-among-the-Hurons. It was here, on the shores of Lake Huron, where they attempted, with heroic ambition, to establish a community where whites and aboriginal peoples could live in concord, each fed by the traditions of the other and all under the banner of the Gospel and *ad majorem dei gloriam*. But the Huron mission failed. Although the Blackrobes brought their learning, skills, and theology to New France, they also brought smallpox, measles, and other European diseases that ravaged the native tribes, to say nothing of the traders and schemers who took unfair advantage of their influence. Because they were supported by the Crown, they were seen as partners in the Huron-France alliance against the British. As such, the Jesuits were particularly vulnerable to the incursions into Huron territory of the powerful Five Nations Iroquois Confederacy. The Jesuits chose, in a sense, to align themselves with the losing side.

In 1649 Ste. Marie and other Jesuit missions were attacked by the Iroquois, and many of the Hurons and Blackrobes were killed or captured. The Jesuit experiment, like the once proud Huron Nation itself, had come to an end.

For several centuries of Jesuit missionary activity—with rare exceptions—the missiological model used was one that either obliterated the culture and spirituality of the would-be converted or attempted to form a fusion between the indigenous and the foreign. Systematics theologian and missiologist Carl Starkloff has long been associated with native communities in the United States and Canada. He directed a large mission in Wyoming for six years and has been actively involved with the native ministry programme in northern Ontario for many more years. In both his academic and in his pastoral work he has found himself drawn to a radical re-evaluation of Jesuit missionary undertakings both current and past.

> We have had conflicting notions of mission in the Order since Francis Xavier. I find it considerably helpful to use William Ernest Hocking in this regard. An American philosopher who headed a Protestant task force to study missions, he outlined a typology that involved three models of mission. The first is the radical displacement model which involves the sundering of the convert's personal and cultural history. To embrace Jesus Christ involves the repudiation of your tribal memory and history. When this model is employed we force people to become Western, European, and white. For centuries this was the Jesuit evangelizing tactic—although Matteo Ricci, Roberto De Nobili, and the Jesuits involved in the

> Paraguayan Reductions tried to get beyond this model, with little success.
>
> The next model is the synthesis model whereby the religions come together and you draw on the good qualities of each, although one religion is usually in the ascendent. Negative critics of this model refer to this process as syncretism, which is for them a kind of ten-letter four-letter word.
>
> The last model Hocking calls the reconception model, whereby scholars and missionaries come to accept the truth that there is salvation outside the church, and that all religions need to engage in a mutually tolerant and supportive conversation about the essence of their own particular creed, without necessarily jettisoning the unique for the universally held. I rather like this model because it doesn't require that I reject the idea of my faith in Jesus as the universal saviour but cautions me that I don't know everything that that means and that I need to listen to and learn from other faith traditions.

Starkloff argues that Brêbeuf was inclined to the synthesis model, trying to effect a marriage of some tribal traditions with a eurocentric Christianity, but post-Tridentine Catholicism was highly defensive about its own conception of Christian truth and not at all inclined to be sympathetic towards non-Christian cultures. The prevailing theological mentality was eager to see the elimination rather than the absorption of non-Catholic customs and traditions. Baptism into the Holy Roman and Apostolic Church was baptism into the Latin culture of Europe. The Blackrobes were the agents for such a wholesale baptism. The native peoples were taught to despise and distrust their own spiritual traditions, to forsake their native tongue, and to abandon the wisdom of their elders. The tribal memory was quite simply erased.

The Jesuits are, however, if nothing else, resilient. They continue to work with the native peoples to the present day—save for the some forty years when they were virtually expunged from pre-Confederation Canada primarily because after the British conquest they were not allowed to accept novices or recruits. The Christianizing of the native peoples of Canada has not, in great part, been a happy affair and, as a consequence, many North

American Jesuits are continually reassessing their service to the aboriginal communities.

In 1980 the Upper Canada Province of the Jesuits built the Anishinabe Spiritual Centre to develop and strengthen native leadership. This ministries training centre is situated on Anderson Lake near Espanola, in northern Ontario. It is a log structure, in perfect harmony with its wilderness environment. Workshops, retreats, theology courses, and sessions for alcoholics and adult children of alcoholics, all contribute to building up and not eradicating the unique aboriginal cultures that constitute an undervalued component of the Canadian fabric. It's a form of redress, of restitution. At least, that's the dream.

George Leach is a former doctoral student under Carl Starkloff who has been much occupied with the vexing problem of inculturation: incarnating or impregnating a culture with Christian values and spirituality in such a way that they do not distort or eliminate indigenous truths and customs. As a result of his scholarship, and of his close pastoral involvement at the Anishinabe Centre, he has concluded that

> the work of the Centre was begun as the continuation of Brébeuf's dream, which is enfleshed in the letters that he wrote back to France in the 1640s, wherein he said that he hoped the Jesuits would develop a native clergy and that they in turn would run their own church. In addition, the work of the Centre involves an act of reparation, incorporating healing ceremonies; we have also had services on some of the different reserves at which time we have tried to surface some of the pain. At one elders conference on Birch Island at Dreamer's Rock, with everybody present, I just very simply said that: "on behalf of my Jesuit brothers of history I am sorry for what happened; I don't want to continue to look in the rearview window of the car; I need to say to you that I am sorry; I hope that I have not offended you; and I hope that we can work together to create a new future, both human and divine."

Leach would be the first to say that it is he who has been converted. In helping the native peoples recover their lost memory, in helping them to see the value of their own indigenous spirituality, in helping them to achieve a creative integration of the Gospel with native culture, George Leach has become one of them:

> These people have become my friends. As a result, whether I am white or native seems no longer to matter. I don't look upon them as native people; I see them as individual persons, as Isaac, Ursula, Dorothy, etc. I was honoured by being drawn into the community of Manitoulin by a group of elders who called me by name, by my new Indian name. I was overcome. I knew then that I was loved and that these people had honoured me in such a way that I am now an adopted son of the Ojibwe, Odawa, and Potawatomi First Nations known as the Anishnabec. I am very proud to be named Brightening Cloud, the one who brings light to the communities. They told me: "You travelled from community to community and you brought us light and you loved us."

It is precisely because the Canadian Jesuits were resolved to understand the native peoples that they established the Anishinabe Spiritual Centre and began on their long road to mutual respect and trust between the races and the traditions. It hasn't been easy. In 1990 reports of the sexual abuse of native boys by George Epoch, a Jesuit priest who served the Chippewa community on Cape Crocker, Ontario, began to come out. The Jesuits immediately set up a counselling program for the abused and their families, provided cash compensation for each valid claimant (as well as additional monies for therapy and education for the victims and their families), and issued a public apology to all the victims and to the community as a whole:

> I speak to you today as the Provincial Superior of the Canadian Jesuits . . . . I come here in sorrow, in regret and in humility, acknowledging the wrong that the late Father Epoch [who died in 1986] did to you, expressing my sorrow and apologizing on my own behalf and that of all Canadian Jesuits for his actions and for the devastating consequences those actions have had in your lives and in the lives of your family and community . . . . I ask you to allow us to work side by side, Native People and Jesuits. Along this pathway I hope and pray that we

> may continue, as in the past, to trust and respect each other as together we approach a challenging future.[15]

Although a financial and reconciliation agreement was reached by most parties in 1994, there is still a lot of pain and discontent among the injured native groups so that the Jesuits face a future more bleak than challenging when it comes to repairing the breach of trust symbolized by Epoch's disabling pedophilia.

Yet, this work of repair must be done and the redress embodied by the work of the Anishinabe Spiritual Centre furthered, for it is the continuation of the work of Xavier, Ricci, De Nobili, and Brébeuf in a different time and with different theological and spiritual tools. Carl Starkloff and George Leach are part of that tradition, their very formation in the Spiritual Exercises made them so.

The spirituality that nurtured Leach and Starkloff in their work with the aboriginal peoples is a social justice spirituality, a spirituality that is not confined to the missal, the choir, or the grotto. It is a spirituality that demands response. It is Ignatius's spirituality.

> We have to become what Ignatius Loyola recommended for activists. We must be contemplatives in action. Contemplatives. Oh, not stargazers, not searching for God in outer space. Rather the contemplation . . . described as "a long loving look at the real."
>
> Here the "real" is not some far-off "pie in the sky." The real is all that is: the sun setting over Western waters, a sparkling glass of burgundy, a child licking a chocolate ice-cream cone, a striding woman with windblown hair, yes Rwanda and Serbia and the sub-Sahara—whatever comes within our ken, whatever we see, hear, touch, taste, smell—all this we "look" at . . . . Another way of expressing this type of contemplation: Try to find Christ in all things, in all people. You see, Christ is present not only in the word proclaimed, not only in the eucharist, not only in my graced soul. Christ is present, is active (like a laborer, Ignatius says), in every last fragment of his universe. . . . especially in the disadvantaged.[16]

To work with the disadvantaged in the starkest terms is the lot of Jesuits like Dean Brackley, a U.S. citizen working in San Salvador who finds that his struggle for justice would be rendered inexplicable and unendurable were it not for Ignatius.

> To be perfectly honest, it would be hard for me to get through the day without reflecting on the *Spiritual Exercises* of Ignatius of Loyola. Ignatius has two key meditations in the *Exercises* and one of them is the two standards. Ignatius talks about life as a struggle between good and evil. He says, "Let's not be naive, we can't be good unless we really struggle against evil." It's not just like buying apples rather than oranges. He says, "Know that there is a power of evil out there, there's a strategy of evil and that strategy is basically a strategy of greed and lust for power. Jesus has another strategy, and that strategy is a strategy of poverty and solidarity. It's a strategy of downward mobility." Not that everybody has to live in misery, by any means, but Ignatius argues that typically the enemy will try to undo us by getting us to have too many things and to think of ourselves too highly. The best strategy to avoid the pitfalls is one of humility and humble service and solidarity with the poor. I find that Ignatius is right.
>
> His other great meditation is the meditation on the reign of God, the idea that God really is at work in the world and has a project, and the project is that we all live more humanly and in community. That we enjoy the fullness of life. It seems to me that this walking in solidarity, this taking one's place among the people is where one gets a glimpse of that reign of God, that hope, that project of God. It's where we see God working in the world.
>
> Those are the two key meditations that help me get through the day.

Although finding Christ in the barrio is different from finding Christ in the drawing room, the spirituality of Ignatius of Loyola, as distilled in the *Exercises* and as witnessed by directors throughout the world, is a spirituality that humanizes, liberates, focuses on the possible, and responds to the actual. Found *in* a handbook, it is not a spirituality *of* the handbook. It is primarily a spirituality to be lived in its fullness. The *Exercises* was

> at first a series of loose notes, detached remarks, and sketches. These were preserved, used, and completed during the years. Finally they were gathered into a whole of potent interior logic but with no carefulness of composition. . . . His entire thought was to gather together the counsels and the materials which the lights he received and the experiences he underwent had furnished him; and he assembled these materials for the precise purpose he had in mind, to help souls to seek, find, and embrace God's will for themselves.[17]

From its inauspicious beginnings—a rude assembly of notes only painstakingly transformed into a manual at a later date—the *Exercises* remains blunt in its purpose "to help souls." It is not a self-help programme with an easy step-by-step remedy; it is, however, replete with psychological insights designed to lead the earnest exercitant into the virgin territory of self-discovery. But first we must attend to those feelings, moods, stirrings of the soul that lead us to feel either consolation or desolation. This attention invites us to discern the spirits and

> discernment means to reflect, in prayer, on our lives, our actions, our thoughts, and to notice the moods and feelings that follow, in such a way that we are led to concentrate on those things that give us deeper satisfaction. It is all, in the end, about doing what we want, but first we must find what it is that we really want, what really satisfies us at the deepest possible level. It is a spirituality of fulfilment, not one of miserable abnegation, even though it may involve such sacrifice and hard work and generosity.[18]

Ignatian spirituality is a spirituality of right-knowing and of making things just. It does not so much proscribe experience, which other traditional spiritualities tend to do, as much as it invites one to sift and gauge its true measure.

And one can do that changing nappies, dodging grenades, or remaining still in the relative quiet of one's room. It's a spirituality for all seasons, fully and essentially Jesuit, but not exclusively so. One senses that Ignatius wouldn't have it any other way.

III

Jesuit as Liberationist

IT DOESN'T PAY to be a Jesuit. The cost of Ignatian discipleship can be steep. Being a Jesuit and a liberationist (and after 1975 these are inextricably linked) places one at odds with the structures of power, property, and privilege.

Gene Palumbo, a veteran reporter based in El Salvador, contributed a news piece to the July 1, 1994, issue of the U.S. Roman Catholic newspaper *National Catholic Reporter*, in which he exposed a new wave of death threats. It would appear that the abolition of the dreaded death squads—which were to be dismantled as a consequence of the peace process that ended the twelve-year civil war in 1990—has yet to come to pass. Various ecclesiastics and lawyers received threats, but those directed toward the Jesuits were particularly pointed.

The Jesuits were being targeted "for getting involved in national political problems." They were warned that if they failed to leave the country they would be "executed," presumably in a manner not unlike that of their six murdered confreres in the 1989 massacre at the Universidad Centroamericano (UCA). According to Palumbo's source, "an additional threat was phoned into a residence of Jesuits who teach and study at the UCA. Seminarian Estudo Garcia, who answered the telephone, said the caller said, 'Some Jesuits are going to die'."

The Jesuits of El Salvador have heard all this before. Palumbo notes that, according to Michael Campbell-Johnston who has returned to El Salvador following a six-year term as the London-based provincial of his order, "We're moving into a period when any work that is concerned with justice and with greater support for the poor and underprivileged is going to be dangerous work once again." It is familiar and deadly turf.

But it is not only in Central America that one continues to hear of the plottings, political chicanery, and liberationist ideals of these meddlesome Jesuits. Following the uprising of the native peoples of Chiapas in southern Mexico on New Year's Day, 1994, spearheaded by the Zapatista National Liberation Army, various critics of Jesuit involvement in human rights issues have attempted to smear the name of the Society along with that of the bishop of San Cristobel de Las Casas, Samuel Ruiz Garcia. The bishop has a long history as a spokesperson and advocate for the native peoples, and the Jesuits are nationally known as critical supporters of the principles of liberation theology. Both are feared by the status quo. Determined to discredit Bishop Ruiz by undermining the credibility of the Jesuits, various and powerful factors within the Mexican establishment realize that as the foremost exponents of liberation theology in the hemisphere, the Jesuits need to be brought to heel. The establishment is desperate.

These two contemporary instances highlight the ongoing struggle the Society of Jesus faces in its international struggle to promote justice. The promotion of justice has become a constitutive dimension of Jesuit life and self-definition. How did this come to pass?

The Roman Catholic Church's commitment to justice is of relatively recent vintage; just over 100 years in fact. It began with the publication in 1891 of the first great social encyclical, *Rerum novarum*, by Pope Leo XIII. Over the following years a body of social teaching has evolved that embraces many principles, critical positions, and contributions to the universal cause of justice. Irish writer and theologian Donal Dorr provides a succinct summary of the cardinal strengths and deficiencies of this body of teaching in his magisterial *Option for the Poor: A Hundred Years of Vatican Social Teaching*:

> Among the strong points of Catholic social teaching are its humanistic character, its practical emphasis on participation and solidarity, its refusal to become identified with any

> political party, the fact that it identifies structures of sin, its biblical aspect, and the fact that it is radical in its commitment to the poor and is therefore evangelical and inspirational. Among the least well-developed aspects of Catholic social teaching are a failure to be adequately ecological and cosmological, an unduly Western and centralising character, a lack of emphasis on alternative models of development, an inadequate treatment of justice for women, an unduly simple distinction between politics in the broad sense and party politics, an insufficient use of social analysis to reveal the class structures of society, a playing down of the importance of contestation in the struggle for justice, a failure to focus on issues of justice in the Church, and a lack of adequate consultation processes which would enable many Christians to play a full role in articulating the teaching.[1]

Clearly, the social teaching of the Roman Catholic Church has undergone significant changes over the last century. During the pontificate of Pope John Paul II it has experienced a radical amplification, including the most detailed critique yet of both doctrinaire Marxism and laissez-faire capitalism.

Jesuits have been major players in the development of Catholic social thought and can be found shaping some of the cardinal insights of the tradition. For instance, the Catholic social principle of subsidiarity—that no larger or higher association should "arrogate to itself the functions which can be performed efficiently by smaller and local societies"—was first expounded in 1931 by Pope Pius X1 in his encyclical *Quadragesimo anno*, an encyclical whose principal architect was the Jesuit Oswald von Nell-Breuning. In addition, Jesuits in both the late nineteenth and early twentieth centuries were influential in developing a social theory that attached considerable importance to the concept of society as an ordered and cooperative system à la Dante.

The Jesuits have helped to shape the Roman Catholic social tradition, and it is not surprising that they should have done so. After all, justice concerns were not foreign to the ministry of Ignatius of Loyola. And this commitment to justice is itself rooted in Ignatius's *Spiritual Exercises*:

> If the Good News is not proclaimed in a practical way to the poor, the message of the *Spiritual Exercises* is vain and lacking in authenticity. Thus we see Ignatius and his companions sheltering 400 homeless people during the harsh winter of 1538–39 in Rome. Ignatius established in the city associations among the laity and the clergy for organising assistance to the hungry and the sick. He considered closeness to the poor essential to the Society's charism. Accordingly he gave instruction to the Jesuit theologians at the Council of Trent to go out to them regularly. In several passages of the Society's *Constitutions*, Ignatius refers to the inspiration that comes to religious life from this closeness with the poor. . . . Of course, in his time, Ignatius could not think in long term solutions which require dealing with socio-economic institutionalised processes causing poverty and injustice. There is, however, an inherent potential in the *Spiritual Exercises* for inspiring justice ministry.[2]

These are the words of the superior-general of the Society of Jesus, Peter-Hans Kolvenbach, and they reflect current Jesuit thinking about the spiritual rootedness of the Jesuit commitment to justice. Although Kolvenbach and historians of the Order can trace the present passion for justice to the very origins of the Society and its foundational documents—the *Spiritual Exercises* and the *Constitutions*—the institutional and spiritual priority now given to justice is a mid-twentieth-century development.

Papal social teaching for the first seventy years—1891 to 1961—is organic and consistent. But beginning with Pope John XXIII's encyclical *Mater et magistra* (1961), which initiated the dismantling of the close association of socially conservative powers with the Roman Catholic Church, and followed two years later by his *Pacem in terris* (1963), which raised several fundamental questions on the issue of human rights, papal social teaching underwent some important changes. Human rights issues, involving matters such as the duties of the individual in society and of the state towards the individual, became a major plank in the social programme of the church.

Subsequent church documents, including such a major work as the Second Vatican Council's pastoral constitution on the church,

Gaudium et spes (1965), underscore the church's eagerness to take seriously, to engage in meaningful dialogue with, the contemporary world, "the theatre of humankind's history." In rapid succession, social encyclicals, synodal documents, and statements issued by episcopal conferences advanced the justice agenda on the universal church's priority list for pastoral action. Justice was in: theologians wrote about it; missionaries preached it; activists died for it.

The Society of Jesus embraced the cause of justice with a passion both inspiring and disconcerting.

The person responsible more than any other for the Jesuit commitment to justice was the 28th General or Black Pope of the Society of Jesus, the diminutive and controversial Basque Pedro Arrupe. Born in Bilbao on November 14, 1907, the last child and only boy of five children, he had a traditionally pious upbringing. And when he chose to enter the Society of Jesus, although the circumstances were unusually dramatic, he nonetheless couched his decision in conventional religious terms. A medical student in Madrid, he found himself stationed in Lourdes for three months:

> I was witness to three miraculous cures from the moment they took place in the midst of the faithful praying to the Virgin Mary, through the verification carried out by doctors who were atheists. This impressed me very much, because I had often heard my professors speak of the "superstitions of Lourdes." There was born my vocation, in that atmosphere of simplicity and grandeur at the feet of the Virgin Mary, midst the prayer of the pilgrims and the murmurings of the River Gave.[3]

His words capture the genuine simplicity of Arrupe's devotional life, the uncomplicated openness of spirit that marked his years as a Jesuit. The style never left him.

He joined the Society of Jesus in 1927, but because of the order of expulsion by the Republican government of Spain, all Jesuits were sent into exile. Arrupe pursued his philosophical and theological studies in Belgium and the Netherlands. Ordained a priest in 1936 and sent off for doctoral work in medical ethics in the United States, he was unexpectedly sent as a missionary to Japan in 1939—not the most propitious year.

He had wanted to go to Japan for some time, but the authorities refused his offer. When he was sent suddenly and unpredictably, he immersed himself in a full year's intensive study of Japanese language and literature at the Jesuit Sophia University in Tokyo. Sent as a parish priest to Yamaguchi, he found himself imprisoned by the state for thirty-three days on a charge of spying. Japan was on war footing and not inclined to view with equanimity the arrival on its shores of a citizen of the West and a Jesuit to boot. It proved to be one of the most determinative moments in his life:

> An important personal event was my imprisonment for one month in Yamaguchi. Japan was at war and I was suspected of espionage. That, however, I didn't learn until the very end. Without anything except a sleeping mat I spent days and nights in the December cold, alone. I learned during this time the science of silence, of solitude, of austere poverty, of inner dialogue with the "guest of my soul." This was the most instructive month of my entire life.[4]

Appointed Jesuit superior and the master of Jesuit novices at their novitiate in the suburbs of Hiroshima in 1942, he was in the ill-fated city when the atomic bomb fell on August 6, 1945, "a permanent experience, outside history, engraved on my memory." He employed his medical skills in the service of the wounded and dying, transforming the novitiate into a makeshift hospital for 200 grievously scarred human remnants. Out of this experience, noted one of his General Assistants, Cecil McGarry, in a memorial sermon delivered in Nairobi, February 14, 1991, "he committed himself to building a civilization of love, in a world of division and destruction."[5]

He remained in Japan after the defeat of the country by the Allied powers in 1945, eventually becoming provincial superior of the Japanese province, which included some 300 members from 20 countries, a veritable missionary potpourri.

At the 31st General Congregation of the Jesuits in 1965, he was elected General by an absolute majority on the third ballot. The Order claimed the highest enrolment in its history: 36,068. The Second Vatican Council was coming to an end. The church was fired by the spirit of renewal and its most impressive religious congregation of men was poised for new tasks under a new leadership, the leadership of a man marked by the dual experiences of Lourdes and Hiroshima.

Vincent O'Keefe, an assistant general to Arrupe and a man who knew him well and was thought by many Jesuits to have been his rightful successor as General, observed in his 1991 obituary of Arrupe in *The Tablet* that he was providentially positioned for leadership in the Society:

> The programme of renewal indicated by Vatican II involved both a continuous return to the original inspiration and charism of the founder, St. Ignatius, and openness to the signs of the times. Pedro Arrupe combined these two processes to a remarkable degree in his own person, and thus was able to launch and sustain a renewal in word and in act. For him adaptation and renewal in religious life were linked to an effective apostolate in a world of unbelief and injustice.[6]

To remain faithful to the charism of the founder, Arrupe placed a heavy emphasis on the centrality of Ignatian spirituality and on the indispensable role of the *Exercises* in the life of the Society as a corporate body, and in the life of each Companion of Ignatius. Arrupe understood that the heart of Jesuit spirituality is finding God in all things, a spirituality that is earthbound, time conditioned, historically conscious. It is not a spirituality cocooned in rubrics; it is not a spirituality confined to monastic choirs, regulated prayer, and the rhythms of common worship. Contemplation and communal prayer have their vital place in Jesuit spirituality, but for Ignatius the hustle and bustle of our mundane lives is the arena in which we discover and grow towards God.

The Ignatian vision is concrete, apostolic, activity oriented, worldly, and marked by a remarkable freedom from proscriptions, rules, and rituals. But it changed over the centuries and it was Arrupe, according to one well-informed ex-provincial, who righted the direction of the Society.

> In later years, this vision was lost as succeeding Jesuit superior generals and general congregations institutionalised St. Ignatius's charism by drawing up rules for their subjects. Their cumulative effect has been satirised as follows: "Ignatius set up

> the Society of Jesus as light cavalry; Borgia turned us into infantry; Aquaviva put us into barracks; Roothan cancelled all leave; Ledochowski set up a concentration camp . . . and Pedro Arrupe said: 'Break ranks'."[7]

And so Arrupe set about to alter things, irrevocably. He travelled extensively throughout the Jesuit world (which *is* the world); he established within six years of his election an international commission to prepare for a comprehensive review of the Order's response to the "apostolic challenges of the ages"; he listened to the cry of the poor and resolved to act on the increasingly pointed and prophetic justice statements coming from Rome and Latin America.

Beginning in 1967 with Pope Paul VI's encyclical *Populorum progressio*, in which he wrote of the injustice of certain situations crying out for God's attention, the official position of the Roman Catholic Church regarding systemic and institutionalized violence was becoming increasingly critical and intolerant of abuse. In his 1971 apostolic letter *Octagesimo adveniens*, Pope Paul admitted that particular situations require particular remedies and that the political dimension is essential given that economics alone is incapable of resolving certain injustices. This was papalspeak for "the development model hasn't worked and political and structural changes are necessary."

In addition, the Roman Synod of 1971 produced a document, *Justitia in mundo*, in which the church fathers go so far as to say that:

> Action on behalf of justice and participation in the transformation of the world fully appear to us as a constitutive dimension of the preaching of the gospel, or, in other words, of the Church's mission for the redemption of the human race and its liberation from every oppressive situation.[8]

Justice and faith are inextricably bound together, never to be sundered. This was music to Arrupe's ears, following as it did the 1968 Medellín Conference of the entire Latin American episcopate, known by its acronym as CELAM II. At this conference the Latin American bishops and their theological advisers, or *periti*, publicly deplored the history of injustice in the hemisphere, acknowledged that class struggle was a social reality in their respective countries, and admitted to the sometimes sad history of church compliance with dictatorial rule. In an important way, the 1971 Synod with its theme of "Justice in the World" was a validation from the centre—Rome—of the Latin American church's Medellín thrust.

Arrupe was there: both at Medellín and at the '71 Synod. He saw and he approved. And he linked, in a quintessentially Jesuit manner, the *Exercises* with the universal church's increasingly aggressive commitment to justice. As the late vaticanologist and papal biographer Peter Hebblethwaite, himself a onetime Jesuit, noted:

> It seemed right that such a man should guide the redefinition of Jesuit identity the Council called for. He quickly inaugurated a new style. The old tight-lipped and awesome impersonality of the Jesuit curia in Rome was changed overnight. The remoteness went. Arrupe trusted his fellow Jesuits to be good Ignatian Jesuits, imbued with the spirit of discernment taught by the *Exercises*.[9]

That spirit of discernment, which in effect means the capacity to see with lucid self-knowledge what is necessary to be done, is not a rarefied spiritual skill. It is not cultivated in isolation from human commerce; it is refined with involvement in the all-too-human world of muck, muddle, and misery. It is a practical skill, a way of being in the world. And Jesuits need it in their work for justice in order that they won't be misdirected in their zeal to serve ideologies hostile to the Gospel, in order that they won't forget that in finding God in all things they are charged to be skeptical of doctrinaire positions that place Christ on the periphery rather than at the centre of their apostolate.

It was the General's own act of discernment that prompted his letter of December 12, 1966, to the Latin American provincials:

> We must take into account the fact that socio-economic structures, by reason of their mutual interdependence, form a kind of global social bloc or system. The intrinsic inadequacy of certain fundamental structures for the establishment of a just social order is mirrored in the global inadequacy of the existing system, which is in contradiction to the Gospel.
>
> From this situation rises the moral obligation of the Society

> to rethink all its ministries and every form of its apostolates to see if they really offer a response to the urgent priorities which justice and social equity call for. Even an apostolate like education—at all levels—which is so sincerely wanted by the Society and whose importance is clear to the entire world, in its concrete forms today must be the object of reflection in the light of the demands of the social problem. [10]

When the moment arrived to move the Society forward in the direction of justice, fully in keeping with the church's growing consensus for a justice component in the contemporary preaching of the Gospel, Arrupe was more than ready. The moment was at hand; it was called the 32nd General Congregation.

Out of this Congregation would come the famous Fourth Decree, *The Service of Faith and the Promotion of Justice*, in which the Society of Jesus unequivocally declares for justice, in which it makes clear, in the language of the 1971 Roman Synod, that justice is a constitutive dimension of the preaching of the Gospel. Jesuits throughout the world are henceforward pledged to work for justice in the name of faith:

> From all over the world where Jesuits are working, very similar and very insistent requests have been made that, by a clear decision on the part of the General Congregation, the Society should commit itself to work for the promotion of justice. Our apostolate today urgently requires that we take this decision. . . . fidelity to our apostolic mission requires that we propose the whole of Christian salvation and lead others to embrace it. Christian salvation consists in an undivided love of the Father and of the neighbor and of justice. Since evangelization is proclamation of that faith which is made operative in love of others, the promotion of justice is indispensable to it. [11]

The Jesuits, signed with the authority of the Gospel and commissioned by the Vicar of Christ, are now promoters of justice in a world wracked by inequality, inhumanity, and despair. Their 32nd General Congregation, presided over and inspired by their General, provides little leeway for the fainthearted.

Arrupe had worked long and assiduously for GC32; it was the culmination of his dreams for the Society, for an Order in the vanguard of conciliar renewal, spearheading that dialogue with culture that Pope John XXIII and Pope Paul VI had inaugurated. The Jesuits, once again, were to be found on the frontier and not safely ensconced in the citadel. They were called to lead. Arrupe liked it that way. It's what his brother Basque, Ignatius of Loyola, would have wanted.

But the cost was great, both for Arrupe and for the Society. So enthusiastic and passionate a commitment to, indeed identification with, the poor is bound to disturb those Catholics, clerics and lay, who see in any programmed service for justice a concomitant diminution of spirituality. One of the most strenuous and perduring of these critics is the highly intelligent and articulate English peer, Peter Lord Rawlinson.

Former attorney-general, a distinguished barrister, and a jurist renowned for his involvement in many of the most notorious political and pathological crimes in modern Britain, Rawlinson is a devout Roman Catholic educated by the elitist Benedictine monks of Downside Abbey. He knows the Roman Catholic tradition intimately. And he doesn't like what the Jesuits are doing to it. And so in the late 1980s he undertook what he calls "a personal investigation" for both the British Broadcasting Corporation and his publishers. The result: *The Jesuit Factor*.

This work, controversial and polemical, does not shy away from calling the Jesuits to task for failing to serve the church in the manner intended by their founder. Rawlinson sees GC32 and Pedro Arrupe as the prime reasons why the Order has become politicized, electing to pursue justice at the expense of faith, embracing with un-Jesuit-like naiveté the dangerous utopianism of Marxism.

> They were back on top. But on top of what? To seek faith and justice, especially the latter, was the new trumpet call which summoned the Society back into the field, back metaphorically into the van of the Church, back in some instances literally into the jungle, but above all back into the great affairs of the world which so many of them had always believed was the natural place for the followers of Ignatius Loyola.[12]

These socially engaged clerics seem not terribly otherworldly for Lord Rawlinson. Quite the contrary. Their spirituality and their politics are distasteful to him because they smack of the time-conditioned and the modish. There is little in the way of discernible piety, little in the way of traditional loyalty to the pope, hitherto a defining mark of the Jesuit charism. And a great measure of this lamentable decline in the ranks of the church's premier Order is, in Lord Rawlinson's mind, directly attributable to Pedro Arrupe himself:

> Arrupe was much loved, of course, especially by those who viewed his reign with great approval because he had given *them* opportunities. He was much loved by *them*, and even by those, undoubtedly, who, even though they didn't agree with his actual leadership, recognized his powers of leadership. Even his critics have paid great tribute to his personal character, his personal holiness. But they worried that the Society under his leadership drifted, that he allowed everyone great license to do what they wanted to do, and that he failed to keep a proper control over the Society at a time of great trouble in the church. He was a poor diplomat and created for the Society insuperable difficulties with the papacy.

Lord Rawlinson's indictment of the Arrupe years is not without its insight and its clarity of judgement. Although *The Jesuit Factor* is error-ridden and although Rawlinson is no theologian, he nonetheless succeeds in highlighting, in his entertaining broadside, the contradictions and contests that followed GC32, the time, as he would have it, of the Jesuits' civil war. The Arrupe profiled in both Rawlinson's book and his BBC radio script is neither dim witted nor malevolent. He is simply misguided; a rather easy dupe for neo-Marxist zealots, for dialectical materialists who have confounded the Kingdom of God with a classless society, and for the message of liberation fervently preached by missionaries who themselves have been converted by the new gospel of revolution. Arrupe, Rawlinson is persuaded, has attended to all these voices and he has been undone by them. But, more tragically still, he has allowed these voices a hearing in the chambers of the Jesuit Curia, in the halls of the Jesuit academy, and in the pulpits of Jesuit churches.

The Service of Faith and the Promotion of Justice is the magna carta of the Arrupe years, and it has charted a new course for the Ignatian barque. For the critics, Rawlinson principal among them, this magna carta is a devil's document crafted in the fires of liberation theology.

Not since the Modernist crisis of the turn of the century has the Church of Rome faced such a challenge to its traditional way of doing theology as it faces now with the rise of liberation theology. Although its major proponents are Latin Americans—it is in many ways an indigenous theology—it is essentially transportable to any culture, particularly a culture that has a history of oppression as a determining feature of its life.

Liberation theology, as the name implies, draws first on human experience as the stuff of theological reflection. As a theological system, it repudiates the classical *a priori*, propositional, and ahistorical approach typical of conventional theology. It accepts as normative in the lives of most human beings structures of oppression that need to be overcome in the name of the Gospel. Liberation theology, then, is engaged in a rigorous critique of the structures of oppression from the vantage point of biblical justice and of the liberating message of Jesus of Nazareth. Although there are now many schools of liberation theology, it is possible to identify certain salient characteristics. Leonardo and Clodovis Boff, Brazilian liberation theologians, provide a succinct overview of these characteristics:

> Liberation theology is the first theology worked out on the periphery but with universal implications. . . . Liberation theology puts on the agenda for discussion questions that concern all human beings, whatever their ideological bent or religious adherence. . . . There is a prophetic call coming from liberation theology, in that it denounces the causes that produce oppression, and inspires an outpouring of generosity destined to overcome destructive relationships and build freedom for everyone. . . . Liberation theology belongs to contemporary history. . . . Liberation theology forces theologians to think in terms of specific actions, of the real problems of life, instead of the classic themes established by theological tradition. . . . It is by nature a popular theology, for the masses of the oppressed are its most congenial recipients and most of

> them understand and embrace its aims. . . . Liberation theology set out to be the servant of the "faith that works through charity," inspired by hope.[13]

With little interest in the philosophical categories and discourse of European-generated theological systems, the liberation theologians, the majority of whom received their advanced education from such European centres of learning as Muenster, Munich, Frankfurt, and, most importantly, Louvain, nonetheless acknowledged their indebtedness to the schoolmasters at the same time as they broke loose from the Euroshackles that bound them.

It is generally conceded that the foundational work that ushered onto the scholarly floor the newest theology was the 1971 *Teología de la liberacíon. Perspectivas (A Theology of Liberation)* by the Peruvian Indian priest-theologian, Gustavo Gutiérrez. Theology was formally and directly enlisted in the war against poverty and oppression, and would itself be critiqued. The church must jettison its neutrality; align itself with the oppressed classes; forgo the privileges of conquest. Liberation theology declared itself a theology of solidarity, a theology of compassion, a theology that embodies a "preferential option for the poor" and whose perspective "recognizes society as divided between 'the powerful,' who have arranged in their own favour the structures that distribute wealth and honour, and the 'powerless,' the victims, who constitute the great majority of the world's population."[14]

This is the language of revolution. Rome trembled. From the perspective of the Tiber, this talk of class struggle, structures of oppression, and solidarity was talk laced with Marxist categories of understanding and expression. It was difficult to see the traditional tools of theological inquiry being applied. It all looked rather dangerously like a social science impregnated by neo-Marxist sympathies and terms of analysis. It didn't look like a theology at all, or at least not like a theology that could give comfort to Rome.

The immediate and potent impact of Rome's displeasure could not have escaped Arrupe. Although Gutiérrez and the Boff brothers were not Jesuits, many of the leading teachers and activists associated with liberation theology were, including the most impressive systematician of them all, the Uruguayan theologian Juan-Luis Segundo.

But in the early days of the skirmishes—prior to the election of Karol Wojtyla as Pope John Paul II in 1978—there were no formal denunciations of liberation theology, only cautious warnings, nuanced directives, traditional execrations over the perceived unorthodoxy of some of the new theology's emphases.

The Arrupe of GC32 could not help but be relieved that even in the midst of the cauldron—he was after all stationed in Rome—he had to deal more with suspicion and fear than outright repudiation. Such is a Jesuit's lot.

But being the General of GC32, and one who had made explicit since his own election in 1965 his personal commitment to justice in the context of a lived faith, Arrupe found himself on a collision course. He was not unaware of this. Arrupe understood the consequences of Jesuit efforts to inculcate the strategies of *The Service of Faith and the Promotion of Justice*, and as early as December 20, 1974, just two months before the Congregation's approval of Decree Four, he asked with prescience: "Is [our General Congregation] ready to enter upon the more severe way of the cross, which surely will mean for us a lack of understanding on the part of civil and ecclesiastical authority and of our best friends?"[15]

Two years later he gave his own answer. A letter from Arrupe addressed to the whole Society and dated March 19, 1977, reminded his fellow Jesuits of the dreadful price of commitment:

> The recent murder of Fr. Rutilio Grande, in the Central American republic of El Salvador seems to be a clear sign from the Lord. Father Grande is the fifth victim that God has chosen from our ranks in the past few months. The other victims were Fr. João Bosco Burnier, murdered on October 11, 1976 in Brazil, and Frs. Martin Thomas and Christopher Shepherd-Smith and Brother John Conway, murdered on February 6 in Rhodesia. The Lord speaks to the Society through the pouring out of this blood, as through the blood of Abel, as through the blood of Christ on the Cross. . . . These are Jesuits of the mold that the world and the Church need today. Men driven by the love of God, to serve their brethren without distinction of class

> or race. Men who are able to identify themselves with those who suffer, who live with them, and even give up their own lives on their own behalf. Strong men who know how to defend human rights in the gospel spirit even to the sacrifice of life itself, if that be necessary (John 15:13).[16]

In this letter—subtitled "paying the price of the GC32 commitment"—Arrupe appropriately begins his list of a modern Jesuit martyrology with the most recent murder, that of Rutilio Grande. For it is in El Salvador, the land of the Saviour, where the greatest and most dramatic price would be paid.

The world was shocked when the Archbishop of San Salvador, Oscar Arnufo Romero, was gunned down while saying mass. It was barely two days after he had been identified as an enemy of the state by the powerful politician Major Roberto D'Aubuisson, founder of the Nationalist Republican Alliance Party (ARENA). It was 1980. Romero, by temperament and training a conservative churchman, had been hesitant to denounce the government on human rights infractions because of his fear of unlawful insurgency. He was inclined, as is the case with the majority of Roman prelates, to view the spirit of revolution with detestation. The overthrow of legitimate authority, irrespective of the genuine abuses of that authority by those exercising power, is the court of last resort. Rome abominates the usurpation of established authority, most especially since 1848, the "year of revolutions," with the subsequent self-incarceration of Pope Pius IX in 1870 following the annexation of the Papal City States by the Italian Nationalists. Still, the Roman Catholic tradition does allow for a revolutionary uprising should all the conditions apply: "[a] manifest, and long-standing tyranny which would do great damage to fundamental personal rights and dangerous harm to the common good of the country."[17]

Arguably, such a state of affairs existed in El Salvador during the leadership of Archbishop Romero, but Romero would never have adopted a policy in favour of violent insurrection. His preferred path was that of Christian nonviolence. And he came to this choice—of nonviolent opposition to the governing powers and their allies—after the death of his adviser Rutilio Grande, a Jesuit. Grande's death sealed in blood Romero's own resolve to oppose actively and explicitly government malfeasance. A professor at the metropolitan seminary, a spiritual formation director for many of the young clergy of El Salvador, a social activist in the rural districts conscientizing the poor and helping them organize and indeed unionize, Grande represented to the authorities the worst features of the post-Vatican II, post-Medellín, post-GC32 spirit—the spirit of Arrupe.

Salvator Carranza, a Jesuit friend of Grande, recounts the priest's last hours:

> I was working with Rutilio in his parish the very week he was assassinated. He ordered me to stay in our house in Santa Tecla rather than to come to help him on the weekend. It was at the time when the government was expelling all foreign priests and he was afraid that if I came to his parish I would be captured and exiled. So, he celebrated mass in my place. The night before his death, a night that I remember as his last supper, he insisted that I stay away because he didn't want me expelled to Guatemala. They killed him because they wanted to send a message to all the clergy and bishops and missionaries working with the campesinos to restrict themselves to a sacramental ministry and not to inciting revolution.
>
> Up to his death, the authorities only killed non-Salvadorans. They warned him repeatedly. Early in the week that he died they had marked a cross on the back window of his truck. It was through this same window that the bullets that murdered him were fired.
>
> Although he was feared by the authorities because of his influence in the seminary and amongst the diocesan clergy, he was assassinated because of his involvement with improving the conditions of the peasants, of helping them grow in awareness of their own dignity and of the oppressed circumstances of their lives.

Grande was slain, along with an old man and a teenage boy, on March 12, 1977, on the road to El Paisnal, the village of his birth.

Four months after the death of Rutilio Grande, the White Warriors, one of many right-wing death squads plying their lethal trade, issued a death threat against all the Jesuits in El Salvador. It was a comprehensive threat that gave the Jesuits just one month to choose either exile or death. This was the time when the slogan "Be a patriot: kill a priest" became fashionable. The priests they had in mind were Jesuits.

But the Jesuits didn't leave.

It was Arrupe himself who said that "to defend justice in the world is really to proclaim a sign of contradiction." He knew that there would be many for whom the Jesuit commitment to justice would be anathema. They would see any threat to the status quo as partisan political activity and, ipso facto, not the work of professionals of the spirit.

In addition, many in the educated and established classes would expect the Jesuits to continue their elitist mode of education, providing a future for the sons of the ruling families. It all sounds rather feudal, but in several countries of the world the Jesuits still provide an entrée to power—social, political, and economic—by means of their network of exclusive education. Along with many other apostolates, as a consequence of Arrupe and GC32, this too is changing. In a major address to the International Congress of Jesuit Alumni of Europe on "training agents of change for the promotion of justice," delivered in Valencia, Spain, on July 31, 1973—the Feast of St. Ignatius Loyola and eighteen months before GC32—Arrupe noted:

> Today our prime educational objective must be to form men-for-others; men who will live not for themselves but for God and his Christ—for the God-man who lived and died for all the world; men who cannot even conceive of love of God which does not include love for the least of their neighbours; men completely convinced that love of God which does not issue in justice for men is a farce.[18]

Translated into action, this summons to educate men-for-others ("men" is not used by Arrupe in a gender-specific way given that Jesuit schools are not all single-sex academies) has resulted in some radical initiatives that have contributed to the unease many feel towards Jesuit redefinition following GC32. For instance, the Salvadoran Jesuits took Arrupe's call to integrate social justice into the very curriculum of Jesuit schools by taking the insights of GC32 and liberation theology and applying them in their school for privileged boys, the Externado San José. The parents and alumni were outraged. They accused the Jesuits of being subversives and delated them to Rome as communists. Many withdrew their sons from the college. Lesson learned; justice costs. As Arrupe said it would.

And it cost more still at the university, the Universidad Centroamericana José Siméon Cañas, where the Jesuits are the deciding presence. Named after a Salvadoran priest who, as a scholar and politician, obtained emancipation for the slaves of Central America in 1824, UCA is a Jesuit-run Christian university. Since 1976 it has been bombed on several occasions, raided by military and paramilitary groups, its students and faculty threatened and forced to flee, its financial aid terminated, and on November 16, 1989, several of its Jesuit faculty and administrators slaughtered with their housekeeper and her daughter. As one of the murdered Jesuits had earlier observed: "Our history has been that of our nation."

Long feared for its work in social and political analysis, its careful chronicling of human rights abuses, its commitment to educating for justice, its advocacy of nonviolence, and its sympathy for the cause of the FMLN (Frente Farabundo Martí Liberacíon Nacional)—although hardly neutral on the matter of guerrilla atrocities—the university and its Jesuit leadership faced their day of reckoning with dignity. Four of the priests were murdered on the lawn in front of their residence and the other two in their beds. The women were brutally gunned down in order to eliminate all witnesses. The Jesuit martyrs of El Salvador are: Ignacio Ellacuría, theologian and rector of UCA; Ignacio Martín-Baró, psychologist and vice-rector of UCA; Juan Ramón Moreno, preacher and assistant director of the Oscar Romero Centre; Amando López, theologian and former rector of the University of Central America in Managua; Segundo Montes, sociologist and superior of the community; Joaquín López y López, catechist and director of the *Fe y Alegria* (Faith and Joy) Movement. Elba and Celina Ramos, mother and daughter, innocents, were also martyred.

Of them all Ellacuría was particularly loathed.

> He was a tireless supporter of peace, but he was also on close terms with rebel leaders, whom he sometimes met outside the country. In November, 1980 Ellacuría was forced to flee El Salvador for his life. He returned in April, 1982, but the threats against him persisted.

To his enemies, Ellacuría was a hugely sinister force. Some may even have viewed him as the *autor intelectual*—the mastermind—of El Salvador's violent rebellion.[19]

The lords of the death squads and paramilitary syndicates were right to fear Ellacuría. As rector of UCA he knew what had to be done, and he was prepared to do it. He articulated his philosophy of education in a convocation address he gave at the Jesuit-run Santa Clara University in California on June 12, 1982, a talk he titled "The Task of a Christian University":

> A Christian university must take into account the gospel preference for the poor. This does not mean that only the poor study at the university; it does not mean that the university should abdicate its mission of academic excellence—excellence needed in order to solve complex social problems. It does mean that the university should be present intellectually where it is needed: to provide science for those who have no science; to provide skills for the unskilled; to be a voice for those who do not possess the academic qualifications to promote and legitimate their rights.[20]

Helping the unschooled discover their rights, and working diligently with all parties to bring peace to El Salvador—but a peace grounded in the principles of justice—marked the policies of the Ellacuría administration, policies that would not be compromised.

Rodolfo Cardenal is a Jesuit, former vice-president for Social Outreach at UCA and a member of the community of the slain fathers. He knows the university well and is unmistakeably bound to the Ellacuría tradition.

> I lived in the community house at UCA, but two days prior to the massacre I left to live with another community because I was nervous over the military's anticipated response to the rebel offensive. I chose to change communities for a few days to let things calm down.
>
> It is difficult for me to give voice to what I feel. Suffice it to say that I am still here, I want to be here, and I will continue my work with enthusiasm and dedication.
>
> The university has to serve the people in El Salvador by

> training professionals and educating rich people, yes, but the main role of UCA is to *change* society, to build a community on the principles of justice and peace.
>
> At UCA we charge according to the family income. We don't have a fixed table for charging students. This allows any student in El Salvador the opportunity to come to UCA to study.

Cardenal is still at UCA; Jon Sobrino, the internationally celebrated liberation theologian and prolific author, is also at UCA (he, too, was spared the night of November 16 because he was in Hua Hin, Thailand, teaching a course in Christology); and also at UCA are other, foreign Jesuits who responded to the loss of their confreres by volunteering to serve in their place. These include Michael Czerny, a Canadian Jesuit and ethicist, now serving on the Justice Secretariate at the Jesuit Curia in Rome, and Dean Brackley, a U.S. Jesuit who has worked with the poor in the Bronx. The legacy, the witness, of Ellacuría remains.

For Brackley, UCA provides the best context imaginable for living out his two passions—social justice and solidarity with the poor—in a manner that is stark, honest, vital, precarious, and not without humour.

> I remember the sisters in our parish telling me once that the local commandante of the civil defence had indirectly threatened my life. We felt the need to bring the pastoral team together to discuss the issue when we discovered, quite by accident I'm sure on both our parts, that the commandante had shown up. The commandante denied everything. Someone at the meeting very astutely said: "Well, if they are saying all these things about you, commandante, perhaps you should go back to the people who have been spreading these calumnies about you and set the record straight." The commandante, of course, felt trapped by this mode of interrogation, so all he could do was agree to go to these people who were accusing him of denouncing the church as an agent of subversion and its priests for taking up arms, particularly Jesuits like me.
>
> At this point, one sharp, young, Jesuit scholastic observed: "Well, commandante, given that you are willing to set the

record straight, perhaps you can start here by saying your piece at the mass we are going to begin in five minutes."

"Oh no, I couldn't do that," said the commandante, "for it is much better that the priest say that." "Not at all," said the priest, "for it is much better that you say it rather than me because I am always saying this kind of thing."

The commandante was trapped and he knew it. For the first time in Salvadoran history, as far as I know, we had a commandante standing up in the front of the congregation telling the people that he supported the work of the church and that what they had been told about him were lies.

A flummoxed commandante is an easy victory, though sweet. Other victories are more difficult to come by. They require stamina, both spiritual and physical, and they require the kind of personal power that is generated and nourished by commitment. For Brackley, that commitment itself, the GC32 commitment, means that it is necessary to

> allow the suffering of the poor to break our hearts. That's really the condition for hope. Ignacio Ellacuría said once: "The eyes of all the world seem to be focussed on El Salvador. Why is that?" His explanation was that in El Salvador, and in Central America generally, we see being lived out in stark and graphic terms what is really the drama of our lives, and that drama is a dying and a rising. That is really what is going on in all of our lives and in all of our communities. What I think the poor people of the Bronx and the poor people of El Salvador have taught me is that we really can't share their resurrection and their hope unless we somehow share their pain. It is not a question of loving pain. It's walking with these people and rejoining, in a way, the human race. Rejoining that crowd that marches along, struggling against death and struggling for life. I think that is the place where hope is to be found, and I'm really grateful to the people of El Salvador for helping me to see that a little more clearly.

This struggle *with* the poor and *alongside* the poor is grounded in compassion, what theologian Sobrino calls that "shaping principle of the human and of the Christian." The UCA martyrs, Rutilio Grande, and all the Latin American idealists motivated by their faith to serve others, were killed because they were people of compassion.

> Compassion is not. . . . something peaceable and inoffensive. It cannot be sentimentally sweetened. It is essentially dialectical and thus conflictive and combative, as with many other traits proposed by the gospel. . . . The exercise of compassion . . . is directly to defend and to save victims; indirectly, but necessarily, it is to denounce and attack tormentors. As a consequence, and scandalously, the compassionate are in turn made to suffer, to be attacked and persecuted by the tormentors, and even to end up on the cross. That persecution is a sign that true compassion has been exercised, and not just "works of mercy" which might have short-term beneficial effects, but which do not liberate the victims from the roots of oppression and, therefore, are easy for the oppressors to co-opt.[21]

Philanthropy doesn't work. Only a substantive justice can effect the kinds of structural and attitudinal change that are necessary, and this kind of justice requires social analysis, a theology of liberation, an action-oriented commitment to the poor, and personal courage, all embodied in people like Jaime McPolin, an Irish Jesuit and director of El Despertar (The Awakening), a training centre for basic communities in one of the poorest parts of San Salvador. *Communidades de base* (basic communities) inspire terror in the hearts of those who fear the conscientizing of the poor and disenfranchised—the secular powers—and they inspire a great deal of anxiety in the hearts of those church figures who fear a diminution of hierarchical authority—the ecclesiastical powers. But these small, decentralized parish communities are the wave of the future as they link social needs with religious celebration, justice with faith, politics with the cross. They are often caught in the crossfire of warring parties, easy fodder for soldier and guerrilla alike. McPolin, a former biblical studies professor in Dublin, recalls the vulnerability of El Despertar in the days of the last major offensive of the FMLN, those same days that preceded the slaughter at UCA.

All hell broke loose. You could see from our roof that the civilian population was being systematically destroyed. Every night we would see helicopters moving right into the most populated areas and just blowing the guts out of them. One night the fighting moved directly outside our main door and we could see the boots of the military as we lay pinned to the ground. They were blasting away at the FMLN with mortars and as many as 90 people sought sanctuary in our small kitchen.

What really maims and kills is the shrapnel, so we got sacks of maize and barricaded the windows and hid under the tables. The military had identified us long ago as Red—they sent in the tanks a few years ago and wiped out the parish priest and five young men with him—so it was not surprising when a military plane began bombing our periphery and moving slowly and methodically towards us. I knew then that we were all in the same boat, that I needed to be calm, and that only divine intervention now could spare us from being bombed. And then the most extraordinary thing happened.

The bombing stopped. Evidently, an S.O.S. was sent to California, and thence to Managua, and then to the Minister of Foreign Affairs in Madrid, and finally to the Salvadoran government, which issued the order to call off the bombing of El Despertar.

And then the military began its many searches and I had to sleep elsewhere and then, oh then, the UCA murders.

The UCA assassinations cast in bold relief the dramatic consequences of Decree Four and of the Arrupe passion for justice. He warned that there would be a price, a dear price, for Jesuit testimony, that GC32 would make demands in blood. He was right. But it isn't a matter of adding to the Jesuit martyrology, of vindicating the General's premonitions, of sealing in blood the "service of faith and the promotion of justice." As Daniel Berrigan understands it, what matters is the defeat of the victors:

In San Salvador as elsewhere, noble tongues are silenced, but the truth must continue to be told. The truth of their death, the cruelty and injustice of it, the precious connection

> between their death and the integrity of the gospel. This is judgement, the heavy tolling, not of a passing bell, but a presentiment of the last day itself. The bell tolls for the defeat here and now of the violent victors, for the triumph of the victims.[22]

For that to happen, for "the triumph of the victims" to occur, the Society of Jesus, a body of men who "can sing in the furnace of tribulation," must become wholly identified with the suffering of El Salvador, must become Salvadoran. And for Jon Sobrino, a survivor of the UCA massacre and the premier liberationist in the country, becoming fully Salvadoran is more than an exercise in sympathy, more than a metaphor:

> Tragically, but fortunately, the Jesuits are not alone in this sea of blood. Which means that maybe for the first time in years, as far as the Salvadoran Jesuits go, we can call ourselves truly Salvadoran. Some people have the impression, and I think rightly so, that somehow Jesuits are people different from other people. Well, maybe that is the way it is—it's not the way I would like it to be. . . . When we participate in the same destiny as the majority of the Salvadorans, that means that we have become Salvadoran, and that for me is one of the most important challenges and one of the greatest joys we can have: to be real human beings in a country.

The legacy of elitism has been overturned. And by the Jesuits themselves.

The collision in Central America of the Arrupe Jesuits and GC32 with the structures of power and the antiliberation lobby in the official church, although played out with panache in El Salvador, is more decisively realized in the neighbouring country of Nicaragua.

It is of this country, riven by contesting factions who play out their tragic game under the eye of their superpower overlords, that Berrigan would note in his 1985 "journal of peace and war in Central and North America":

> How the Jesuits cling to the mind! Strangely, and not always consolingly. Meeting them in the most diverse conditions and circumstances, from the university to the remote barrios,

> touched me to the quick. It was as though they held in hand a burning glass—focussed on me.[23]

Jesuits throughout the world found themselves focused on by the burning glass of Nicaragua during the '70s and '80s in ways that divided the Order and pitted Rome against the Society. It was perilously reminiscent of the politics of the eighteenth-century Suppression. Both enemies and friends of the Society were aware of the parallels and the stakes were high.

But why Nicaragua?

Following the defeat of the corrupt government of Anastasio Somoza in 1979 by a movement and party known as the Frente Sandinista por la Liberación Nacional (FSLN) things for a while looked promising. Although the Sandinistas were feared as crypto-Marxists—their founder was the revolutionary Augusto Cesar Sandino who was treacherously executed in 1934 by the National Guard —their leadership was philosophically eclectic, admitting of hardline socialists, doctrinaire Marxists, liberals, Christians, and others. But very soon after the Sandinistas formed the government, the Roman Catholic hierarchy (with two notable exceptions), particularly as embodied in the person of Miguel Cardinal Obando y Bravo, the Archbishop of Managua, began to express its disapproval of the Sandinista Administration. The core of the disapproval, at least publicly, would revolve around the membership of four ordained priests in the cabinet of this government of reconstruction. Pope John Paul II was adamant that priests and those consecrated to religious life must not hold elected office. The revised 1983 *Code of Canon Law* made his intention explicit. Throughout the world priests who held elected public positions were required to tender their resignations or to decline renomination following the completion of their term of office. Canadian New Democrat parliamentarian Robert Ogle of the Saskatoon diocese, and the Massachusetts Democratic congressman Robert Drinan, s.j., were the two outstanding North American politicians affected by the new canonical directives and papal instructions. Both men acceded to the ecclesiastical imperative.

But things were different in Nicaragua. The historical and political context made them so. The country was the product, liberation theologians strenuously argued, of the first truly Christian revolution, and therefore should enjoy the support of the church. Others saw the matter differently, including John Paul II.

The four priests who held office—Maryknoller Miguel D'Escoto, Minister of External Affairs; diocesan priests Ernesto Cardenal, poet and Minister of Culture, and Edgar Parrales, Minister of Social Welfare; and Fernando Cardenal, Ernesto's brother, a Jesuit, and the person responsible for the National Literacy Campaign—were required to resign their seats or forfeit the right to exercise their priestly functions. The incident, which was to consume many years of political and ecclesiastical intrigue, reprimands, and rhetoric, resulted ultimately in the suspension of their active priesthood and in the expulsion of Fernando Cardenal from the Jesuits. The Holy See won and Managua lost.

In the case of Fernando it was an especially difficult affair, if for no other reason than because it became a test case for the pontificate of John Paul II and his resolve to bring to heel the wayward Society of Jesus. With the immobilization of Pedro Arrupe—felled by a stroke on August 7, 1981—and the subsequent intervention of John Paul II with his appointment of a delegate and assistant to run the Society until the next General Congregation could be called and a new General elected, the Jesuits found themselves in a dilemma unprecedented in their history: the Pope had run roughshod over their constitutions; by tradition and vow they were obligated to pay special heed to papal instructions; and their own much-loved Arrupe was powerless to intercede on their behalf. Most likely, he was greatly responsible for the papal displeasure itself.

And so to Nicaragua and Cardenal.

Paolo Dezza, Papal Delegate to the Society and himself a Jesuit, wrote to Cardenal in January 1983 ordering him to withdraw from his work with the Sandinista youth. The message was courteous, blunt, and clear:

> As you know, I have communicated to Fr. Provincial the confirmed desire of the Holy Father that all the priests, not only the Jesuits, withdraw from the type of collaboration with the government in which they are committed to being part of official organisms. The post you are holding, though not directly part of the government, is very closely aligned to it because it

> deals with a political organization of the Sandinistas. And though it is possible to exercise a real apostolate in the position like the one you hold, the Holy Father has over and over manifested his will that such offices not be performed by priests and he hopes that the Jesuits will be an example of obedience in this matter. It is necessary, therefore, that we follow the will of the Holy Father promptly and in a spirit of faith.[24]

Cardenal's response was to appeal, Newman-like, to conscience and to his personal fidelity as a Jesuit to the Order's own commitment to the poor. He understood the Society's canonical effort to enjoin him to submission or expulsion as a politically motivated action on the part of the Vatican. The sabres were drawn.

> To leave the revolution precisely at this time would be like deserting my commitment to the poor, and I would have difficulty convincing myself that at this time my withdrawal could be anything but a betrayal of the cause of the poor and even a betrayal of my country. . . . The order which I am being given obliges me to make decisions of conscience, but I have come to realize that the pressures which are provoking this order do not originate in theological reflection, nor in evangelical inspiration of pastoral necessity. . . . From my point of view and personal experience, it is possible in my situation simultaneously to live my fidelity to the church as a Jesuit and as a priest and also to dedicate myself to the service of the poor of Nicaragua from within the Sandinista people's revolution.[25]

Rome thought otherwise; Cardenal was expelled from the Society of Jesus. But he continues to live with the Jesuits at their residence on the university campus, and the General who presided over his expulsion, Peter-Hans Kolvenbach, derives no satisfaction over the departure from the Jesuits of a nationally revered priest. But he remains firm in his conviction that there was little alternative.

> It is a fact that I wrote to Father Cardenal's mother, at his request, to explain to her my decision to release him from his vows in the Society of Jesus. Father Cardenal's much-appreciated commitment to the poor is supported by many statements of the Church, in spite of its political implications.

> But the Church—and this means first of all her official representatives, the priests—in order to be at the service of all, cannot and should not be identified with a particular political party, or program, or regime. Father Cardenal was sincerely convinced that his service to the poor had to take the form of serving as a minister in the Sandinista government. While fully respecting the position he took, it seemed impossible that he act on it while remaining a priest and a religious; and so, though it was painful to all concerned, it was inevitable that he leave the Society.

Others would share the same fate. William Callahan—a U.S. Jesuit and physicist who had worked at NASA and as a university professor prior to his involvement with the controversial Quixote Center (an activist organization engaged in various justice undertakings)—found himself, because of his pro-Sandinista and anti-Reagan position, at odds with his own province. He was destined to repeat the Cardenal pattern. Although Callahan's public endorsement of several positions at variance with the Vatican, including the ordination of women to the ministerial priesthood and homosexual rights, contributed to the demands for his expulsion, pressure for his dismissal, in his estimation, arose over his Sandinista sympathies.

To do justice, then, has become a perilous Jesuit enterprise, with antagonistic forces coming from within as well as from without. In a widely distributed letter to the friends of the Quixote Center Callahan made public his anxiety over Jesuit self-contradiction:

> We call ourselves to make the service of faith and the promotion of justice our highest priorities. Yet, when individual Jesuits attempt to live these values and authorities complain, as they inevitably do, we lack mediating structures to handle the fallout. Termination, muting of the ministry or dismissal become the only alternatives. Any of these choices, especially dismissals, have a chilling effect on the work of justice.[26]

The work of justice is itself at the heart of the maelstrom generated by GC32 and Decree Four. Callahan and Cardenal took the service of faith and the promotion of justice seriously. They didn't die like Grande and the UCA martyrs; they were purged from within. There are limits to interpretation and limits to implementation. And there is the pope. They are, after all, Jesuits.

But if the critical left is dissatisfied with the Jesuit resolve to be in solidarity with the poor, to partake of that social critique that invites hostility and even repression, the critical right is no more satisfied by the Jesuit determination to link justice with faith. For instance, Lord Rawlinson deplores the politicization of religious symbols and the admixing of spirituality with partisan credos; James Hitchcock, a historian, professor at the Jesuit St. Louis University in Missouri, and author of *The Pope and the Jesuits* (1984) holds out little hope for the Society's reversing its disastrous commitment to justice via GC32; and the ex-Jesuit professor at Rome's prestigious Biblicum, Malachi Martin, excoriates the Society in a monumentally inventive polemic that identifies Decree Four as "a pitiable model of false doctrine in which sound theological underpinning is replaced by sociopolitical aims conveniently stitched together with the trill-notes of spiritual-sounding mush."[27]

For critics of the left and of the right both El Salvador and Nicaragua became flashpoints of controversy demonstrating either the miscreant and flawed genius of Pedro Arrupe and his ilk or, conversely, the dread consequences that followed upon the eclipse of Arrupe and the "restabilizing" of the Society under his much safer successor, Kolvenbach.

But there are regions of the world where debates over GC32 are virtually nonexistent, where Jesuits have moved from theory to practice with little care for theological and political niceties, and where the service of faith and the promotion of justice are pursued without dramatic flourish. One such place is West Kingston, Jamaica, in an utterly non-Catholic country with a history very different from that of Imperial and Most Catholic Spain.

The Archbishop of Kingston, Samuel Carter, is a black native Jamaican Jesuit who walks a fine line in a country where wealth is restricted to the few, the middle class is fledgling and timid, and the poor constitute an expanding and increasingly desperate mass. A member of the Maryland Province of the Society, Carter had a very direct encounter with racism while studying in the United States and entertains no illusions about the crippling and august power of systemic discrimination. The plight of the poor is at the core of his episcopal and Jesuit ministry and this ministry is seldom easy. Jim Webb, a Canadian Jesuit who knows Carter well, recognizes the value of the Archbishop's quiet but granite-like courage.

> Carter is very committed to the preferential option for the poor; he's very intelligent and understands what the phrase means and what it demands. Some of the very rich people in Jamaica think that he is a Communist, although he is really a middle-ground bishop in most of his positions, except on the issue of the poor for whom in his public utterances and pastoral letters he has declared his solidarity.
>
> To give you one example of what I mean: at one point some justice activists and Jesuits identified all the companies operating in Jamaica that had links with the South Africa of apartheid fame and brought the information to his attention and for his disposal. He called a meeting of church leaders and then summoned the press. That same evening I happened to be with him for a Confirmation class and when it was concluded we watched television to see how the press conference would be handled. They identified the list of Jamaican companies with South African connections—Gillette, Nestlé, etc.—and he looked at the list rolling down the screen, smiled, and said: "Well, there goes my charity drive this year."
>
> He knows. He knows that when he has to face the people who have just seen their companies on the TV that they are not going to be pleased with him. His stand will cost his charity drive money. But he will not be swayed.

Webb has been in Jamaica since 1980, and he currently works with his fellow Canadian Jesuit Brian Massie, a novice and scholastic or two, several sisters, and a number of Jamaican laypeople at St. Peter Claver parish, a community of some 500 families in West Kingston. The parish has a women's housing cooperative; a catechetical programme; a primary school; numerous outreach programmes that involve working with free zone workers—women who work in the garment factories in Kingston for slave wages—sewing, English, and mathematics classes; AIDS, nutrition, and cholera information workshops and clinics; as well as many other social and pastoral endeavours. There are twelve base communities in the parish; it is a successful experiment in liberation theology.

For Webb, steeped in the philosophy of Decree Four and an Arrupe Jesuit, St. Peter Claver is a laboratory in which to test the ideas of GC32, a sacred place in which to erase a notion of God that is anti-life and un-Christian, even if hallowed by official religious practices.

> When Hurricane Gilbert hit Jamaica a large majority of the people, including many preachers and priests, took this as a sign of God's punishing the people for their wickedness. But when you looked around and saw that the average poor person's house had been levelled by the hurricane with little chance ever to rebuild it, how could you ever imagine that this destruction could be willed by God? What kind of a notion of God do these people hold which would have you believe that God could so rapaciously punish the poor and innocent? When you start asking the question you discover that indeed many Jamaicans labour under a theology that justifies, explains, natural disasters as divine punishment for human misdeeds—by the poor and uneducated principally.
>
> Where does such a theology come from? More importantly, why is it maintained? There are 21 families in this country who are immensely wealthy by world standards, and they control 50 percent of the wealth of Jamaica. They are laughing all the way to the bank and the masses are convinced that they are poor because they are wicked. People need to be liberated from this kind of theology; they need to know that God is with the poor.

The God of the poor is the God that Arrupe pledged the Jesuits to serve and not an isolated trinket encased in a tabernacle or a divinity remote, ineffable, and enwrapped in transcendence. But it would be folly to think that Arrupe was therefore a man unaccustomed to traditional prayer, or that he had transformed the God of Ignatius into a humanist's deity of good deeds and noble sentiments. Arrupe was fully Ignatian in his spirituality, conventional in his devotion to the Virgin, and incontestably Rome's servant.

When he died on February 5, 1991, an era of revolutionary import came to an end. Although Alain Woodrow, a journalist on the staff of

Le Monde and author of *Les Jésuites*, has observed that on the essentials—the promotion of justice and solidarity with the poor—Arrupe's successor "does not hesitate a second in toeing the Arrupe line," Kolvenbach is made of different stuff. There is a different agenda to be faced. Yet Kolvenbach knows that the course set by Arrupe as early as the '60s and ratified by GC32 in the mid-'70s is as substantive a shift as the Jesuit enterprise in education in the 1540s and the post-Restoration theological conservatism of the mid-1800s.

The Jesuit as liberationist is here for the millennium.

IV

Jesuit as Educator

It would not be an exaggeration to observe that, from the outset, Ignatius of Loyola's chief ambition was the education of youth and the formation of the unenlightened. Indeed, the teaching of catechism to the young was a passion with the newly converted Ignatius and became a primary responsibility for all of the Companions of the early Society. *Regimini militantis ecclesiae*, the 1540 founding document of the Society of Jesus, captured the essence of Ignatius's intent: "Above all things let them have at heart the instruction of boys and ignorant persons in the knowledge of Christian doctrine, of the Ten Commandments, and other such rudiments as shall be suitable, having regard to the circumstances of persons, places, and times."[1] It is a directive that Ignatius enjoined upon Diego Laynez "in virtue of holy obedience."[2] As for the formative capacity of instruction, Ignatian education conducted through the Spiritual Exercises not only ignited Ignatius's Parisian converts and in so doing established the basis for the Montmartre vows, it also attracted adherents to the nascent Company and repeatedly drew the censorious attention of the Inquisition.

Still, as Ignatius conceived of the Society, as described in its founding documents, formal education as such was reserved for the preparation of the Society's recruits and was not envisioned as a ministry to society at large. Ultimately, it was Francis Xavier's nagging insistence on support for his secular college at Goa (and his frequent epistolary celebration of its successes) combined with the Society's

1547 transformation of Francis Borgia's college at Gandia into a secular university (a *studium generale*) that launched the Jesuits into an extended educational apostolate that was to become the hallmark of the Society. It was in Messina, Sicily, in 1548 that the Jesuits founded their first full-fledged classical college, but only eight years later in 1556 the Society had increased that number to thirty-five colleges; by the end of the sixteenth century their number had escalated to 245, and when the Society was suppressed in 1773 the network of Jesuit schools had multiplied to the point that "the extinction of the Order meant the closing of 546 colleges and 148 seminaries in Europe alone—145 in Italy, 124 in France, 117 in Spain, and nearly 300 in Germany, Austria, Belgium, Bohemia, Poland, and Lithuania. It meant in addition the closing of 123 colleges and 48 seminaries in missionary provinces of the Order, chiefly in Hispanic America and in India."[3]

Mindful of his own haphazard educational experiences in Spain, Ignatius looked rather to his alma mater at the University of Paris for the Society's original model of curriculum development and pedagogical effectiveness. At Paris Ignatius was moulded by a carefully organized system of education that was both traditional and contemporary. It presented the best of the philosophical Middle Ages, but without the cerebral aloofness of the postscholastic logicians; the University of Paris also explored the humanistic and more worldly concerns of the Renaissance, complete with the exuberant rediscovery of classical Latin and Greek writers, and especially of Cicero's rhetoric. There was also an appreciation of the philosophical and theological precision of Thomas Aquinas and an eschewing of the simple sophistical idolatry of rhetoric as an end in itself. Ignatius learned much at Paris both with respect to the means and the method, the form, and the content of a sound education. In his Constitutions (IV, 14), he directed that Aquinas should replace Peter Lombard as the philosopher's touchstone, and the Fifth General Congregation of the Society of Jesus, Decree 41, recorded that "by unanimous opinion, the congregation decreed that our professors were to follow the teaching of Saint Thomas in scholastic theology as being more sound, more secure, more approved, and more in accord with our Constitutions."[4] Indeed, for Ignatius and the early Jesuits Thomas Aquinas was the unparalleled angelic doctor (i.e., teacher):

"In teaching," the fathers of the Congregation added, "let it be our care first to strengthen faith and nourish virtue. Wherefore in matters that Saint Thomas does not explicitly teach, no one should teach anything that does not accord with the sense of the Church and with accepted traditions or which would in any way lessen a firm and solid piety." While advocating the superiority of the Thomistic theological compendium, Ignatius completed his educational design by also pressing the Augustinian appreciation of Ciceronian rhetoric as a practical tool for inculcating virtue and changing social values, of plundering Egyptian gold to grace the Christian temple. Contemplation in action was an educational as well as an ascetic principle.

At Paris Ignatius found a rationally ordered approach to intellectual and professional progress. Though it incorporated Renaissance humanistic concerns and classical ideals, the curriculum at Paris grew out of and adapted for its own use the traditional seven liberal arts, the trivium (grammar, rhetoric, and logic) and quadrivium (mathematics, geometry, music, and astronomy) so central to the medieval university. Sensitive to the Renaissance emphasis on the human, the colleges at which Ignatius studied at Paris provided an essentially person-centred emphasis on the learning experience. The student's progress from one intellectual plateau to the next depended more on the individual's own capacity to learn than on systemic lockstep movement from a lower grade to the higher. The learning experience was more interactive than passive. Real value was placed on disputation and repetition. And student discipline was prized.

The person-centred nature of the Paris model is one that the untutored Ignatius understood intuitively; indeed, his Spiritual Exercises move precisely from that starting point. As a result, several students of Ignatius have observed that his educational philosophy springs quite comfortably from the Exercises. John English, a spiritual director at the internationally admired Ignatian Centre at Guelph, Ontario, sees the Spiritual Exercises as the absolute bedrock of Jesuit educational philosophy:

> What the Exercises are about is experience reflecting on experience, articulating experience, and interpreting experience and making a decision out of the experience. That is in the Exercises and I think that's the basic Jesuit pedagogy in those

five steps. The *Ratio Studiorum* [the traditional handbook of Jesuit pedagogy] was just a technique to move people through experience to reflection, to articulating, to interpreting, and to deciding. That's how I understand the Ignatian pedagogy that's in the Exercises and which gets transferred into the school system. As it happens, in the last thirty or forty years, experience has become very, very significant; so people now are trying to get in touch with their story, my story, or our story. What is present in my story, what is present in our story that is pulling us into the future? That's really, from my point of view, Ignatian pedagogy that you actually see directly in the Exercises. I would think that in good Jesuit schools and universities this should be uppermost. They should be working with this dynamic.

The biggest danger with that is individualism. In today's world when you say "person," for many people that says the isolated individual. I don't think that's Jesuit. I think that the individual is constituted by relationship and therefore there has to be a communal component in the educational system. It's focusing on person, but not so much on an individualism. Not on collectivity either. These are little distinctions that are very necessary.

Ignatius's model for his educational system incorporated the best of the Parisian, though he imbued it with a Christian rather than a merely secular humanism. For Ignatius, education had both a personal and a social dimension, all aimed at the complete "care of souls," so that the Constitutions of the Society of Jesus record that "[v]ery special care should be taken so those who come to the universities of the Society to obtain knowledge should acquire along with it good Christian moral habits" (*Cristianas costumbres*, IV, 16). As a result, the Constitutions specify that Jesuit education is open to all, and free to all: "just as the Society teaches altogether gratis, so should it confer the degrees completely free" (IV, 15). The Constitutions also have a good deal to say about the specifics of a Jesuit education, outlining principles with respect to content, structure, and the individualized, person-centred character of the educational ministry. In the Jesuit university, young boys began their studies at approximately the age of 10 and they entered with an assumed ability to read and to write basic Latin. Ignatius's university provided youngsters aged approximately 10 to 13 with a careful and thorough grounding in Latin grammar, taking them through an intensive two-year programme of rhetoric, poetry, and history. The objective was to develop in the student a facility for reading and writing Latin with ease and grace while imbuing him with classical culture and aesthetics, enriched by Renaissance and Christian insight, while simultaneously preparing the young man for study in philosophy and the related arts. But Latin was not only the *lingua ecclesiastica*. It was also the language of commerce, government, and culture; hence, to become thoroughly conversant with the Latin language and conversationally adept in the Latin tongue were not only the means of assimilating classical Latin and preparing the aspiring student for a career in the church, it also ensured a route to personal success and social influence.

The Constitutions placed a heavy emphasis on debate, disputation, and public defence of contentious theses. Not only the students, but the professors too were to dispute publicly with one another. Cicero's rhetoric and the Renaissance admiration of eloquence, right reason, and oratorical style (of *eloquentia perfecta*) combined to make the Jesuit a formidable adversary in confrontations with the Reformers, and gained for him both a respect and a suspicion for effective use of rhetorical schemes and tropes. Not surprisingly, the public nature of discourse and debate soon evolved into dramatic form and Jesuit theatre quickly became an integral part both of the student's practical education in the art of Latin eloquence as well as a practical means of transforming society by inculcating proper Catholic values. The dramatic production, therefore, moved quite naturally beyond the accustomed fortnightly and monthly debate into the classical realm of Aristotelian catharsis and Horatian *dulce et utile*: drama could not only inculcate self-confidence and style in the orator (be he 12 or 20), but could move the frequently teary-eyed audiences to avoid vice and to embrace virtue. Little wonder that Jesuit theatre (usually produced in Latin) flourished in spectacular form and attracted the patronage of townspeople, the moneyed classes, and royalty.[5] Spectacle does not come cheaply, and the unlettered in particular relied on spectacle since Latin dialogue was generally beyond their comprehension. Indeed, precisely because Jesuit drama had become so complex and so expensive, the 1591 preliminary formulation of the *Ratio Studiorum* carried the directive: "In regard to staging comedies and tragedies, let the Rector come to a decision with the Provincial in good season; nor should he allow all the work of training the actors, gathering the costumes and preparing the stage to devolve upon the author of the play [normally either a member of the faculty or of the student body], but should see that his burden is lightened by the co-operation of others."[6] As part of the spectacle, the tradition of Jesuit theatre extended also to dance, a form of artistic religious expression that lives on even today in various forms, the most inventive of which is no doubt Robert VerEecke's Boston Liturgical Dance Ensemble whose lavish visual celebration of the Christian message has been received with both joy and scorn.[7]

The typically successful student of the trivium and quadrivium spent his fourteenth to sixteenth years immersed in logic, physics, metaphysics, mathematics, and the study of morals, after which he received the bachelor of arts degree. For those destined to pursue higher studies, the faculties of theology, law, and medicine awaited, with theology being the queen of the sciences. It was a system to become enshrined in the Jesuit method of studies, their *Ratio Studiorum*.

Ignatius's decision that the Company should embrace the educational apostolate forced him not only to turn to Paris for a curricular model and a pedagogical method, it also caused him to turn his attention to the shaping of a system of education that would embrace not just one school, but a network of schools. It was a task with no precedent. And it was an ongoing task to be initially completed more than forty years after Ignatius's death. Typically, in designing their programme of education, the Jesuits set out to study the varied experiences shared by their companions from the four corners of the earth. Following some fifty years of experience and reflection beginning with the founding of the Jesuit university at Messina, the first codification of Jesuit educational philosophy and educational practice was formally accepted and promulgated in the *Ratio atque Institutio Studiorum Iesu* of 1599.

During a December 1992 interview, John Padberg, the Director of the Institute of Jesuit Sources at St. Louis University in St. Louis, Missouri, outlined the nature of the *Ratio*.

> The *Ratio*, to put it in its simplest term, was a handbook on how to teach. But, it's much more than that. It was basically a handbook that grew out of the experience of Jesuit teaching and a very rapid expansion of Jesuit teaching in the last years of Ignatius's life and for a few decades after his death. By the 1580s, the then General of the Society, Father Claudio Aquaviva, decided in a way to gather that experience and almost to codify it into a manual of practice whereby adequate teachers might learn from good teachers, and good teachers might learn how to become excellent teachers. As a result, first and foremost, the *Ratio* is a manual of practice on how to conduct a class, what courses were to be taught year by year by year in the Jesuit schools, what classroom method was to be like, what books were to be used, what authors were to be treated. It's especially that and it prevailed in the Jesuit schools from after 1599 when the definitive edition of the *Ratio* was promulgated all the way up to the temporary suppression of the Society in 1773.
>
> One of the things that's most important to remember about Jesuit education falls within the purview, the ambit of the *Ratio*, and that is that it was the first organized system of education in the Western world. In two ways: first of all, you could go from Montreal, for example, in Canada to Monreale in Sicily, or you could go from Cuzco in Peru to Krakow in Poland and have the same system of Jesuit education, an international system where people could easily move from one place to another. For example, towards the end of the sixteenth century, Edmund Campion, after leaving England, coming to the continent, joining the Society, taught briefly in Rome, then taught in Prague and from there was called to go to England. He could do that because there was a coherent uniform system throughout all of the Jesuit educational enterprises. The internal system was such though that year-by-year, step-by-step, students entering a Jesuit school could progress in an orderly and intelligible manner from the lowest classes up to the highest.

We take for granted, at the present time, that a person enters a school at a particular month, most often September or October, goes to an organized course of studies, completes that at the end of spring or the beginning of summer, and presupposing that he or she has done successfully, is advanced to the next year. That kind of thing really didn't exist as such, a system of progression in secondary education, until the Jesuits developed it and popularized it and propagated it.

That's what the *Ratio* is all about, but there's something even more important about the *Ratio* which I would like to mention. At the beginning of one of the trial editions of the *Ratio*—and remember, it grew out of the tried and true experience of the Jesuits—Diego Ledesma, who is one of the Jesuits' great educational theorists, asked why Jesuits had schools. In response, he gave four reasons which are pretty well, it seems to me, the same kind of reasons for which Jesuits would run schools today. He said, first of all, that Jesuit schools provide a way in which people can effectively, practically earn a living; that is, there is a practical reason for education. Secondly, they provide for the right governing of society and the proper making of law and public affairs. In other words, there is a social reason for education. Thirdly, he said that Jesuits have schools because they provide (I'm using his baroque term, now) for the ornaments, splendour, and perfection of the rational nature of man. In other words, there is the liberalizing effective end of education. Finally, he said, and this is almost a quotation although I don't have it in front of me, "What is most important, is that education helps lead humankind, men and women, most securely to their last end, God our Lord." In other words, there is a religious motive for the Jesuit educational enterprise. So you've got a practical, a social or civic, a cultural or liberal, and a religious motive for Jesuit education. I think most Jesuit educational enterprises today would say, given all due consideration of their circumstances and the kind of school they have, that's why we're in it.

Indeed, the official *Ratio* of 1599 outlines in no little detail the expectations of every Jesuit university no matter its home country.

Within the *Ratio* there are rules for the Jesuit provincial, for the rector, the prefect of higher studies, for the professors, and for the students; rules for the beadles and rules for the academies, rules for the Jesuit students and rules for the externs; rules for examinations, rules for prizes, and rules for punishment. As for the curriculum, it is carefully laid out both with respect to content and with respect to pedagogical performance. In sum, the *Ratio* contains a comprehensive design intended to ensure an immersion into classical culture, mastery of material, quickness of mind, sensitivity to individual ability, and personal discipline. The method is preeminently efficient and wholly utilitarian. Not surprisingly, several of the early General Congregations exhorted the Society's schools to be faithful to the letter of the *Ratio*; Decree 23 of the 1649 ninth General Congregation captures both the nature of the *Ratio* and the Jesuits' concern for sound pedagogy: "The complaints of several provinces against philosophy teachers were reported. They are said to waste time on useless questions. They treat their subject matter in jumbled order. They take unto themselves excessive license to offer their opinions. However, in accord with the judgement of the commission on studies, the conclusion of the congregation was that in the *Ratio studiorum* there is sufficient provision for this kind of undesirable practice in the rules of the Prefect of Studies and of the Professors of Philosophy."[8]

Although the Enlightenment had changed radically the way the educated elite viewed the world, and also changed the education that helped shape the way they looked at the world, the Society of Jesus hung on too formally to the philosophical and hierarchical view of the world at the heart of the *Ratio* of 1599 with its narrow stress on Aquinas, Aristotle, Plato, Homer, Hesiod, Pindar, and the like—spiced as it was with a sprinkling of hagiographic and doctrinal texts. Indeed, the 17th General Congregation, which was held in 1751, affirmed the conviction of the previous congregation that "even in general physics the system of Aristotle must be taught and defended, and that the more attractive and experimental physics very well conforms to it."[9] Although the 1785 General Congregation, which convened in Russia, confirmed the need to review the *Ratio*, only after the suppression and restoration of the Society in 1814 did the Jesuit Curia in Rome seriously and formally revisit the Aquaviva formula that had served them so well for so long. There was a real need, as Ignatius would have said, to transform the old formula in light of the practical need to have "regard to the circumstances of persons, places, and times." Nonetheless, talk about revisions to the *Ratio* persists like a well-worn leitmotif well into the mid-twentieth century. It was an exercise never to be completed.

John Padberg notes the impossibility of a single, formulaic post-Enlightenment approach to the educational enterprise:

> When the Society of Jesus was restored in 1814, the world had changed dramatically: a political, social, cultural, intellectual, religious, artistic revolution had taken place. Not just the French Revolution in its political terms, but the change to romanticism, for example, the beginnings of the industrial revolution, et cetera. The Jesuits' first General Congregation, or general chapter, or general legislative meeting after the restoration, asked that a new version of the *Ratio* be prepared. One was prepared and publicly sent out to Jesuit institutions in 1832, but it was never adopted officially or promulgated officially for all the schools of the Society by any later general legislative assembly, because it became quite clear that the world had changed so drastically that you couldn't set down such a handbook of teaching methods for places as different as —well, let's take today—Kathmandu, on the one hand, or the University of Sudbury, on the other hand.

Although Ignatius had long conceived of the formation of the *Ratio* as a desirable objective and although Aquaviva had made it a matter of pressing concern for his administration, it did not come easily into being, nor did it arrive without a groundswell of concern and some expressed discontent from several of the international provinces. Even from the beginning it was clear that the needs of time, place, and persons made so comprehensive an approach to educational homogeneity quite a questionable proposition. Which is not to say that Aquaviva had not provided for variation at the provincial level. He had. Nor is it to suggest that the Society had ignored entirely the shifting emphases from the deductive to the inductive, from the reasoned realm of the medieval schoolmen to the more tangible, mathematical, and empirical world of the Renaissance experimentalist, from the world of ideas to the world of matter. Indeed, the Society boasts an impressive list of presuppression Jesuit scholars of mathematics, physics, astronomy, anatomy, and the like. As one indication of the Jesuit Curia's concern to reach beyond the traditional curriculum outlined in the *Ratio*, Allan Farrell recalls General Lorenzo Ricci's 1764 letter to the province of Mexico: "There is no doubt that you have among you competent theologians and moralists, but I wish to make sure that you have teachers equally competent in the humanities, in experimental physics, mathematics, and history, with its auxiliary sciences, such as numismatics, historical criticism, epigraphy, and archeology. I do not mean that everyone needs to become a master of all these branches, but that there should be outstanding scholars in each of them; that in some all should be instructed, in others, of a more specialized nature, only the chosen few."[10]

Although the proposed *Ratio* of 1832 did indeed make concessions with post-Enlightenment education theory by placing a renewed emphasis on physics and mathematics in their proper place, Jesuit education could not accept the wholly human-centred, amoral, and essentially atheistic emphasis of that education. Nor could the Jesuits abide its liberalizing directions either with respect to content or to the growing diversity of elective subjects of study. Indeed, the newly formed emphasis on state control of the educational undertaking by its very nature was undermining the essence of education as Ignatius and his companions had envisioned it and, indeed, had pioneered it. Jesuit General Jan Roothaan embraced the practical aspects of nineteenth-century educational theory, but he was unwilling to relinquish the essentially moral characteristics of a sound human development and the absolute centrality of Latin, Greek, and philosophy. Roothaan lamented both the dismantling of the progressive Parisian curricular plan adapted by Ignatius and the reduced emphasis on honing students' critical abilities to think clearly and to argue convincingly—the abandoning of *eloquentia perfecta* as a noble formational objective:

> In the higher schools or in the treatment of graver studies, it is a subject of lamentation with prudent men that there is no solidity but much show; that there is an ill-arranged mass of superfluous knowledge, but very little exact reasoning; that

> the sciences, if you except Physics and Mathematics, have not made any true progress, but are in general confusion, so that it is not clear where the final results of truth are to be found. The study of Logic and severe Dialectics is almost in contempt, whence errors come to be deeply rooted in the minds of men who are not otherwise illiterate; and these errors, by some fatality or other, are made much of, as if they were ascertained truths, and they are lauded to the skies, because nothing is treated with strictness and accuracy, no account is made of definitions and distinctness of reasoning. Thus, tasting lightly of philosophical matters, young men go forth utterly defenceless against sophistry, since they cannot even see the difference between a sophism and an argument. . . . [11]

Driven by the necessity of adapting to persons, places, and times, since the Society's nineteenth-century efforts to renew the *Ratio* the Jesuits have proven typically inventive, typically practical, typically accommodating. Indeed, the recent appearance of *Conversations on Jesuit Higher Education* published in the United States through the Institute of Jesuit Sources under the sponsorship of the National Seminar on Jesuit Higher Education is one tangible sign of the Society of Jesus's continuing efforts to find its own characteristic voice in the contemporary field of post-secondary education. And so, *Conversations* struggles with the traditional and the practical in Jesuit education by publishing theme issues on topics such as "Helping College Students Make Moral Decisions" (Fall 1992) and "Preparing for Service: Professional Education in Jesuit Colleges and Universities" (Spring 1993). John Padberg encapsulates the transition from the 1830s to the 1990s when he observes:

> Ignatius had said in the Constitutions that normally we wouldn't have faculties of medicine and law in which the Jesuits were engaged, but he also said in the Constitutions that that, of course, also depends upon the circumstances of time and place. And so in 1992 we celebrated the four hundredth year of the founding of the first medical faculty at Pont à Mousson, a little town in modern France not too far from the city of Nancy. The Jesuits got into professional education especially after the 1814 restoration of the Society of Jesus when

> that kind of education advanced beyond the baccalaureate and when a not exactly simply academic doctorate came into vogue. It came into vogue especially in the New World in the United States and Canada. So, we have the kind of schools that would be business administration, law, nursing, we even have very recently founded a school of public health at St. Louis University. We have a great variety of professional education because the Jesuits are convinced that all things can contribute to the glory of God, the service of humankind. Given the increasing professionalization of the world today, it's important, it seems to me, that we take seriously the professions, every one of them, as a way in which to help men and women in this world.

These are developments with which Ignatius could not have been unhappy. As the Jesuit guru on Jesuit education, George Ganss, observes time and again, Ignatius was a practical man whose selection of subjects for his curriculum "was their usefulness, either for studying or for living in his era."[12] For Ignatius there was also the concomitant need to adjust to present needs. Ganss argues that Ignatius had learned the lesson that many of his contemporaries had not: "adapt yourself to the tastes and needs of your own age, or you will atrophy while your new competitors thrive."[13] Indeed, Jesuit education has been persistently admired as an effective formative model from the day the Spanish viceroy invited the Society to establish a university in Messina in 1547 for the lay people of that city. Acting from similar motivations, Frederick II of Prussia and Catherine II of Russia were motivated in no small manner by their unwillingness to abandon the Society's educational structures when they refused to extend the suppression of the Society to their territories; and decimation of the educational systems of Spain, Portugal, and France resulting from the suppression has historically validated those refusals. With the restoration of 1814, the Society began its efforts to reconstruct what had been destroyed, but they achieved only a partial success. The golden days of Jesuit education had passed. Nonetheless, the original intention of educating the uninfluential without cost has been generally accepted as a socially and humanly responsible objective; on the other hand, the Society's efforts to educate the influential so that they might in turn become the reshapers of a new society has enjoyed a checkered success.

Contemporary figures such as Cuba's Fidel Castro, the United States' Bill Clinton, Canada's Pierre Elliott Trudeau, and Holland's Ruud Lubbers provide vivid examples of the Jesuit attempt to influence the influential as a means of initiating social change. Fidel Castro was the son of a landowner who was hardly wealthy but did have the wherewithal to provide the future revolutionary with a sound education. Castro came under the influence of the Jesuits in the fifth grade at Colegio de Dolores in Santiago de Cuba, a school that he characterizes as "a prestigious upper-class school." Castro's reflections on his jesuitical training are not wholly unlike those captured by James Joyce's unflattering depiction of Father Butler in his story "An Encounter" or Father Arnall in *A Portrait of the Artist as a Young Man*; but Castro also colours his criticism with genuine gratitude and undisguised admiration. In the Jesuits he found "teachers and other men who were interested in moulding the students' character. They were Spaniards. In general, I think that . . . the traditions of the Jesuits and their military spirit—their military organization—go with the Spanish personality. They were very rigorous, demanding people, who were interested in their students and in their character and behaviour. In other words, I acquired ethics and norms that weren't just religious. I got a human influence from the teachers' authority and the values they attached to things."[14]

Motivated by his experience with the Jesuits at Colegio de Dolores, Castro decided to continue through high school with them and enrolled at the Colegio de Belén in Havana, which he calls "the best Jesuit school in the country." Although he found the Jesuits at Colegio de Belén to be "very backward politically," many of them being pro-Franco, they were nonetheless well trained and impressively dedicated, he thought. The programme contained echoes of the *Ratio* with the inclusion of logic and philosophy as well as the heavy stress on repetition and mental drill. Jesuit meditation was, for Castro, "a form of mental terrorism." But through it all, he was imbued with characteristics he credits with shaping the successful guerrilla revolutionary. "Undoubtedly, my teachers, my Jesuit teachers—especially the Spanish Jesuits, who inculcated a strong sense of personal dignity, regardless of their political ideas—influenced me.

Most Spaniards are endowed with a sense of personal honor, and it's very strong in the Jesuits. They valued character, rectitude, honesty, courage and the ability to make sacrifices. Teachers definitely have an influence. The Jesuits clearly influenced me with their strict organization, their discipline and their values." [15]

Pierre Elliott Trudeau, Canada's fifteenth prime minister (1968–79, 1980–84), who governed like a modern-day philosopher king, was widely recognized for a quickness of mind, combative rhetorical style, and ready wit that often led to his being characterized as jesuitical. The term is not misplaced. Trudeau's early training at Collège Jean-de-Brébeuf in Montreal thrust him into an environment and a traditional Jesuit programme where his natural talents were to blossom. In his book *Memoirs*, Trudeau celebrates the exceptional teaching skills of his Jesuit mentors, noting in particular their encouraging of the cut and thrust of effective debate. In Trudeau's mind, the Jesuits were extraordinary men with extraordinary inclinations, especially during the repressive years of Maurice Le Noblet Duplessis's leadership in Catholic Quebec. "In an era and in a society where freedom of speech was not held in high regard," Trudeau records, "they encouraged their students to speak out. They insisted, of course, that the discourse be focused on what they were teaching, but we were able to go beyond this framework without incurring too great risk. For someone like me, who for a long time had always wanted the last word, it was a joy to constantly test how far I could go without going too far." [16] His rallying cry in the 1968 general election—"The Just Society"—represents a passion that might seem to echo the social teachings of the Second Vatican Council and the mind of Good Pope John, and it is an election theme for which many a post-32nd General Congregation Jesuit might naturally want to take credit, but the influence is in fact more France's darling of the Catholic left, Emmanuel Mounier, and the 1891/1931 papal encyclicals on social justice (*Rerum novarum* and *Quadragesimo anno*) that represent the source of Trudeau's philosophical hunger for justice.

As for Bill Clinton and his student days at the Society's Georgetown University law school in Washington, D.C., the Jesuit influence is in fact more likely to be displayed in this southern Baptist's penchant for social justice and his understanding of the religious dimension of faith and justice than in a clever turn of phrase or subtlety of mind. But the jury is still out on Clinton.

Interestingly enough, both Castro's and Trudeau's education predated the social justice emphases of Vatican II and the 32nd General Congregation that followed it. Yet it was these two events in the modern history of the Roman Catholic Church that shook the vision of the Society of Jesus and of Jesuit education to their very roots. During the 1991 celebrations marking the five hundredth anniversary of the birth of Ignatius and the 450th anniversary of the founding of the Society, Assistant General Giuseppe Pittau, quoting Pedro Arrupe, characterized his companions as "Rooted in the Past, immersed in the present, set out for the future."[17] The observation nicely captures the nature of modern Jesuit education, though its definition remains as elusive as the individual Jesuit's acceptance of the 32nd General Congregation itself.

Doug McCarthy, past novice master of the Jesuit house of formation in Guelph, Ontario, observes that

> with the 32nd General Congregation we left the courts of the kings and moved into the courts of the poor, and unless we remain on the courts of the poor and do our ministry from there, we are not going to meet the needs of this time. I know that there are people who can't do that, who can't move to the courts of the poor. I don't think we can get the message across without being there. I think we have to be on the margins of society to be able to speak to the mainstream of society. We can't speak to a mainstream society living the way mainstream society lives. I don't think we are heard. We have no credibility, we have nothing to say if we're in the mainstream. So, we have to go to the courts of the poor. I don't mean just the financially disadvantaged here. We have to be with them and they will mould our message for us. Until we do that, I think we will plod along, keeping our institutions going and meeting needs and doing good work, but not meeting that hunger that I talked about in the way it has to be met.

As for the Ignatian traditional incentive to shape the leaders of society, McCarthy's point of view is consistent with his social gospel, though not universally shared: "It never worked for the past

500 years. We've been shaping them for 500 years: a trickle down doesn't happen in economics, and it doesn't happen in leadership."

The social principles that Doug McCarthy outlines have been thoroughly absorbed by pastoral academics like Jon Sobrino and Dean Brackley at the José Simeón Cañas campus of the University of Central America in San Salvador, and they are at the heart of the 32nd General Congregation's motivating thesis, which holds that "the service of faith and the promotion of justice cannot be for us simply one ministry among others. It must be the integrating factor of all our ministries; and not only of our ministries but of our inner life as individuals, as communities, and as a world-wide brotherhood."[18] Both the letter and the spirit of the documents emanating from the 32nd General Congregation echo Arrupe's observation of the order as being "rooted in the past, immersed in the present, set out for the future"; indeed, there is in the records of that Congregation a constant harkening back to Ignatius and to the formative statements from which the Society took its early shape.

Although the theory is clear, it would, of course, be naive to assume that all Jesuits and all Jesuit institutions have eagerly embraced the justice dimension of the 32nd General Congregation or that all Jesuit educational institutions reflect its principles. One need only walk the streets around the Lone Mountain Campus at the Jesuit University of San Francisco and note, for example, the provision for instruction in military studies to get a sense of the difference between the spirit and the letter of the law. Nor does one need to engage in detailed discourse with the Jesuits' conservative renegade at the University of San Francisco, Joe Fessio, to know that there are still deep divisions between thought and practice within the Society. And, indeed, there is many a modern Jesuit who exudes the air of a Boston politician or New York businessman. Ignatius himself cultivated the wealthy, the powerful, and even royalty in his service of the poor—it is an approach used by many a churchman and, as *My Father's Business*, the biography of Gerald Emmett Cardinal Carter, past cardinal archbishop of Toronto, testifies, it is a practical approach that leaves one open to sometimes bitter controversy. As a matter of realpolitik, it is difficult nonetheless not to observe with the goodhearted prostitute in Morley Callaghan's *Such Is My Beloved* that prayer does not pay the rent. The tension between serving the poor and tending to the needs of the well-to-do is hardly new. It would be more than surprising if the Jesuits could solve the matter with the promulgation of a document, and it would be nothing less than astonishing not to find the tension (or is it a contradiction?) very much an issue within the Society. It is, therefore, a tension very close to the surface in much of what is to follow.

In its effort to read the signs of the times, the 32nd General Congregation struggles with the need to be of service, to be contemporary, to be faithful to the past, and to be realistic. There is a call to reassess "traditional apostolic methods, attitudes and institutions with a view to adapting them to the new needs of the times. . . ."[19] With respect to education, that reassessment suggests a number of explicit challenges:

> —We must be more aware of the need for research and for theological reflection, carried on in a context which is both interdisciplinary and genuinely integrated with the culture in which it is done and with its traditions. Only thus can it throw light on the main problems which the Church and humanity ought to be coming to grips with today.
> —Greater emphasis should be placed on the conscientization according to the Gospel of those who have power to bring about social change, and a special place given to service of the poor and the oppressed.
> —We should pursue and intensify the work of formation in every sphere of education, while subjecting it at the same time to continual scrutiny. We must help prepare both young people and adults to live and labour for others and with others to build a more just world. Especially we should help form our Christian students in such a way that animated by a mature faith and personally devoted to Jesus Christ, they can find Him in others and having recognized Him there, they will serve Him in their neighbour. In this way we shall contribute to the formation of those who by a kind of multiplier-effect will share in the process of educating the world itself.[20]

As part of its contribution to the ongoing dialogue on the nature and philosophy of Jesuit education, in 1987 the Jesuit Secondary

Education Association in the United States issued a booklet entitled *Go Forth and Teach: The Characteristics of Jesuit Education.*[21] *Go Forth* effectively combines the formative ideas of Jesuit education with the directives of the 32nd General Congregation to produce a handy reference tool for inculcating the spirit of the Society into an environment in which lay people are rapidly replacing Jesuits in the classroom, in the administrative offices, and in the boardrooms. *Go Forth* is an effective vehicle for bequeathing into lay hands not merely buildings and professional positions, but also a philosophy of education that is identifiably Jesuit. The benchmarks are all familiar ones: a systemic commitment to faith that does justice; a stress on *eloquentia perfecta* as determined by local persons, place, and time; the development of an inquiring and critical mind; the formation of the individual as a Christian living practically within a social context; the shaping of a critically responsible individual sensitive to local culture; the inculcation of a spirit centred on service for others in imitation of Christ; the inclusion of a justice dimension in all courses; the placing of service to others above personal material gain; the pursuit of excellence, with human excellence being the highest goal; the education of "leaders in service"; diversification based on circumstances of persons and place; and a rejection of the competition exalted within the *Ratio* in favour of the instilling of a sense of cooperation and community. These are noble ideals, and they are transferrable ideals. They can be found, for example, at England's Stonyhurst College, arguably the flagship of the Jesuit secondary schools.

Set on a campus of some 200 acres of rolling hills, teaming waterways, and verdant woods in beautiful Lancashire in northwest England, Stonyhurst is a vibrant symbol of a Jesuit educational system rooted in its past, immersed in the present, and set for the future. An impressive reflection of the privileged academic life thriving within its walls, Stonyhurst College is housed within a constantly updated and thoroughly modernized renaissance manorial complex that serves as the academic home to some four hundred boys aged 13 to 18 living in its residences, another forty or so students (some of them girls) living in nearby homes, and some fifty faculty. On the surface, the Stonyhurst curriculum is rooted in the *Ratio*, with a Stonyhurst adaptation of the *Ratio's* academic grades so that students proceed in turn through lower grammar, grammar, syntax, poetry, and rhetoric; and the aim of the Stonyhurst curriculum, like that of the *Ratio*, is centred on the fashioning of the socially involved Christian individual, with due consideration given to persons, time, and place. At the same time, therefore, Stonyhurst boasts the most modern of facilities for the teaching of biology, chemistry, and physics, and provides regular as well as additional A-level instruction in mathematics even while preparing for university admission significant numbers of students in pursuit of a time-honoured specialization in the classics. Indeed, the architecture, history, and curriculum of Stonyhurst reflect the incessantly practical doggedness traditionally characteristic of the Society of Jesus in pursuit of the ideal. Stonyhurst also stands as a telling symbol of the Jesuit conviction that it is part of the Society's charism to establish, to inspire, and then to move on, leaving the task to others: even with the constant diminution of formally professed Jesuits among its numbers, Stonyhurst remains thoroughly Jesuit.

The college's first lay headmaster, Dr. Giles Mercer, sums up Stonyhurst's fidelity to its historical roots:

> Are there characteristics which remain essentially the same over 400 years in the College? There are persistent ideals demanding implementation; that nothing can be taught in an ethical vacuum; that education is an apostolate serving families; that the school should foster a strong sense of community; that pupils must always be valued and treated as individuals and every teacher should be a mentor in and out of the classroom; that those who are educated in the College should be taught how to think, not simply what to think, and they should, beginning at school and then through later life, think, judge and act for the good of others and, as the Jesuit motto has it, "for the greater glory of God".[22]

Today's Stonyhurst springs from seeds planted at the College of St. Omers in the northwestern region of modern-day France during the reign of Elizabeth I and in direct response to her government's efforts to Protestantize the motherland. Britain's Penal Laws, variously promulgated in 1571, 1581, and 1593, targeted in particular the recusant Roman Catholic population who refused to attend Church of

England services and who were unwilling to take the Oath of Allegiance to the Crown, an oath which was to become a prerequisite for the reception of a university degree. Both the antipapist tone of Elizabeth's England as well as its expressed anti-Jesuit barbs were sufficient to spur the Society's missionary zeal. But the founding of St. Omers is more specifically a response to the government's stipulation that Roman Catholics were not allowed to educate their children in any but state-authorized schools, be these schools in Britain or abroad, and to the 1593 regulation which, for the purpose of the education of a recusant's children over the age of seven, decreed that such offspring be committed to the care of others. In that same year, Robert Persons, friend and confidant of English Jesuit Martyr Edmund Campion, accepted the generous financial support of King Philip II of Spain and established the Jesuit school at St. Omers where the Jesuits already ran a Walloon college and whose pleasant air reminded Persons of England.

Although 1593 predated the promulgation of Aquaviva's final version of the *Ratio* by some six years, the preliminary versions were by then in circulation, and Persons turned naturally to them when designing the educational path to be followed at St. Omers Jesuit college. Accordingly, Thomas Muir's analysis shows that in 1632 St. Omers's curriculum was progressively structured from Third Grammar, Second Grammar, First Grammar, Humanities, and Rhetoric in appropriate imitation of the *Ratio's* Lower Grammar, Middle Grammar, Upper Grammar, Humanities, and Rhetoric. Also like most Jesuit schools, St. Omers was an instant success. Though it lived through turbulent times its student body quickly escalated from its original 19 to more than 100 boys most years, reaching a high of 200 in 1635. Enrolment quite understandably fluctuated with the ebb and flow of hostilities on the continent, reactions to alleged Popish Plots at home, depletion of family income resulting from the payment of fines imposed by the Penal Laws, and as a result of two destructive fires at the college, at least the second of which was of suspicious origin. As the seventeenth century drew to a close, England became even more inhospitable to Roman Catholics, with legislation being passed to impose heavy fines on anyone convicted of sending a child overseas for Catholic schooling and for anyone running a Catholic school. St. Omers became a relatively safe haven from the persecutions of recusants at home as well as fertile soil for the fostering of priestly vocations.

In 1762 St. Omers's odyssey began, an odyssey that was to terminate at Stonyhurst. On April 1 of that year, the French Parlement moved to suppress the Society by confiscating its lands and closing its colleges. The assets at St. Omers were seized on July 9 and on August 6 Parlement ordered the closure of all Jesuit houses in France. Moving in small groups, the students began their trek to Bruges, Belgium, in what was then within the Austrian Netherlands and Maria Theresa Hapsburg territory, where the college found a temporary safe haven; but the times were tempestuous and the stay destined to be brief. In 1773 the Society was formally suppressed and the St. Omers Jesuits were once again on the move, this time to Liège where the college found a home until 1794 when the aggressive aftermath of the French Revolution spurred the Jesuits once more to seek a more friendly environment. By this time, anti-Catholic suspicions in England had begun to subside, the legal effects of the Penal Laws were being softened, and the English college could finally look to the motherland for a welcome port. Thomas Weld, a Bruges Old Boy, offered Stonyhurst manor for the college's new location, and the final pilgrimage was under way.

The tenacity of the St. Omers Jesuits provides a chronicle reminiscent of the unrelenting determination of Ignatius himself. Along that tortured path, Stonyhurst has accumulated a long list of saints and martyrs, seven Victoria Crosses, and a host of influential Old Boys, many of whom played prominent roles in the early development of the United States, and no few number of whom have assumed influential roles both within Britain and abroad. Despite its upper-class heritage and no doubt because of its Jesuit character, Stonyhurst has been able to embrace the social direction of the 32nd General Congregation as it was captured, for example, in the 1986 document issued by the Jesuit curia and entitled *Characteristics of Jesuit Education*. *The Stonyhurst Magazine* reprinted parts of that document as they relate to matters of justice, social sin, and the preferential option for the poor. The segment designated the Awareness of Social Effects of Sin and Injustice explains:

> A realistic knowledge of creation sees the goodness of what God has made, but includes an *awareness of the social effects of*

> *sin*: the essential incompleteness, the injustice, and the need for redemption in all people, in all cultures, in all human structures, Jesuit education emphasizes the need to be in contact with the world as it is—that is, in need of transformation—without being blind to the essential goodness of creation.[23]

Augustinian-trained historian, Oxbridge graduate, and headmaster of Stonyhurst since 1985, Dr. Giles Mercer has no trouble discerning the Jesuit character of the college, or in delineating its place within the Society of Jesus after the 32nd General Congregation.

> I think there is a great deal of overlap between Catholic schools of any kind, or at least there certainly ought to be, and Jesuit ones. There are special characteristics which arise from the charism of a particular religious order, in this instance of the Jesuit Order which has run Stonyhurst for a very long period of time, and the principles in action at Stonyhurst are those of a Jesuit character and flavour. What are they? Well, I think, first of all, the whole thrust of Jesuit education is towards the education of the individual for others, to serve others in the world be it the family, the church, the community in which you live. The wider dimension involves serving those most in need. So whatever you do in your life, you attempt to improve the well-being of others, not only those around you, but you try to make decisions which are going to affect perhaps a wider group of people, perhaps on a global scale, for the better. That sounds very idealistic, but I think that is a very fundamental aim of Jesuit education. In other words, you're not just simply being educated to do well in a career in a conventional sense; you are being educated to do good. There is a very important difference.
>
> This is very much a continuing element of Jesuit educational philosophy. In fact, I don't of course know precisely what the priorities were in Stonyhurst in the 18th and 19th centuries, but you can look back through our history and you can see a tremendous sense of service in the way that this school arranged its curriculum and arranged its teaching, and you can look at the Old Boys of the college and you can see that underlying it all there is a strong sense of service. But, today,

certainly in my time, and I know well before, there has been a very strong sense of the need to be, in Father Arrupe's phrase, "men for others." How is that worked out? Of course, the question of justice in the world must be an issue which is found in the teaching in the school in various subjects. Secondly, in the way that the school develops its activities, we have a very large voluntary service programme, more than I have ever seen in a school; that is, the boys themselves are engaged in a whole variety of fundraising activities in the furtherance of those causes: handicapped children, famine relief, local projects in this area, some eight or nine community projects that take place every week, quite large projects where the boys go out from the college to help the aged, the sick, the poor, the handicapped—special needs schools, that kind of thing. It is very important for young people to think not only about themselves, but about others. It's this breaking down of selfishness and self-centredness which I think is a key part of Jesuit philosophy in action.

These lessons on justice have in many instances become a matter of life-long habit. In recent numbers of our school magazine, *The Stonyhurst Magazine*, we have had various features on former students of the college and what they have done and you will find quite a strong element of the Old Boy body would be involved in that kind of work. In social work, for example, in prison work—we have a distinguished prison governor; we have those involved obviously in medicine, in overseas aid work, but I suppose, at a more basic level, in every profession or career that a former student undertakes, we would hope that they would see that as a kind of management of God's business. That he entrusted them with one life on earth and they have to use that life as best they can. They are entrusted with a responsibility not only for themselves, but to use their talents to improve those around them. So, if you are in industry or in the legal profession or in medicine or any walk of life, in teaching of course, then it is incumbent upon you to think carefully about what you do, to realize that nothing you do takes place in a moral vacuum, and to heighten the awareness of those around you of some of the deeper moral implications of what you are doing. That sounds very grand, but I think that in practice you can see a kind of Stonyhurst or Jesuit characteristic in many of the former students. Take our Old Boys association: the former students look upon their association as a charity. Much of their work is involved in fundraising and in recent years, for example, they have raised a lot of money to support a Jesuit college in Beirut which was very badly damaged in the wars there. More recently, they raised a lot of money to help an Old Boy who was rendered paraplegic, one of their own. That's only an example of what they are doing for others, but they have raised a lot of money to help handicapped children, both students here and former students. So, there's a kind of continuity in the college.

Is Stonyhurst an elitist institution offering a service to the upper classes, or does the College also embrace the underprivileged in the spirit of the 32nd General Congregation? So long as the College is truly following Jesuit characteristics, then it will survive and indeed flourish. That is a challenge which is placed before me by the Jesuit province in Britain, but that is a challenge I welcome. If we cease to respond to that challenge, then we will die. The College is largely fee-paying. It has had a past which has been tied up with a social elite for quite a long period of its history. That is part of history, and it's a good, valued part of the history of the Catholic community in this country. It's the nature of English history. You have those Catholic families who needed to be educated and to go abroad. They were the people of influence at the time and they largely kept the church alive in this country. So, we must not run down our past. We are proud of it. Indeed, today, February 12, is the feast of the Martyrs of this College, the St. Omers Martyrs. The College was on the continent for 200 years, and we have fifteen martyrs, three canonized saints, and twelve blesseds. This is their feast day, and we are proud of that contribution to our history, and we aren't elite in a narrow sense.

Those who are educated here should become, I hope, we hope, agents of change in the world. We have broadened our entry in the College, so that one day, please God, if we work really hard to build up our own funds for bursaries and financial assistance, there will come a day when money alone will never be an obstacle to entry at Stonyhurst. We must do that to be true to Jesuit principle. After all, St. Ignatius himself laid it down that the Jesuit colleges must not charge fees for tuition. That's a basic Jesuit principle. Now, of course, many have had to do that because there have had to be compromises. The church lives in the world and this school has lived in this country, in a particular country with a particular social structuring, with particular needs, and the Society of Jesus has been quite prepared to make compromises in order to achieve greater objectives.

So, there is always a tension between the ideals of the Society of Jesus and of the church and the reality. So you're moving along, and you know what you want to achieve, but you can only achieve so much, and so all the time you have to break down any barrier, be it social, or be it any other kind of barrier. This school must be, in a sense, comprehensive. Every single student who comes here is on an equal level, an equal standing—we have boys from all over the world—it is an exercise in community living, an exercise in developing tolerance, and a breakdown of any kind of divisiveness which inflicts our society and many other societies in the world, so that boys who leave here, students, who go on into the world, can really get the best out of those around them with no inbuilt prejudices of any kind. It is very important, that. I think that elitism is a word that is misleading. I don't think that it would apply to Stonyhurst in any deep sense. We might be regarded as elitists because many of our parents had to pay large fees for their child's education. But, incidentally, that isn't of our choosing. We would far rather that they didn't have to pay those fees. We would far rather they didn't pay any fees at all. If the school were an island, the staff would be paid by the state. Our particular government, and all political parties in this country, are not prepared to pay teachers' salaries if they work in independent schools. That isn't of our choosing, that is the nature of this society here. In Australia, they do, and in Ireland, and if we were in France, it would be a different system again. As the present Father General says, every Jesuit college is forced to adapt to its local circumstances. So all you can really do is try to do your best, following Jesuit characteristics in the particular environment in which you happen to be placed historically.

Fidel Castro has claimed that his Jesuit education supported him during his struggles as an anti-Batista revolutionary. I suspect that when Fidel Castro talks about becoming an effective guerrilla warrior as a result of his Jesuit education in Cuba what he has in mind is that that education gave him the background to be successful. I suspect he's not saying, "I am an exemplary kind of Roman Catholic." What he is probably saying, I suspect, is that his Jesuit education enabled him to think for himself, to develop his own opinions, to see his own way in the world, to stand on his own feet confidently, and it gave him a strong sense of the necessity and the urgency to make social improvements in a radical way in order to change society as he would see it, for the better. If you like, a strong social conscience. The same, incidentally, I discovered recently might be said of President Clinton who went to Georgetown and he's on record as saying in *The Tablet* that he owed to the Jesuits two things: one was a strong sense of the need for social reform; that what you learn at school doesn't end at school, but you have to apply that in a social environment in actuality to change the world. The second thing he learnt was that there is no discrepancy between faith on the one hand, and the intellect on the other; that you should use your reason and your thought processes in order to serve your faith, for the two go together. Faith underpins reason. He took these principles away with him from Georgetown. Clinton said, actually, that his Jesuit training was unlike his own Baptist background which was that of the individual and God, although it's not a private religion, but one in which there is not a strong sense of social community. Georgetown Jesuits taught him that your religion cannot be individually compartmentalized. It has social consequences. You have got to think in communal terms. So he's not actually so far removed from Castro, although they come from totally different backgrounds and they ended up in totally different

> arenas politically; nevertheless, there is some fundamental point there. And you can apply the same thing to other Jesuit products. The Prime Minister of Holland, Ruud Lubbers, is a Jesuit product. He was making very much the same points as Clinton about a year ago in Ottawa. He's a very impressive man. He has a strong sense of the need to make the social situation for the generality of people in some way more just, to distribute the fruits of wealth in a more even way, and to have some ideals in a society.

The very setting in which Stonyhurst is located, the privileged air that dominates its halls, and indeed the richness of the works of art that decorate its corridors would seem to conspire to give the lie to Mercer's overview of Stonyhurst and its place in the contemporary Society's educational mission. Indeed, it is not difficult to find numbers of Jesuits willing to express their own reservations. Still, as if to prove Mercer's point, British journalist Jimmy Burns provided a tribute to Stonyhurst, published in *The Tablet* in May of 1993; it is the kind of testimonial that would have confirmed for Ignatius the rightness of his vision and the timelessness of its application, especially given Burns's own relatively modest background and the financial sacrifices that Stonyhurst's expenses exacted of his own parents. Burns concludes his reflection:

> I was extraordinarily fortunate that my Stonyhurst years coincided with a period of theological and social liberation and that the majority of Jesuits who taught me were well versed in the teachings of Vatican II. When I am asked what I learnt at Stonyhurst, I think not just of the gratitude I feel towards my parents for saving every penny to put towards my education, but of the lessons I took with me: the importance of justice and sacrifice for others, and the centrality of love in one's personal search for truth and spiritual growth.
>
> My contemporaries at Stonyhurst went on to many and different professions in many parts of the world: bankers, soldiers, journalists, actors, social workers, barristers, priests, from Tyneside to Tierra del Fuego. I have kept in touch with only a few of my old school colleagues, less through choice than through circumstance. One or two of them are the kind

> of friends I will never make again, so much in common binds us, even the kind of women we love. The majority of us remain deeply troubled by the injustices of the world that surrounds us. In Establishment eyes, this is an unreliable asset, and yet it is the kind of value that lasts for life.[24]

Despite its systemic stress on matters of justice, however, Stonyhurst has not forgotten Ignatius's directive concerning the need for recreation. In addition to the active musical component of the Stonyhurst way of life, every boy learns an orchestral musical instrument in his first year at the college: it is an extension of the Jesuit drama, which also finds expression in the school choir, drama, and liturgy. Consistent with the directives of the *Ratio* with respect to societies, though without the exclusivity implicit in the *Ratio*, the students at Stonyhurst are encouraged to join various clubs and societies, not all of which are a natural extension of the academic life as they are envisioned in the *Ratio*. There are, in addition, opportunities for fishing, cricket, soccer, swimming, basketball, clay shoots, badminton, squash, water polo, ju-jitsu, et cetera. But for a symbol of the Jesuits' and the students' ability to combine the serious with good fun, the locals are fond of pointing to the tree house, a project whose inspired peculiarity has fashioned it into a bit of the local folklore. Conceived and brought to fruition through the imagination of James Chaning-Pearce, Jesuit instructor and spiritual father at Stonyhurst, the tree house is an impressive structure imaginatively complete with showers, bedding, kitchen, and place of prayer. Built into a gathering of trees within sight of the college buildings, the tree house is a natural escape, a place for formal and informal retreat and contemplation, a place where young boys can be naturally inspired to find God in all things.

The contention vigorously and convincingly argued at Stonyhurst that it is not an elitist institution is far from universally shared even among other British Jesuits. The question inherent in the apparent contradiction is, as we have noted, a matter of Jesuit charism that has troubled the Society in the past and troubles it still. In Kingston, Jamaica, for example, there are two Jesuit secondary schools, one "down the hill" (St. George's College) and one "up the hill" (Campion College). St. George's serves the less affluent members of

Jamaican society, Campion the more socially elite. Marty Schade, an Ohio-born teacher and the chaplain at St. George's College, acknowledges the difference between the two schools and in diplomatic terms points out that the commitment of manpower from the New England province, which has administrative responsibility for the Jesuits in Jamaica, is expressly to St. George's.

> We raised that question several years ago during the '70s. We had what was called Mammee Bay meetings where we looked at our manpower (and I can use that word "manpower" exclusively because we are only Jesuit) and our apostolate: we had made the option to put any manpower that we have at St. George's College. We haven't left Campion College yet, and there was just the real move from the Board at Campion to maintain a Jesuit presence and vision, to use that word, at Campion. We haven't made a verbal commitment to send men there; we still will send any Jesuits in the education apostolate to St. George's College, but we will work towards maintaining a Jesuit presence and at this time the chairman of the Board is still a Jesuit.
>
> Campion College is certainly one of our more elite schools on the Island. Students are coming from a much socially economic higher class than St. George's. St. George's has been poor, but in the past recent years it's changing. We are finding that more and more uptown boys are coming here, more and more cars are driving through. When I was here as a scholastic between '82 and '83, few cars would drive through here in the mornings or the evenings. Now, a lot more cars are driving through. The social class of the students is changing. Our concern is to try to maintain a school for the poor, but even so our sixth form, where I am directing the religious education programme, regardless of whether they are poor or higher class, need certain academic requirements to get in, so we're dealing with a higher level of intelligence with these men. So, they will still be leaders even though they may be coming from a poor class. In the lower forms, our concern is that as we are seeing the shift towards a higher class of students coming in that somehow we maintain a school for the poor. It's the govern-

ment who determines who comes here. The government is allowing us to run it, but it's the government who determines who comes to this school.

People who have come here from Campion College lower school and then come here for sixth form find it nice to be able to mix like that. There is a tension, there is a recognition of a different class with the upper class, but I think that is a plus of St. George's College in that we do have a diversity of students in the socio-economic levels, so they blend and they mix a lot easier. It's also an element that we want to connect with Campion College through this ministry programme just so that the upper class and the lower class can work more closely together as far as the students go and know that regardless of economic class and social class they can still be brothers and sisters.

Similar questions can be asked about Jesuit secondary schools in Canada, with Loyola in Montreal serving the more privileged classes, St. Paul's in Winnipeg serving the middle class, and Gonzaga in St. John's, Newfoundland educating the less affluent. Len Altilia, President of Loyola High School in Montreal, argues in essence that one must make allowances for differences of times, persons, and places.

I have worked in both Loyola of Montreal and St. John's Gonzaga. There are definitely public perceptions that have to do with the quality of the schools, and I just want to expound on that for a moment.

When I was first assigned to go to Newfoundland, which I asked for by the way because I felt there was an opportunity for me to make a contribution there to a school that was really in need of some assistance, people asked me what did I do wrong, why am I being punished by being sent out to Newfoundland, which was not my perception of it at all, nor the perception of my Jesuit confreres. When I got there I found that many of the people in Newfoundland, many of the students, were very concerned about my perception of them and their school, and they kept asking me over the first couple of years, "Well, how does this compare to Loyola?" because there is a perception of Loyola as kind of the flagship, as it were, and the elite. The truth of the matter is that in our three schools, we have collaborated extensively as school leadership groups trying to ensure that all of our schools remain faithful to the ideals that our Society of Jesus has been promoting over the last many years. It isn't a question of one school being more Jesuit than another school. It's a question of each school attempting to the best of its ability, given the reality that it exists in, to incorporate into the life of the school those activities and programmes that authentically inculcate the values we are attempting to accomplish. I don't think that there would be any realistic way that you could evaluate any of the three schools as being more successful at that than the others. All three schools have done it differently, because their contexts require that. All three schools are emphasizing different aspects because of the nature of the institution, but if you took each of the three schools and analyzed what's happening in them, you would find that in all three of those schools those values are there and they are being expressed in different ways and with different emphasis and so on. But, they permeate the activity of the school. You can extricate from each of those three schools those same values because we worked hard together doing that. We have met to discuss how we would do those things, and we went back to our own schools and said, "Okay, this is where we have to move now." I think our schools work very successfully at developing programmes that really do put into practice what we preach. We share with each other and we also say "How can we help each other?" This has been unique to this particular Jesuit programme because we have sat down and worked with each other. Not in competition, but with the same basic goal. That has been very, very instrumental.

Different places emphasize different aspects and each place because of its unique character has to find its own particular way of inculcating those elements into its programme. Newfoundland is a very, very different environment from Quebec or from Manitoba. The school in Newfoundland is a very different school from the one in Montreal or the one in Winnipeg, and because of that it cannot be a lock-step approach. There has to be a flexibility and an openness, an inculturation—we've been talking about that recently in the Society—an inculturation of not only the Gospel but also the spirituality of the Society of Jesus into the situation that you find yourself in.

Our school in Newfoundland is coeducational. That sets an automatically different context and because of that we have to recognize the reality that we are dealing with a different spectrum of society in that situation. Obviously Newfoundland's recent experience with regard to the conflicts in the news concerning sexual abuse of young boys by clergy and members of religious orders sets another dynamic that we had to deal with. We had to take an approach there that would realize that situation, respond to it honestly, and move the church forward in relation to that situation. We couldn't turn a blind eye to that and say, "Well, that's somebody else's problem." That's our reality, we're living there. Each place has to have its own understanding of that reality. According to my understanding of it, when it came to what Ignatius wanted the Society to do, it was to influence the development of the world and the church for good by dealing with those who could make the changes that were necessary. Don't forget, Ignatius lived in a reality where there was an aristocracy and a peasant class and he had to address both of those realities, so he went for who could change the world, mainly the aristocracy, and at the same time realized that they had to be down in the streets with the peasants who also needed the encouragement and the nourishment. The people of the Society had to identify with the needs of those who were most oppressed and lowest in the ranking, but if they were going to really change the world, they had to go to the top, because the peasants weren't going to change the world in Ignatius's reality. We are in a different context, but we don't shy away from the fact that in the world that we live in there are people who wield more influence than others. If you want to change what goes on in the world you have to address that reality, which means you have to deal with the political, social, and economic reality that you exist in. If you shy away from that, you lose your impact.

Altilia's thesis is certainly consistent with Ignatius's perception of the practical benefits to be reaped socially and personally from a Jesuit education. It is also consistent with the Jesuit Curia's 1986 contemporary analysis of the social aspects of education in their *Characteristics of Jesuit Education*. Still, the problem of the traditional perception of Jesuits themselves as being an elite corps drawn from the social elite is not a simple one to put to rest. Certainly there is nowhere that has more thoroughly embraced the 32nd General Congregation's admonitions with respect to "the service of the faith and the promotion of justice," of cultural integration, conscientization, and service for others animated through mature faith and devotion to Christ than has the University of Central America (UCA). And no Jesuit community understands better the 32nd General Congregation's warning that "any effort to promote justice will cost us something"[25] than does the one at the José Simeón Cañas campus of UCA in San Salvador. Yet, as Amanda Hopkinson points out in her article on the murder of the six Jesuit professors, their housekeeper, and their housekeeper's daughter at UCA San Salvador, even within UCA the debate as to the role of the Jesuit university is not at all settled.[26]

While the San Salvador and Managua campuses of UCA have opted for the prophetic voice encouraged by the 32nd General Congregation, the well-appointed Landivár campus of UCA in Guatemala caters to the "hopelessly privileged"[27] who neither need nor receive financial assistance. It is an assessment one hears repeatedly in San Salvador and Managua, where the universities are decidedly and precariously placed at the service of the poor. Hence, the Spanish-born rector of UCA San Salvador, Ignacio Ellacuría, was martyred on campus along with five of his companions on the night of November 16, 1989, apparent victims of government hostility. His crime? Ellacuría lived by his principles, the principles of the Society. As had the Society, Ellacuría thought that UCA should make a difference. Like the Society's, his definition of a university included the preferential option for the poor; as a result, Ellacuría worked tirelessly and vocally to improve the lot of the underprivileged and to instil a sense of social justice into strife-ridden El Salvador. His intent was seen to be subversive, and the Jesuits at UCA became a target for extermination. Ellacuría's sense of the preferential option also included the conscientizing of the well-to-do, and he argued, therefore, that his opting for the poor "does not mean that only the poor study at the university"; the university, he argued, needs the best minds to solve complex social problems while simultaneously teaching skills to the unskilled.[28] Indeed, even Pope John Paul II (who has shown little affection for Jesuit liberationists in Latin America) has sided with the poor when in his 1990 apostolic constitution on Catholic universities, *Ex corde ecclesiae*, he argued that universities must be prepared to "speak uncomfortable truths which do not please public opinion, but which are necessary to safeguard the authentic good of society."[29] Speaking uncomfortable truths always comes at a price.

The 32nd General Congregation of the Society of Jesus had assured its members that "the Congregation supports our Jesuits who are working in scholarly research, in publishing"[30] and suggested that the communications media would play a significant role in "humanizing the social climate."[31] The Jesuit faculty at UCA San Salvador understood the role of the media; so they established a university press, published periodicals, disseminated monograph analyses of injustice in San Salvador, took to the airwaves, and, as part of the students' programme, they required even the right-wing supporters of ARENA to investigate social injustice, death squad activities, and human rights violations in El Salvador. ARENA concluded that the Jesuits at UCA needed to be taught a lesson and ordered the military to silence the bothersome priests.

Liberation theologian and Basque ex-patriot Jon Sobrino reflected on the prophetic purpose of a university in an article entitled "The University's Christian Perspective," which he published in his testimonial to his murdered companions at UCA, *Companions of Jesus: The Jesuit Martyrs of El Salvador*. Sobrino argues that the Catholic university must provide the incarnation of its Gospel principles. What could be more of an incarnation than to lay down one's life for one's compatriots? During one of our interviews Sobrino expanded on his written reflections:

> The main finality, or principal purpose, of a Christian or Catholic university, is to put forth knowledge: the knowledge of the university at the service of the Gospel, and putting historically

> conditioned knowledge of the truth of the Gospel today means putting the Christian university at the service of the poor. So for me, this is clear. I have nothing, of course, against teaching theology—I do it, and we do it at UCA—and teaching theology in an orthodox way. We try to do it. . . .
>
> My fear is not so much that the Vatican tells Christian universities to be orthodox, to be pastoral, to be catechetical; rather my fear is that they want to make universities tools for the Vatican in order to impose what they want onto society. I don't think we should impose anything on anybody. We should invite people, we should have credibility because of the way we are, the way we act, the way we are persecuted for the sake of justice. Then we can invite people to be Christians or Catholics, but imposing things, no.
>
> Nobody should be surprised that there is a cost in having the university put its knowledge at the service of the Gospel and in serving the poor in this way. We all know that when Jesus of Nazareth walked this earth, he had to pay a price for what he did and said. He was assassinated; he died on a cross. In El Salvador the cost for the Jesuits has been seven Jesuits assassinated. There were the six Jesuits at the university in 1989, and Rutilio Grande in 1977. Of course, together with them there were eleven more priests and North American sisters, and an archbishop, Oscar Romero.

Both the traditional Jesuit theme of inculturation, of meeting people where they are in their own societies, and Sobrino's own sense of incarnation combine in El Salvador and at San Salvador's campus of UCA.

> Now, I have mentioned Jesuits, archbishops, sisters, but if you put together the peasants who were assassinated because they got organized to defend their own rights the numbers go up to 70,000 people. So tragically, but fortunately, the Jesuits are not alone in this sea of blood. Which means that maybe for the first time in years, as far as the Salvadoran Jesuits go, we can call ourselves truly Salvadorans. Some people have the impression, and I think rightly so, that somehow Jesuits are people different from other people. Well, maybe that is the way it is—

it's not the way I would like it to be. Maybe we are different because we have studied more years than other people—but that's not the point. When we participate in the same destiny as the majority of the Salvadorans, that means that we have become Salvadoran, and that for me is one of the most important challenges and one of the greatest joys we can have: to be real human beings in a country.

Dean Brackley is one of several Jesuit priests who volunteered to help fill the void left at UCA with the death of the martyrs of El Salvador. Before coming to San Salvador he had worked in his native United States, serving the underprivileged in the South Bronx and teaching ethics at Fordham University, the Jesuits' university in New York. In San Salvador, Brackley ministers to the campesinos at Jayaque while teaching at UCA. He is in an ideal position to compare the Jesuit charism at work. How would he define the Jesuitness of Fordham and the Jesuitness of UCA San Salvador?

In many ways the difference stands out more clearly than the likenesses. Let's begin with the contrast and the comparison of Fordham with the UCA. Fordham stands in the tradition of liberal Christian Western education. It attempts to provide a Christian form of traditional liberal education. The UCA explicitly defines its objective as the liberation of the poor. The philosophy of Fordham would be to provide a liberal education within the context of Christian values. What would be the difference and what does the UCA mean when it says that its objective is the liberation of the poor? The UCA perceives itself not first of all as training professionals to function morally within a particular social system—which would be basically what Fordham would be trying to do. The UCA judges from a Christian and ethical standpoint that the reality of El Salvador is a contradiction of truth and a contradiction of humanity. And so the University exists not simply to train professionals to function within this, not even to train professionals to transform it, but the UCA's purpose is to transform the society itself from the perspective of a university. The UCA, therefore, tries to be an institution in the service of the truth in El Salvador in such a way that it will transform the society. Another way to put this would be to say that the UCA wants to be a good citizen and it wants to serve the common good, but in El Salvador the common good means the liberation of the poor.

Ellacuría insisted that the UCA is a social reality and a social force with a responsibility to provide a social service; the UCA must perform this service to the outside world, the world outside the campus, not as a political party would do it, not, of course, as a military organization would do it, but specifically as a university. He said the UCA has its centre outside itself. Well, how does a university do that? It serves the truth. In this climate, that means not just pushing back the frontiers of ignorance, or from another standpoint, of knowledge; it means serving the truth within a conflictual situation and it means, therefore, unmasking the lies. It means recognizing that discourse in El Salvador is part of a power struggle, like it or not, and one must declare the truth and defend the truth by unmasking the lies which are being massively propagated through the propaganda of the elite in the media—the means of public communication.

It is not surprising, then, that the principal object of study in the UCA, and the principal object of research is what Ellacuría called *la realidad nacional*, the national reality. He said that we should be the first, we in the UCA, who understand the reality of this country, and no one should understand the reality of El Salvador more than the people at the UCA. It's interesting, because I think what happens often in many of our liberal institutions is that we are first of all studying the literature as such. In the UCA, at least theoretically, we study the literature in order to understand the world. We don't just study the literature for its own sake. The same is true of research. In research that is done in the UCA whether by students or professors, at least theoretically, a person has to make the case that somehow, in the long run, this will have a useful social purpose. It doesn't mean we can't research obscure authors or obscure insects, but somehow it should be of service to the community. Why I say this, it's important to recall that for Ellacuría and for the UCA as a whole, there are three instruments that the UCA uses typically to achieve its objective. One is teaching, the other is research, and the third is the most important of all and it's the one that Ellucaría felt should permeate the whole life of the university including teaching and research. He called that *projección social*, which is imperfectly translated "social outreach," and it has to do with every direct form in which the UCA has an impact on the social reality outside the campus, has a direct impact on helping to form the social consciousness and the national consciousness of El Salvador. It has to do with the nine publications of the UCA, it has to do with the appearances on television and radio for which the UCA Martyrs were killed, it has to do, theoretically, with 600 hours of social service that students are to perform, it has to do with Professor John Cortina building a bridge, an engineering professor building a bridge, up in Chalatenango, and many other forms of social projections: social surveys that are done in the country, the documentation service, the human rights institute. For Ellacuría that *projección social*, in all its forms, was the principal instrument in the service of the liberation of the poor, the principal instrument that UCA could use. Obviously, this is a rupture with the traditional understanding of liberal Western education: it means taking sides, and it means taking sides as an institution. It means that the UCA, as institution, while it tolerates within its own professorial ranks and its student debate and its classes a wide diversity of opinion, declares itself as a university on the general question of liberation of the poor and on specific issues. It takes sides on specific issues within a highly conflictual situation. I think this is a remarkable turn of events. It certainly is open to abuse, but so is neutrality. It seems to me that the UCA has courageously adopted the type of policy which wishes to assume the responsibilities of respecting the tension between respect for plurality and pluralism in education and academic freedom and taking a stand as an institution.

All of this obviously has implications for a Christian university. But Jon Sobrino has made an interesting point about that. He believes that a university, a Jesuit university, is not Christian because it searches for the truth and opens a space for

> people to receive the sacraments on the side. No. Receiving the sacraments on the side is not specifically university work. He believes that the university itself, in its teaching, in its research, in its *proyección social*, must be dedicated to the reign of God, to the liberation of the poor, to the struggle for justice, and cannot content itself with providing the chaplaincy space which is so often characteristic of Christian education in other areas. It cannot simply say that it has a theology department and a chaplaincy and let it go at that. As a university it must work for justice, take a stand, opt for the poor.
>
> I must say that in a case like Fordham, I was pleasantly surprised that although we were certainly within the general context of liberal Western education, and although it still seems to be anathema for the university to take, as a university, a stand on political issues and on important moral issues, especially in the areas of politics and economics—indeed, in the North, issues are much more ambiguous and the injustice is not quite as blatant as we find here in El Salvador—the issues are not quite as clear cut. I do see as well in Fordham, and many Jesuit institutions, a significant body of Jesuits, professors, administrators—Jesuits and lay people—with a fairly clear vision of how we need to help the students break their hearts to introduce them to the world of the poor and allow that to raise the questions which are much more fundamental than the answers that we are all too ready to give to them. Often, they come from an experience-poor background in which they do not have the questions and we continue to provide them with answers in which they find they have very little interest. I think that we are seeing important changes in Jesuit education in the U.S. and in Canada in that respect.

Of course it is widely assumed that many of the problems in El Salvador could be solved with different decisions being made in the United States. Since Jesuits, especially in New York and in Washington, are in a position to transform society by transforming the thinking of those who ultimately shape society in the United States, one might well wonder about the extent to which the Jesuits have in fact fulfilled their commitment to their ideals in the Society's institutions like Georgetown and Fordham. Brackley does not shy away from the problem:

> We have to be honest here, and we have to recognize that most Jesuits come from middle-class backgrounds and the fact is that we, people of middle-class background, live in our middle-class world and until the poor break our hearts and break that egg-shell world that we have constructed, the question of the poor is not that alive for us. It's on the horizon, it's on the fringe of our consciousness, but it is not central to our agenda as Jesuits and as university people. We have to be honest that not all Jesuits have the promotion of justice as an integral priority of their service of faith. And that profoundly affects Jesuit higher education in the United States. That fact is that the question of the poor in the Third World is not a burning and vital issue. I say this not to condemn people who have not had this experience happen to them and who have not made that a central priority—many are victims of our North American culture which convinces them that they are at the place where the pulse of history is beating. I think it's where the pulse of history is rather weak, and the pulse of history is really beating among the poor. But that awareness is not sharp among the majority of our brothers and our university people. There are many for whom it is without question a burning priority, but they are, I think, still a minority among our university people.

Explaining the Fordham situation and relating it to the Society's vision of education, Jesuit president Joseph O'Hare points out that Fordham transfers about 14 percent of its tuition income into student aid, that 1991 tuition at Georgetown is approximately $23,000 a year compared with Fordham's $17,000, and that at both the Lincoln Centre and the Bronx campuses of Fordham there is a heartening degree of enthusiasm for community service. The theme is very familiar. Just as the *Ratio* of an earlier era provided the broadly based touchstone for the presuppression Society, so the 32nd General Congregation's directives with respect to education can be found in almost every Jesuit institution in its embrace. And so Joseph Schner uses GC32 terminology in defining the university mission for Campion College at the University of Regina in Saskatchewan and so does Winston Rye in outlining his vision of Loyola High School in Montreal. Jesuit professors Paul Locatelli, Gerald McKevitt, James Reites, and Steve Privett of Santa Clara University in California confirm that the 32nd General Congregation has reshaped the way Jesuits and like-minded professors approach the content of their research and the examples they use in the classroom; distinguished Cambridge Jesuit astronomer Christopher Moss would sooner talk about his interest in liberation theology than in his research as an astronomer. Rodolfo Cardenal, Jesuit rector of the José Simeón Cañas campus of UCA and past director both of the UCA San Salvador press and of communications at UCA, sees the inspiration for his university's media activity in exactly the same light. Similarly, in his inaugural address as the 22nd president of Loyola University in Chicago, John J. Piderit, s.j., assured those assembled that "at Loyola University Chicago, we transmit our tradition by showing it in action." And Basque-born Jesuit Director of Managua's Central American Institute, Inaki Zubizarreta, laments the declining interest in social justice among his student body since the electoral defeat of the Sandinista government of Nicaragua. In a very real way, the 32nd General Congregation has become the *Ratio* of the modern Society.

Membership in the Society of Jesus, much like formal membership in the church itself, has decreased dramatically since Vatican II, reaching a high of 36,038 in 1965 (the final year of the Council) and apparently levelling at its 1991 component of 24,049, spread throughout 114 countries.[32] More telling still is the fact that the majority of the Society's members live in the United States, Canada, and western Europe, whereas over 70 percent of the Society's younger companions and seminarians live in Asia, Africa, and Latin America. What do the new numerical realities mean for the Society's educational apostolate? In the United States, most Jesuit universities have been transferred into the hands of lay boards, and the Society in the United States is apparently resigned to the fact that it will be forced to abandon some of its 28 colleges and universities. The observations offered by the late Timothy Healy, past president of both Georgetown University and of the New York Public Library, are representative:

> The numbers of Jesuits are declining, not precipitously, but steadily enough so that I think the Society really is going to have to reach out to lay colleagues on the faculty and make certain that they understand the structure and the background and the spiritual base of the institution. When you get a phenomenon that lasts for twenty or thirty years, one of the real conclusions is that the Holy Ghost is trying to teach you something. What will happen to these institutions? My hunch is that they will all stay Catholic, that those Catholic colleges now in sensible shape, that is most of the Jesuit ones, will not slip off or drift into secularity. I think the form of that Catholicism will be sharply different from what it was when I first showed up at Fordham in 1947.

For the most part, Jesuits in the United States, Canada, and western Europe are convinced that they have established a legacy that is embraced by large numbers of lay people who are fully suited to carry on with the mission. The Society's Superior General, Peter-Hans Kolvenbach, notes that the addition of new members does not compensate for the numbers of Jesuits lost through death or resignation. As a result, he acknowledges that the Society cannot do everything it has done in the recent past, but he adds that the decline in professed Jesuits and the increase in competent lay people "means a shift from, let us say, the commitment of the religious to the commitment of lay persons, and this is very sensitive, especially in the educational sector where in an excellent spirit lay persons take over from what was the monopoly, especially in the Middle Ages, of the clergy and later on of religious life." Although Christopher Jencks and David Reisman's *The Academic Revolution* certainly calls into question the ability of Catholics in the United States to retain an educational system that is in fact Catholic, most Jesuits persist in their optimism. Marty Schade notes that "another word since General Congregation 32 is 'collaboration.' Collaboration is not something we should do out of necessity; it's something we should do out of mission."

Today's Society seems to be relatively at peace with the fact that Ignatius's vision and the imminent inversion of the constitutional requirement that "all the teachers, if possible, should be members of the Society, although there may be others according to necessity."[33] The next few decades will be the proving ground of the Society's current optimism that it has built an educational foundation that can withstand the buffets of twentieth-century secularism, and the testing of whether today's "necessity" can indeed be translated into tomorrow's "collaboration" in the sacred enterprise of the shaping of minds and the reshaping of society.

V

JESUIT AS WORDSMITH

THE PREACHING OF the Word, and communicating by word, are perduring marks of the Jesuit tradition. In the first written charter, "The Formula of the Institute," submitted to Pope Paul III in 1540 and subsequently incorporated into his *Regimini militantis ecclesiae* (1540), and followed ten years later with an edited version in Pope Julius III's *Exposit debitum*, you have the primordial delineation of Jesuit ministries:

> to strive especially for the defense and propagation of the faith and for the progress of souls in Christian life and doctrine, by means of public preaching, lectures, and any other ministration whatsoever of the word of God.[1]

Although the Formula goes on to embrace several other ministries, their ordering is not insignificant. The Word is foundational.

Preaching, teaching, catechizing—all these activities involved the Jesuits in the cultivated arts of articulation and persuasion. It is but one reason why they became the most skilled controversialists of the immediate post-Reformation period.

The centrality of the Word—in preaching and teaching—also had a direct influence on Jesuit architecture with its positioning of the pulpit in the middle of the nave to ensure that all the congregants could hear the homily. This can be seen very clearly in the case of the Gesù, the mother church of the Jesuit Order. For Thomas Lucas, the Gesù,

> which became the prototype for churches all over Europe and all over the New World, was designed not to be a place of mystery, but to be a place of communication. This is very different from the medieval cathedrals with their dark and vertical ambience. The thrust of the Gesù, and of the Jesuit churches in general, is horizontal with a long, wide, and unencumbered nave, which was itself used as an auditorium for preaching and teaching. Because the Jesuits don't sing choir like the monks and friars, there is no need for a long choir to separate the altar from the nave; the people must be able to see and hear. The communication of the word of God through the preaching of the Word all point to this kind of incarnate realism: that God is present in time and space, here and now, and that the Word has to be heard and preached and celebrated in holy places by holy people.

But the homily itself was generated out of the Jesuit conviction that

> God worked directly within the human heart. . . . The proclamation of the Gospel was more like mid-wifery than artificial insemination, and had to identify the way God was already working in human lives.[2]

To discover God in all things, to attend to the divine presence at the heart of all matter, to hear the chords of transcendence in the midst of the mundane, has always constituted the unique Ignatian insight that fuels a spirituality both apostolic and contemplative. Schooled in the *Exercises* from the beginning of their training, Jesuits are compelled by the inner logic of their evangelical zeal to transmit in a vital and credible way the creed of the Christian faith and the humanizing and liberating values of the Gospel. Such has never been an easy task.

To communicate their Christian witness, Jesuits need to rely on more than text, pulpit, and sound bite: they need to communicate their understanding of a truth that cannot be contained in script and logic. Walter Ong, the distinguished Jesuit communications theorist, literature professor, and friend of media guru Herbert Marshall McLuhan, opines;

Brad Reynolds s.j.

Dale Buckman of the Spokane Indian tribe reviews liturgical texts with Jesuit Tom Colgan at the Kateri Institute.

D.R. Letson

Canadian Jesuit Brian Massie, Pastor of St. Peter Claver Church in West Kingston, Jamaica, is also the death row chaplain at the city's St. Catherine's Penetentiary.

D.R. Letson

Jim Webb, Jesuit priest and social justice activist, is stationed in the slums of West Kingston, Jamaica.

D.R. Letson

Christopher Llanos, a Jesuit student of the Upper Canadian Province of the Society of Jesus, is serving his regency in the Caribbean.

The UCA Martyrs: a memorial billboard at the San Salvador Campus at the University of Central America.

Mark Raper

Jesuit Father Deradoss in Somalia engaged in the often perilous work of the Jesuit Refugee Service.

Continuing the tradition of Jesuit drama, Indonesian Jesuit scholastics demonstrate their Thespian skills at the International College in Rome.

P. Proulx s.j.

J.A. Loftus s.j.

Jesuit Robert Ver Eecke in full flight with his Boston Liturgical Dance Ensemble.

Queen Elizabeth II being welcomed by Dr. Giles Mercer, Headmaster of Stonyhurst College, the prestigious Jesuit public school in Lancashire, England.

D.R. Letson

James Chaning-Pearce s.j., stands at the foot of his famous treehouse, a student retreat at Stonyhurst.

D.R. Letson

Inaki Zubizarreta s.j., Director of the Central American Institute at Managua, Nicaragua.

Peter Levi, poet, biographer, past Professor of Poetry at Oxford University, and former Jesuit relaxes in his centuries-old cottage in Frampton-upon-Severn.

D.R. Letson

Winston Rye s.j., at his presidential desk at Loyola High School in Montreal.

D.R. Letson

Stan Obirek s.j., the Rights Manager at the Jesuits' WAM editorial house in Krakow, Poland, reviews a freshly printed bookcover.

D.R. Letson

D.R. Letson

Joe Fessio, a U.S. Jesuit, is the controversial editor and publisher who founded and manages the Ignatius Press from his home base in San Francisco.

D.R. Letson

Dean Brackley s.j., chats at the spartan lodgings he shared with several Jesuit seminarians in San Salvador.

John Padberg s.j., Director of the Institute of Jesuit Resources in St. Louis, Missouri, discusses a recent Institute publication.

D.R. Letson

Timothy Healy s.j. in his office at the New York Public Library during his tenure as president.

D.R. Letson

Walter Ong, Jesuit communications theorist and English professor, is the eminence grise of U.S. Catholic intellectual life.

D.R. Letson

Jesuit astronomers at Vatican-owned Observatory.

> You might ask the question: If Jesus were alive today, would he be on television? My answer to such a question would be that is why he lived when he did. The church is something implanted in the world—it's here rooted on the planet. Many people have the impression that all truth communicated by this church is propositional, that you can simply state it. Now, if this is so why did Jesus not leave us a list of propositions? He never even wrote anything. He said: "I am the Way, and the Truth, and the Light." Truth is personal. We communicate truth not simply by means of verbal and written communication but by means of our pauses, our silences. Words alone never explain anything. Propositions are an invitation to ask further questions, because you don't get at the truth in a statement but in a statement in context. Jesus is the Way, the Truth, and the Light: he communicated himself. That's where the truth is. The Jesuits educate and preach to that end.

In order to effectively communicate the "truth" that is Jesus, the Society consecrated to his name faces challenges in our contemporary context very different from the Reformation world of Ignatius and his companions, and very different too from the still largely homogeneous, eurocentric universe of the post-Enlightenment era. The Jesuit of today is confronted with diverse challenges on several fronts: the "practical atheism" of the consumer-driven, materialistic culture that dominates in North America and Europe, an atheism very different from the "scientific atheism" of dialectical materialism or any other philosophical system that excludes the divine—because the atheism that is practical simply dispenses with God as a determinative factor in the search for human meaning and happiness; the rudimentary life-and-death struggle conducted with increasing ferocity in the Third World where talk of God disengaged from human rights and just government is meaningless and incredible; and the mounting potential for new religious wars as the once nominally Christian nations face increasing numbers of non-Christians eager to practice their faiths in often hostile and intolerant societies. To communicate the Gospel in the global village necessitates new evangelizing strategies.

Pedro Arrupe understood the importance of mass communications and directed the Society to undertake greater work—analytical, practical, and experimental—in the whole area of mass media. He saw the catechetical possibilities inherent in the rapidly evolving world of communications, and he wanted the Companions to move from simply manning the library stalls and the editorial offices of learned journals to the new frontier of film and fax. Kolvenbach credits Arrupe with initiating a communications awareness in the Order worldwide:

> Father Arrupe founded JESCOM, an organization to coordinate and help Jesuits working in this sector [mass media], and an Institute, with its seat in London [Centre for the Study of Communication and Culture], to train Jesuits and other Christians who intend to involve themselves in the modern means of social communication. . . . In our universities too, including the Gregorian, we now have research centers dealing with the mass media. . . . I should also mention that several Jesuit universities run Departments of Communication, which train graduates and non-graduates in the production techniques of the mass media.[3]

Although Peter-Hans Kolvenbach personally regrets the tardiness of Jesuit reaction to the many complex challenges of mass communications—he argues that the Jesuits were a bit slow in getting into the mass media field—he credits Arrupe with propelling the Order into the fascinating, morally ambiguous, and limitlessly influential arena of social communications. In an address given at a meeting of communications experts held in Villa Cavalletti in Rome in March 1973, Arrupe noted:

> Today we cannot afford to be so weighed down by old practices as to lose the flexibility and adaptability of our original charism. It is my judgement that we can accomplish much more for the service of souls if we learn how to use correctly these modern instruments of the apostolate; if we consider those mass media and all who toil in them as part of our present day apostolate; if, finally, we offer them our cooperation in preparing, aiding and directing them in their efforts in mass media.[4]

Enjoined by Arrupe to use the "modern instruments of the apostolate" in the service of humanity, Irish Jesuits like John Dardis, director of the Dublin-based Jesuit Communication Centre, have come to understand that the departure from simply print-based enterprises into broadcasting is motivated by an effort

> to find a language that speaks to people today, and to discover and employ meaningful symbols of the faith, because much of the language we use, and the images we draw upon to articulate our experience, are tired, old, shop-worn. We need to find symbols that can speak to the hearts and minds of Irish people today, that can move them to action, and convince them that faith is both important and relevant.

To "move them to action," Dardis and his associates have decided that nothing less than a fully honest dialogue with Irish political culture is necessary, and this means placing on the national agenda GC32 concerns such as solidarity with the poor and the promotion of justice. In a country that is beginning to taste economic prosperity —Ireland has benefited more than all the other members of the European Economic Community from the new trade arrangements —and that has a preponderantly youth-dominated populace increasingly uninterested in traditional religious practices, Jesuits have the twofold task of conscientizing the newly affluent—a particularly difficult job given that until recently Ireland was the second poorest nation in Europe—and injecting a charged meaning into the atrophied symbols and images of this hitherto most pious of countries.

For Marc Gervais, a Canadian Jesuit and professor of communications at Montreal's Concordia University, the Jesuit commitment to communications is hardly new: it is a mark of their charism. After all, he reasons, in the sixteenth and seventeenth centuries there was the flourishing pedagogical and evangelizing instrument known as "Jesuit theatre"—though no one is prepared to argue for the lasting artistic quality of the dramas—and a strong Jesuit interest in the study and cultivation of arts and letters all employed to the apostolic end of expanding God's kingdom.

> In its day, Jesuit theatre was a way of proclaiming the reign of God. The notion that the spirit of God can be found in our

> culture—creating; working; vivifying—is at the very heart of Jesuit engagement with society. Art is one of the supreme, most privileged aspects of culture because through art one comes across the question of the sacred, of the ineffable, paradoxically expressing itself in a most dialectical and ambiguous manner. Art—its creation and its study—are the proper preserves of Jesuit activity, whether, as in the early centuries of the Order's existence with its indigenous theatre, or now, in the age of the cinema.

Having earned his doctorate in aesthetics from the Sorbonne by writing on the films of the French cinema auteur Jean-Luc Godard, Gervais understandably sees film as the genre par excellence of the century, the premier art form of our time. It is too easily neglected by Jesuit educators, perhaps even despised by some critics because of its populist appeal, but for Gervais cinema is the crucible in which a culture struggles to know itself, and the principal players in the world of cinema—the directors, actors, cinematographers, and writers—can be shaped, however indirectly or implicitly, by Jesuit values. To understand the spirituality—tortured, ironic, and strangely luminous—in the work of the British director Alfred Hitchcock (*Psycho*) or the Québécois director Denys Arcand (*Jesus of Montreal*) one needs to know something of their Jesuit education, and of those individual Jesuits who helped shape their sensibility.

> When I teach a course on Hitchcock I try to experience the films with the students. I try to respond *directly* to the individual film, not as mediated by the critics and commentaries. Then, after this initial experience, I introduce my students to the various critical approaches: the psychoanalytical; the feminist; etc. Then I say, "But what I personally think is. . . . ", and introduce them to the various ways of telling a story, of the unique path of film language, about the rhythms and the like. This is my way of incarnating the Christian story and in so doing communicating my own convictions and those I understand Hitchcock to have shared. I resent the efforts of petty and ideologically driven biographers to picture Hitchcock as nothing more than a dirty old man, a misogynist, seducer,

misanthropic, guilt-ridden voyeur. Their whole approach is reductionistic. Art as muck.

But art is dialogue and so is education. I converse with my students; I articulate in the course of my film criticism the essential me. I could be a Sartrean absurdist, or a Marxist, but I happen to be a Christian who really believes in the Christian myth as the richest answer to the whole human mystery. By coming to grips with a film you reveal yourself. This is communication as self-disclosure. As grace, if you like.

The Jesuit resolve to both employ and study mass communications is merely a continuation of their centuries-long educational enterprise. Although, now, they operate the impressive Radio Vaticana network, serve as consultants to film directors, staff communications study centres and projects, and maintain departments of communications in their universities, their involvement in the print media is of longstanding duration.

Most Jesuit provinces in the world publish two or more journals—one of which will invariably have an academic or scientific orientation and one a pastoral or catechetical thrust. Very often these publications enjoy a special place of prominence in the province's history, like *The Month* for British Jesuits, *Studies* for the Irish, and *America* for the Americans. The Swedes have *Signum*, the Canadians *Compass* and *Rélations* for their English and French-speaking provinces, respectively, the Australians *Eureka Street*, and the Germans, *Canisius, Geist und Leben*, and that bearer of light in the darkness of the Third Reich, *Stimmen der Zeit*. It was this latter journal, suppressed by the Nazis in 1943, that published the work of the Jesuit philosopher Alfred Delp, Dachau prisoner #1442, a man who once preached:

> No hopelessness or lack of prospect of success dispenses a person from saying what they have to say, or compels them to say what is false. . . . Once you start thinking about the success or efficacy of your decision, then you are lost.[5]

Delp was hanged by the Nazis for the crime of "defeatism" on February 2, 1945; the publishing quarters of *Geist* and *Stimmen* in Munich are now named Alfred-Delp-Haus. He spoke the truth as he saw it; he earned the wrath of the Gestapo; and his pen was permanently stilled.

Delp isn't the only Jesuit writer or editor who has been censored, fired, or killed. During the pontificate of John Paul II the Jesuit editors of France's *Etudes* and Spain's *Estudios* were removed from office by their respective provincials because of pressure exerted on them by a nervous hierarchy sensitive to Rome's displeasure. The sacked editors were theological liberals. And then there is the Fessio phenomenon.

Joseph Fessio is a theology professor at the Jesuit-run University of San Francisco and a member of the California province. A graduate in civil engineering from Santa Clara University, Fessio decided to study for the priesthood and entered the novitiate at Los Gatos, California, in 1961. He returned to Santa Clara for his regency and organized, with another Jesuit, a summer programme for the poor and disadvantaged called Project 50, grew a beard, wore bermuda shorts, and dispensed with collar and cross. He was your model '60s Jesuit. But it didn't ring true somehow. Fessio felt "disjoint and out of frame." Summoned by his provincial to discuss his future, Fessio made protestations, both ironic and earnest, that he wanted to be a good and not rebellious Jesuit. He shaved his beard. And then he went to France to study theology.

When it was time to do his doctorate he sought out the advice of Henri de Lubac, the eminent theologian, Vatican Council expert, and esteemed Jesuit master, who told him to go to the University of Regensburg in Germany to study under "a wonderful German theologian who will do great things for the church," Joseph Ratzinger, now the Cardinal Prefect of the Sacred Congregation for the Doctrine of the Faith, orthodoxy's able defender, and, post-1968, a theological reactionary with little taste for Jesuit radicalism à la Arrupe and the liberation theologians. In addition, de Lubac encouraged Fessio to do his dissertation on Hans Urs von Balthasar, "the greatest theologian of our time, perhaps of all time." A systematic theologian of encyclopedic magnitude, von Balthasar, an ex-Jesuit, is indisputably a thinker of the first order. Fessio found himself in singular company. His liberal phase was definitely over.

Upon completing his work in Europe, Fessio returned to California and was appointed to teach at San Francisco. It was 1974. Within a year he was working with some fellow Jesuits and like-minded lay people to find a way to serve the church in a new and more intense manner. After a period of reflection, prayer, and pilgrimage, Fessio and his associates decided on a plan of action that would result in the St. Ignatius Institute, an alternative form of undergraduate education. An integrated liberal arts programme with a markedly Catholic focus, the Institute was conceived as a countermeasure to the diluting of Catholic content and tradition by the post-Vatican II theological zealots. Predictably, the Institute and Fessio encountered opposition. Fessio found himself increasingly alienated from his own province, constantly at loggerheads with his Jesuit administrators and confreres, and at one point, as he would have it, struggling to survive a Jesuit-inspired effort to have him removed from the university for reasons of psychological disability.

And then in 1978 Fessio launched the Ignatius Press, an ambitious undertaking that has produced volumes of classical reprints, the publication of major works in translation by past and contemporary thinkers, and an increasingly elaborate marketing network that has turned a modest national press into a significant international player. The Institute on the local scene and the Press on the global are Fessio's grandiloquent expressions of loyalty to the tradition, and at the same time a statement of defiance against those rogue Jesuits and postconciliar Catholics who have betrayed, or at least compromised, the Faith. Not inappropriately, both the Institute and the Press are named after the founder of the Society of Jesus. Fessio's companions understand the ploy.

Fessio continues his labours as editor in the modest office of his Ignatius Press, to be found in the very shadow of the mighty chapel at the University of San Francisco, poised on its hill, disapproving perhaps of Fessio's sustained pose of rebellion—an apt visual metaphor, this David and his Goliath. But there is a particular poignancy in that this time, unlike the biblical archetypes, Fessio and the San Francisco Jesuits are members of the same tribe.

Fessio communicates the word, but more often than not it is at some variance from that of most of his confreres. The Jesuits, in their turn, seem more inclined during the Kolvenbach years to allow a place for his voice—a voice often discordant and accusatory, seldom mellow or conciliatory—but a voice better heard than suppressed. By means of this political legerdemain the Order tolerates the enthusiasms of the right while keeping a tight rein on the enthusiasms of the left, all with an eye to that ubiquitous monitor, the Roman Curia. The editors of *Etudes* and *Estudios* may well envy Fessio's carte blanche, but the situation is different in both kind and degree. Fessio's operations are not Jesuit-owned, Jesuit-run enterprises. Fessio is *the* Jesuit; it is a one-man undertaking, ambitious and largely successful, but in great part dependent on the energy, charisma, and conservative contacts of the indefatiguable civil engineer turned theologian/editor.

Zealous in his war against those who would tamper with the scriptures by using inclusive language, resolutely antifeminist in taste and conviction, and deeply suspicious of any ecumenical dialogue that could dilute the essentials of the Roman faith, Fessio may be a thorn in the side of U.S. Jesuits, but he is utterly orthodox, and unlike William Callahan and John MacNeil, both of whom are expelled Jesuits, he has neither contested received doctrine nor confronted Rome. He has Cardinal Ratzinger's blessing. No more is necessary.

Jesuit editors and writers have been plying their trade for centuries. They are practised at it. They neither fear nor avoid controversy. In fact, they welcome it, even when the controversy involves their own membership in the Society or casts a cloud on their loyalty to Rome. It is all part of that intellectual cut-and-thrust approach to knowledge that reflects the best of an ideal Jesuit education. But we can expect something different from the Jesuit poets. Or can we?

In a 1930 historical study of the Society, author René Fülöp-Miller observes:

> that the ranks of the order itself produced relatively few poets of importance may, in a large measure, be attributed to the preponderating influence of Latin; in those days, the beginning of modern times, Latin had become too stiff a vehicle and was too far removed from active life for any artistic literary work to be possible in it.[6]

This is an astounding claim. It may be true of some Jesuits, but as a universal judgement it fails miserably. Certainly, in Tudor and Jacobean England there are enough examples of Jesuit poets—Robert

Southwell, Jasper Heywood, John Brerely, and Henry Hawkins—and Jesuit-influenced poets—Richard Crashaw and John Donne—who wrote with enough distinction in their native tongue to easily repudiate Fülöp-Miller's sweeping assessment.

Following the Counter-Reformation several Jesuit critical theorists and poets struggled to articulate a notion of literature wholly consonant with the Jesuit programmme of evangelizing and catechizing.

> It can be reasonably said that, in essence, Jesuit poetic theory reworks the classical notion of literature as bringing both delight and instruction to the reader. Through affective imagery and, more broadly speaking, the appealing cleverness of his artistry, the poet is to reveal to the mind and impress upon it the moral laws which should structure the individual's life and which can be discerned as organizing and informing the creation. From that imperative in Jesuit poetic theory emerge three things: first, that poetry is seen as manifesting an affective asethetic . . . ; second, that the moral principles embodied in human art are considered as identical to those embodied in the divine art of the creation; finally, that true poetry is thought to achieve a reconciliation of pleasure and virtue. . . . [7]

In addition to the theory, there is the direct influence of Ignatius himself as mediated through his highly influential *Spiritual Exercises*, in which work he

> directs that one must . . . use the image-forming faculty to provide a concrete and vivid setting for a meditation on invisible things. . . . Whatever the subject, he insists, we must find "some similitude, answerable to the matter." [8]

The *Exercises* are designed to employ all the faculties of the mind, to engage the entire person in the art of meditation. Ignatius, no poet himself, nonetheless attached great importance to the role the imagination could and should play in the act of praying. Unlike some Spaniards, he was not disposed, like that unequalled love poet of the golden age of Spanish literature, San Juan de la Cruz (1542–91), to forego the image-forming power of the mind in favour of the apophatic tradition in mysticism with its emphasis on the stilling and emptying of the mind: the dark night.

Although the German Jesuit poets Johann Scheffler and Friedrich von Spee added some lustre to the Jesuit literary tradition, it was not until the Victorian period and in that most un-Roman of sovereignties, Great Britain, that there appeared on the scene a theoretician and a poet of the first order who would singlehandedly, though posthumously, set English poetics on its head: Gerard Manley Hopkins. Jesuit poetry would never be the same again.

Norman White, a Hopkins biographer, provides in this telling scene from Hopkins's days at a Jesuit public school in Lancashire a wonderful example of the poet's utter eccentricity:

> At Stonyhurst College in the early 1870s, Hopkins came downstairs to the refectory for breakfast one morning, and was asked why his hair was arranged in such a peculiar style. He replied that he wished to resemble Dante.[9]

Hopkins was born in Stratford, Essex, in 1844, the first of eight children. He early demonstrated his skill at language by winning the poetry prize at Highgate School in 1860. And his formidable gifts as a scholar were similarly in evidence at a precocious age, culminating with an exhibition at Balliol College in 1863.

While reading classics at Oxford he fell under the influence of the Tractarians, those zealous proponents of Anglicanism's Catholicity who continued to be a shaping force at the university despite the conversion to Rome of their most celebrated intellectual, John Henry Newman, in 1845. Although for a time Edward Pusey, the premier Anglican leader of the Tractarian or Oxford Movement, exercised the greater influence on Hopkins, the latter eventually turned Romeward and to Newman. In fact, it was Newman himself who received Hopkins into the Roman Catholic Church on October 21, 1866. The Hopkins family was devastated. Barely two years later he compounded the shock by entering a Jesuit novitiate—and this in a society deeply fearful of Jesuit intrigue and chicanery. Hopkins biographer Robert Bernard Martin places the radicalness of Hopkins's decision in historical context:

> Informed public opinion about the Society was becoming slightly more tolerant, but middle-class England still

> distrusted it; when hard fact was unavailable, its place could be taken by prejudice and actual falsehood. There were many scurrilous books about the Order, of which one typical example was called *Plan of the Jesuits for the Seduction of Religious Women*, and Jesuits were stock villainous characters in such novels as Kingsley's *Westward Ho!* or the less well-known story by Catherine Sinclair, *Beatrice: or The Unknown Relatives*, a "moral tale, purporting to show the joys of Protestantism contrasted with the miseries of Popery" that "features a vile Jesuit with the usual 'bland smile,' 'insinuating voice,' 'diplomatic skill,' 'noiseless velvet step' (Jesuits always 'glide' through Victorian novels), and the habit of 'emptying people's purses with a face of brass and dividing their families with a heart of steel'."[10]

Even William Gladstone, the great British prime minister, churchman, and controversialist called the Jesuits "the deadliest foes that mental and moral liberty have ever known." Hopkins could not have elected a more un-Victorian mode of life than that of a Jesuit, for clearly it was not the life for a gentleman. But a Jesuit he would be in spite of the national prejudice and the domestic opposition.

Following his two years as a novice at the Jesuit house at Roehampton, Hopkins was sent to study philosophy at Stonyhurst College, where he happened upon the work of the medieval philosopher Duns Scotus, a Franciscan thinker who attached marked importance to individuality and personality and whose concept of *haecceity*, of "thisness," selfhood, of the utter, irreplaceable uniqueness of a created thing, appealed to Hopkins, who had himself originated the terms *inscape*—an "individually distinctive" form consisting of the integrity of a natural object—and *instress*—that energy of being that allows created reality to cohere. Scotus was his soul brother. Not so, however, for his Jesuit confreres who remained attached to the teachings and methodology of that other great medieval thinker, the Dominican theologian Thomas Aquinas.

The influence of Scotus, an eccentric and innovative thinker who flirted with heresy, lasted throughout Hopkins's life. In a journal entry of August 20, 1880, several years after his ordination, while commenting on the *Exercises* of Ignatius, Hopkins returns to his own poetic and spiritual principle of individuation, of *inscape* and *instress*:

> Nothing else in nature comes near this unspeakable stress of pitch, distinctiveness, and selving, this selfbeing of my own. Nothing explains it or resembles it, except so far as this, that other men to themselves have the same feeling. But this only multiplies the phenomena to be explained so as the cases are like and do resemble. But to me there is no resemblance: searching nature I taste *self* but at one tankard, that of my own being. The development, refinement, condensation of nothing shews any sign of being able to match this to me or give me another taste of it, a taste even resembling it. [11]

The charged uniqueness of matter, sensation, and impression are fundamental doctrines in Hopkins's poetics, shored up by the Subtle Doctor (Scotus), and enfleshed in craft and vision. Exquisitely attuned to nature's myriad voices, Hopkins the poet found ample evidence of creation's singular resplendence and plenitude. This is the poet as psalmist, the lyrical celebrant of nature's majesty:

> Glory be to God for dappled things—/For skies of couple-colour as a brinded cow; /For rose-moles all in stipple upon trout that swim; /Fresh-firecoal chestnut falls; finches' wings; /Landscape plotted and pierced-fold, fallow, and plough; /And all trades, their gear and tackle and trim. ("Pied Beauty")

There is in Hopkins—to draw on the distinction author and critic George Woodcock used when discussing the work of the American monk-poet Thomas Merton—the poet of the desert as well as the poet of the choir. This is the poet of the "dark night of the senses" if not the "dark night of the soul," the poet of the "terrible sonnets" written in his last years, the poet who tasted the bitter gall of despair, abandonment, ennui, and emptiness of purpose:

> I am gall, I am heartburn. God's most deep decree/Bitter would have me taste: my taste was me; /Bones built in me, flesh filled, blood brimmed the curse. /Selfyeast of spirit a dull dough sours. I see/The lost are like this, and their scourge to

be/As I am mine, their swearing selves; but worse." ("I Wake and Feel the Fell of Dark, Not Day")

While at Stonyhurst Hopkins wrote very little poetry. Such would not be the case, however, when stationed at the Jesuit theologate at St. Beuno's in northern Wales. The college is built into the side of Moel Maenefa, one of the hills of the Clwyd range, and close to the small medieval town of St. Asaph. It was here, in the idyllic Welsh countryside, that Hopkins wrote his magnificent experiment in "sprung rhythm," the revolutionary "The Wreck of the Deutschland." In a letter to Canon Dixon Hopkins describes how it came about:

> What I had written I burnt before I became a Jesuit and resolved to write no more, as not belonging to my profession, unless it were by the wish of my superiors; so for seven years I wrote nothing but two or three little presentation pieces which occasion called for. But when in the winter of '75 the Deutschland was wrecked in the mouth of the Thames and five Franciscan nuns, exiles from Germany by the Falck Laws, aboard of her were drowned I was affected by the account and happening to say so to my rector. He said that he wished someone would write a poem on the subject. On this hint I set to work and, though my hand was out at first, produced one.[12]

Produce one he did. But the editor of *The Month*, the Jesuit publication to which it was submitted, found it unreadable and another Jesuit reader to whom he passed it on for comment found it the cause of a severe headache. The Jesuits were simply perplexed, and Hopkins severely disappointed. The mad dream to re-Catholicize England—the original Jesuit mandate that motivated Hopkins's sixteenth-century predecessors Robert Persons and Saint Edmund Campion—so brilliantly and unconventionally voiced in the concluding canto of "The Wreck," remained incomprehensible to the readers at *The Month*. And not surprisingly:

> Let him easter in us, be a dayspring to the dimness of us, be/ a crimson-cresseted east, /More brightening her, rare dear Britain, as his reign rolls, /Pride, rose, prince, hero of us, high-priest, /Our hearts' charity's fire, our thoughts' chivalry's throng's/Lord.

As if to make amends for Hopkins's contemporaries not seeing what subsequent generations have seen, the editor of *The Month* in 1975 editorialized:

> There is no convincing evidence that the Society [of Jesus] was an enemy to his genius. His fellow-Jesuits were also fellow-Victorians, neither more nor less perceptive than other men of their period and class. They neither helped nor hindered him much. The dark side of his own temperament was a greater enemy. The real trouble was duller but, in a sense, worse. It was the low valuation set on art by the Society after its restoration, and by no means consistent with its own more ancient and grander tradition. It had become, at least in England and more generally elsewhere, philistine, puritanical. Art, except in banal, popular forms, was regarded as irrelevant, a distraction from the main business of preaching the gospel. And its preaching see-sawed between the coldly rational and the sickly sentimental.[13]

Hopkins didn't make sense; his poetical genius was suspect. It was very difficult to find a place for him, and following his ordination in 1877 it wasn't any easier. Hopkins's delicate sensibility, refined instincts, and generally distracted manner prevented him from making a smooth transition to ordinary parochial and communal life. The Society tried many different pastoral postings: London, Oxford, Liverpool, Glasgow, and Chesterfield. But he was obviously unsuited for conventional work as a parish priest. He went back as a Latin and Greek master to Stonyhurst from 1882 to 1884, and was then appointed Chair of classics at the Jesuit-run University College, Dublin (UCD). It was during his Irish stay (1884–89), in so many ways uncongenial to him, that Hopkins wrote his sonnets of wrenching poignancy, the sonnets of terror that earned him the soubriquet, "poet of the discouraged and the self-belittling."

Ex-Jesuit John F. X. Harriott, the late British writer and broadcaster, is right when he detects in the sublime and desolate Hopkins a "poet . . . who encourages [the] conviction that whatever is done because it is good in itself, whatever its immediate consequences, does indeed become indestructible, immortal diamond."[14] The poet who could write, "No worst, there is none. Pitched past pitch of grief, / More pangs will, schooled at forepangs, wilder wring. / Comforter, where, where is your comforting?" is also the poet who could write, "No wonder of it: sheer plod makes plough down sillion / Shine, and blue-bleak embers, ah my dear, / Fall, gall themselves, and gash gold-vermilion."

The poet of the desert is also the poet of the choir. Because of the Dublin years and the "terrible sonnets," Hopkins is incompletely pictured as a near-suicidal Oxonian priest of the Roman tradition helplessly enmired in the gloom, grime, and grittiness of "John Bull's other island."

Irish poet Desmond Egan makes the case for a reconsideration of Hopkins as a happy poet, if only occasionally:

> Perhaps we have been encouraged to remember only the frustrated priest-artist who wrote during his last retreat in Co. Offaly (January 1889): "I am ashamed of the little I have done, of my waste of time, although my helplessness and weakness is such that I could scarcely do otherwise. . . . All my undertakings miscarry: I am like a straining eunuch. I wish then for death; yet if I died now I should die imperfect, no master of myself, and that is the worst failure of all."
>
> But we should place such remarks (not despairing, by the way) in the context of a life devoted to absolute standards, as was that of other laureates of unease including Beckett, Pound and even Virgil, who wished at the end to burn his *Aeneid*. Perhaps we should advert a little more to the hopeful Hopkins (not wholly absent even from the letter quoted): to the prankster who could blow pepper through the keyhole as the governors of University College held a meeting; to the man considered by fellow Jesuits as "always a popular companion" (G. F. Lahey SJ), one about whom another confrere—George O'Neill SJ—could write that Hopkins's "usual demeanour with his house companions—including the 16 or 20 resident students—was cheerful and unconstrained."[15]

Although Egan's effort to alter the portrait of abjectness, self-recrimination, and spiritual despondency predominant during Hopkins's final years is understandable, and marginally successful, it cannot be gainsaid that the Gerard Manley Hopkins of UCD is more accustomed to the dark than to the light.

Although the root causes of Hopkins's sombre moods, and occasionally bizarre behaviour, are more the terrain of the depth psychologist than the literary critic, it would be foolish to ignore them. He was a complex man; a wounded genius; a failed saint. The Society of Jesus did not make him so; they received him as such. The inability of the English Jesuits to fully appreciate the true measure of the man may well underscore deficiencies of imagination in the Jesuit leadership of the day, but it also betrays the larger social and literary conservatism that would find Hopkins's unconventional poetics distasteful. His friend and fellow poet Robert Bridges knew that and protected him. And when the time was ripe he sprung Hopkins on the world. In 1918, nearly thirty years after Hopkins's death, the first edition of his work was published with a preface by Bridges.

Still, Bridges had his blind spots and the Society of Jesus was one. In his biography Robert Bernard Martin is eager to set the record straight on the role of the Society of Jesus in the life of Hopkins, priest and poet:

> Critics and biographers have sometimes followed the lead of Bridges in saying that the Jesuits and the severity of their discipline were his ruin. It was true that he was unhappy during most of his time with the Society, but there is nothing to indicate that he would not have been more so elsewhere. The Order was strict, but it was also solid, and Hopkins needed a firm structure of belief and behaviour within which to move: Newman had known what he was talking about when he said that it was the right spot for him. Even if the Jesuits, like almost everyone else who knew him, failed to recognize his rare quality, they were very kind to him and constantly put up with his awkward but loveable personality. One might ask where he would have been happier.[16]

If Hopkins wasn't a happy Jesuit he is incontestably an influential one. And for every Jesuit poet who has followed him, he is, in the words of the United States Jesuit poet Daniel Berrigan,

> our Gorgon at the gate, for everyone starts with Hopkins and if you are lucky, as I have been, you come back to him. I wept when I read the Martin biography of his tragic and glorious life. The biography inspired me to write poetry again and I put together a new volume as a kind of delayed homage to Hopkins. You have to learn to get away from him before you can come back to him. He remains the main light on my path as far as Jesuits are concerned.

Berrigan, the *enfant terrible* of U.S. Catholicism and the Jeremiah of Jesuits, was drawn to the Society in an utterly dissimilar way to that of the Oxford convert. There was no Newman; no conversion; no dislocation of sensibility.

> I think I chose to become a Jesuit because my closest friend was becoming one. We graduated from high school together and he had been quite clear about the priesthood for a number of years. He was a very single-minded individual and I admired him deeply. We were sort of walking the same path in many ways except that I was quite bewildered about the future and then I began to take him and his direction more seriously. Finally I kind of blurted out: What are we to do about this business of the priesthood? After a period of exploration and inquiry, during which time we wrote to several religious orders requesting information, we both came up with these strange Jesuits as our first and only choice. We were influenced by their cool and noncommittal attitude in the literature they sent us. Their phones were open and we could phone and pursue our inquiries at our leisure. We were taken aback by this take-it-or-leave-it approach. There were no pictures, promos, come-ons, or big athletic facilities. There was nothing promised and this was strangely attractive to us.
>
> One day, which I will never forget as long as I live, I was sitting alone in a moviehouse and it hit me as though the big chandelier had landed on my head, this awe-ful, appalling sense that if I went in it was for life and that the burden, the dread burden, of decision was mine and mine alone. There was no coming home, no giving up, no cancellation. This moment of awareness was both a moment of pain as well as a

> moment of glory for me. I followed in the footsteps of my friend those many years ago and I am still here, still a Jesuit.

Berrigan's years as a Jesuit have been tumultuous. Variously teacher, essayist, chaplain, activist, protester, editor, and poet, he has also been a renegade, exile, war resister, inmate, fugitive, and ecclesial critic. He has challenged the authority of the church, the order, and the state. And he has paid the price of his disobedience—the price of exile!

Following the self-immolation of the young Catholic pacifist Roger Laporte in November 1965 on the steps of the United Nations building in New York—an act inspired by his opposition to the Vietnam War—the official church, in the person of the Cardinal Archbishop of New York, Francis Spellman, who was also chief chaplain to the Catholic forces in the U.S. military, took swift and immediate action. Berrigan was associated with the Catholic Peace Fellowship to which Laporte belonged and what Berrigan dubbed a religiously inspired act of non-military self-sacrifice, the cardinal plainly identified as suicide. Berrigan was served notice of eviction; he was thereafter persona non grata in the Archdiocese of New York.

Sent to Latin America, ostensibly on assignment for a Jesuit publication, Berrigan found exile a "good laboratory":

> For one who chooses to be free today, the choices are strait and biblical. One can be an exile, a prisoner, a condemned man, a Negro, a villager under napalm. A choice is offered. And it is the faces which reveal that the choices have been authentic. In prison, at the point of death, in courtrooms—human faces. Tranquil, bold, finely sculptured by adversity, supple, without extravagance, without waste or superfluity. A people who have passed time and again from life into death, and miraculously back again. Witnesses of what an older tradition would call resurrection; which we translate, more modestly, a people of hope.[17]

Jesuits are men of hope; men, in the telling phrase of Pedro Arrupe, for others. And as the '60s progressed and the United States found itself drawn deeper and deeper into the maelstrom of the Vietnam War, Berrigan, his brother Philip, and several like-minded pacifists committed to non-violent civil resistance in the tradition of Gandhi, found that the stakes were dangerously high. This was a period when "sanity at times looked like madness, where the highest art possible to the artful was simply hanging on."[18] The Berrigan brothers and their allies became celebrities. They poured blood on draft files, symbolically damaged a warhead, defied the authorities to their faces. To many they were heroes; but to many more—the majority of ordinary Catholic clergy and laity—they were a disgrace, criminal priests, outlaws in a society consumed by self-hatred and paranoia.

Again and again Berrigan found himself before the courts, judged and sentenced. He even eluded the FBI, went underground, and lived as a prisoner without walls. He also lived incarcerated in the medium-security federal prison in Danbury, Connecticut, from August 1970 to February 1972, a time of spiritual darkness, emotional crisis, and stunning productivity.

> I think that there are moments when the sky falls in and you realize that, although it's one thing to face the prospect of this or that judicial revenge, it's another thing altogether having it descend on you. You're a little bit like Chicken Little under the sky. This fear, this darkness, takes various forms: it takes forms that might be summed up in the smell of death, of one's own death, a kind of death rehearsal. In fact, I think I experienced something like this early on in Danbury Prison in '72, when I suddenly realized that this was going to be a very long haul in prison. It was very hard for me to breathe because I felt suffocated by the reality of it all. I just had to swallow hard and go on. The moment passed. I picked up whatever debris was around and went on. I wrote three or four books while in Danbury and somehow managed to get the manuscripts out although we were very closely monitored. It was not easy. The writing was not the problem; it was surviving the writing. In a sense, these prison years were very productive years, filled with new insights and imagery, years when I charted the dark side of the moon, mapped it, encountered new flora and fauna —all waiting description. It was not an easy time; but it was also not a sterile one.

Berrigan the lyricist has become increasingly discordant and Swiftian. His poetics have moved from the traditional to the experimental, from a poetics of devotion to a poetics of desperation. His poetry is apocalyptic, deeply rooted in the mad hope of Christian witness, a poetry of stark justice and raw emotion:

> Imagine; three of them. / As though survival / were a rat's word, / and a rat's death / waited there at the end / and I must have / in the century's boneyard / heft of flesh and bones in my arms / I picked up the littlest / a boy, his face / breaded with rice (his sister calmly feeding him / as we climbed down) / In my arms fathered / in a moment's grace, the messiah / of all my tears. I bore, reborn / a Hiroshima child from hell. ("Children in the Shelter")

Berrigan, in spite of his tribulations, declared for life and meaning in a chaotic and dissolute world governed by dangerous certitudes and a crazed reason:

> For now, perhaps we can only make do, not give up, come together in the bleak firelight, make what sense we can of it all. Dwelling as we do, in redawn, that darkest blink of night which seems for a horrid moment, like the blinding of the eye of day . . . we keep intact the code of the nearly lost.
>
> I hear this unquenchable poetry of survival. I hear it, it prevails, even on the winds of a firestorm.
>
> It will decompose, into sweet compost of song even the vile prose of hell.[19]

The easy piety of the young Jesuit poet has given way to a wonderful "complexification consciousness," to use a phrase by fellow Jesuit Teilhard de Chardin, culminating in the sage and visionary poet of the mature years. Berrigan the romantic, Berrigan the outsider, is finally and predictably Berrigan the existentialist, the moralist, the innovative conservative, the supreme Jesuit, shaped, as Berrigan himself would have it, by the imaginative genius of Christ:

> He offers ways, apertures, lights them up, smashes them open even to let in air. . . . We must see him in a kind of nightmare frenzy, moving like a madman down the dry arteries of time,

> tipping over the desiccated properties of the dead, invading the coffinmakers' shops, setting Caesar's coins spinning into corners to lie among the bat turds, ringing the tocsin, crying up the dead under pretext of fire, flood, shipwreck, Hamlet's father's murder, the disappearance of the town children into a mountain in company with a ragged flute player.[20]

This Ignatian insight underscores the fact that "finding God in all things"—in the shocking, the temerarious, the untoward, the blasphemous—is an essential part of the poet's calling, ever attentive to the wild and mad cadences of the divine voice.

And the divine voice for the Berrigan of the post-GC32 generation is neither muted nor gentle; it is a voice of judgement.

> The Fourth Decree—on the service of faith and promotion of justice—is the *magna carta* for the new Jesuit. However, I find that it is much easier to live a recognizable Christian life as a Jesuit in the Third World in comparison with the First. Admittedly, it's a terrible thing to say, but so much depends upon a response within a given culture to the challenge of the faith and justice imperative, and in our culture it's so difficult to move off a dime in the direction of the Gospel.
>
> I have the highest respect for Pedro Arrupe and his call to all of us to live in a manner defined by the spirit of the Fourth Decree, and yet we can't do it. He called us to it in '75 and we couldn't do it then and we can't do it now. The women of the church, the nuns of America to limit it to them, are so far ahead of us Jesuits that there's no race any longer. The combination of property, male ego, clerical pride, and the awful academic atmosphere that enshrouds us stymies our efforts. I'm part of this legacy, although I am not institutionally bound and that is a great relief for me. I teach here and there, write, give retreats, earn my living, pay my rent, and cook for my confreres. I feel the heavy burden of a dying culture weighing on all of us, and it is worse in proportion as one settles into a university community. I think these communities are the dead centre—the really dead centre—of Jesuit life.
>
> I think that there is a death hold on the Jesuits, a death clutch in which we are held by the institutions at the same

> time as we hold them. It is almost demonic the way in which this kind of womb-to-tomb security has people by the throat. To the degree that a religious order has bought into this culture of death, it will itself die. It is not a question of numbers but of the quality of our Christianity, our authentic Jesuit commitment.

Berrigan resists the pull of this culture of death, of spiritual death, by defying the gods of death. He does this by living simply, by avoiding the ostentation and comfort afforded by Jesuit prestige, by refusing to live off his own celebrity status—he is after all an icon for many both in and out of the Society—and by opting for the poor.

And the poor whom Berrigan has chosen as his own are the new lepers, the broken ones, those infected by the AIDS virus. He is their chaplain, the wounded Jesuit who has moved from draft-file burning to comfort the terminally ill in an inner-city AIDS hospice. He is simply there; a predictable presence; a sign of contradiction in the institution he serves.

> They gather about the bedsides of their stricken ones: parents, sons, daughters, brothers and sisters, lovers, wives. Sorrow, disorientation, anger, fear, dread of the unknown. The lovers have it hardest of all, making their unsteady way through the gauntlet of church, state, family, neighbourhood, job, housing, life in sum; including the feral looks laid on them from the corner deli.
>
> And then, as if this weren't enough, in comes this priest—about whom, if one has ear to the ground, one has heard a few things. So what good can come of this?
>
> As to the good, or what remote part I might have in its making, I wouldn't sweat a bet on an inflated nickel. Who could waste a thought on an abstract good? The only good I could understand lay there, a life ill unto death, the human interrupted, normalcy and expectation gone awry.[21]

As he advances in years—he was born in Virginia, Minnesota in 1921—Berrigan neither mellows nor compromises. The hard prophetic edge is still there, the passion unabated. He still seeks the answer to that Blakean question:

> What meaning abides, / when the world's / machinations run amok, / the innocent / swept like debris aside, / irrationality enthroned? ("The Evangelist")

The Word-embedded meaning that Berrigan, poet and Jesuit, will have "easter in us" is the only antidote to the culture of death that seeps into our very marrow and bones. Berrigan, the priest, is the celebrant of life, his poetry a sacrament of salvation. Like the "Gorgon at the gate" he is charged with the beauty of matter, the integrity of creation his sacred trust. He is still, irrespective of chronology and culture, under the sway of Hopkins.

He wouldn't have it any other way.

Such is not entirely the case, however, with that quixotic intellectual tease, the ex-Jesuit polymath Peter Levi:

> Berrigan read English at university and that is why Hopkins worried him. I didn't read English but classics. In fact, I had never heard of him until I became a Jesuit novice and when I did I thought he sounded rather dotty.

Levi delights in playing the iconoclast—"I became a Jesuit because of Oscar Wilde"—so it is not surprising that he would be deliciously irreverent with the memory of Hopkins:

> The obituary for Gerard Manley Hopkins in the privately circulated English Jesuit magazine spoke of him with affection and admiration as one fascinated by pebbles and thrilled by the winds and clouds. A pity, they wrote, that he never brought it all together, that such a clever, scholarly man never amounted to anything. The Jesuits of my day were very conscious of Hopkins, for whose poetry I had personally very little taste until I was close to thirty. I was frightened by him. But I inherited from him one great blessing. The English Jesuits were determined never to be accused again of maltreating poets, so from quite early on I was handled with extreme, rather nervous and edgy liberality; not that I thought so at the time.[22]

The beneficiary of Jesuit guilt, Levi has prospered as a poet *both* as a member and as an ex-member of the Society. And he readily acknowledges that it was his years as a Jesuit—both pre- and post-ordination—that made him "a poet and a kind of scholar."

In love with the English countryside, imbued with a taste for the elegiac, nurtured by dreams of Celts, Druids, and the pre-Roman peoples of Britain, Levi found in his Jesuit formation a freedom to explore, excavate, and revel. His Jesuit training would encompass seventeen years; its aim

> to produce a perfect inner freedom, a conscious freedom in which God, life, death, oneself and the world and the Crucifixion of Christ, are all tranquilly and completely accepted. The theory is that to serve Christ, to become a saint, a person needs only to be set free: freedom and the operation of grace make a heaven even of earth.[23]

It is this earth, with its plenitude of riches, its contours, cadences, and mysteries, that continues to feed the imagination of the once-wandering Jesuit. And wander he did: throughout the length and breadth of England and Wales, and, as an archaeologist-writer, to Greece and Afghanistan. "Religion for me was like a flock of birds moving across the winter fields and among the stony villages." Hopkins would have said as much.

Taught first by the Jesuits at Beaumont, a respected boys' grammar school, Levi then decided to enter the Society and began a more intimate association that would last twenty-eight years, from 1948 until 1976, during which time he described himself "as attempting and finally attaining a more or less classless condition, in which I was outside the rat race, a benign observer and private friend of mankind."[24]

This "private friend"—schooled at Heythrop and Oxford—tried his hand at serving humanity in a trifold manner: as priest, as poet, and as archaeologist.

> For me, each of the three always led back into the others. I ought to make it clear that my position as a priest was peculiar. I had no parish work unless I sought it out, I seldom administered the Christian sacraments, few of my private friends were believers, my studies were not theological, and my journeys were seldom missionary journeys. But I believed perfectly in

> everything I did and said: I gave public sermons and often spoke about religion. What I believed then I believe now.[25]

Gifted, atypical in his interests, and eccentric by disposition, Levi early found himself supported in his efforts "to find God in all things," no avenue proscribed, no edict or convention hostile to the poetic sensibility enjoined. The Jesuits had learned their Hopkins lesson well. History wouldn't repeat itself in the English province. Itinerant scholar, journalist, classicist and archaeologist more amateur than professional, poet, occasional tutor, and translator, Levi kept himself busy as a Jesuit for nearly three decades until exhaustion and a vocational crisis took its toll. He resigned from the Society of Jesus in 1976.

Following his departure from the Jesuits, he has been, variously, Fellow of St. Catherine's College, Oxford; biographer of Shakespeare and Tennyson; professor of poetry at Oxford (1984–89); literary critic; poet; and a translator of Russian and Greek verse. In addition, he has tried his hand at fiction and has written the conclusion to Cyril Connolly's posthumously published and incomplete mystery novel, *The Head in the Soup*. He also married Connolly's widow, Deirdre. He has proven to be as prolific a writer outside the Society as inside.

He remains informed by the Jesuit sensibility in ways reminiscent of Hopkins—of whom he writes "his constant urge is to outsoar his own mind's boundaries, to race towards a receding horizon, to come close to saying what cannot be said"[26]—and he knows that poetry, released from its transcendent moorings,

> withers . . . is undone: / the world hovers round it with kind advice, / but poetry's as lost as paradise.[27]

In this regard it is important to note the singular role, the "powerful underground influence" on the life and spirituality of Peter Levi exercised by the twentieth-century Welsh painter, poet, and visionary David Jones. In Levi's estimation, the Blakean Jones was both the most isolated and most free of modern poets. An epic poet and a visionary artist, Jones encapsulated those qualities of genius Levi admired; and Levi shared with the Welshman common interests like pre-Roman Britain, the 1914–18 cataclysm, and the sublime accomplishments of Latin and Catholic culture. They also shared a common respect for Hopkins (even if Levi's was late in maturing). Indeed, Jones is reputed to have said that "Hopkins comes closest to the achieved intricacy of Welsh verse."[28] No mean accomplishment in Jones's eye.

Like Hopkins, Levi's "praises of God are abundant and irregular"; like Hopkins, he is a pastoral poet, but with a preference for the elegiac over the melancholic:

> Slowly the universe expires, / blue plum blushes with dewy fires, / all that God's hand can hold / is a mere sand of gold, / a drifting glitter, a wreckage, / the boneyard of age after age, / a cloud of dust that dies: / all this lives in my eyes, / and the wet lamps are lighted now, / they lean down like an apple-bough / over the grass of love / and star we were made of. ("Mountains stalk naked from their sleep")

Levi shares Hopkins's rapturous sympathy with nature, his almost Wordsworthian insertion into the "mind" of nature, but he doesn't share his taste for metaphysics. He would rather scrounge like the archaeologist, pry like the historian, and dream like a mythmaker than probe the *ens* and *essentia* of created matter. That kind of Hopkinsesque interest is best left to other poets of Jesuit moulding and sensibility, like the Canadian Tim Lilburn.

A member of the Upper Canadian Province of the Society of Jesus for nearly a decade until his departure in the late 1980s, the Regina-born Lilburn has earned a deserved reputation as a poet of mature and significant standing. He is recognized as a major and original voice by both Margaret Avison, Canada's foremost "spiritual" poet, and Dennis Lee, the country's foremost "philosophical" poet. And these two strains, the spiritual and philosophical, are the direct legacy of his Jesuit formation. Although Lilburn's philosophical and spiritual interests are deep and expansive—they embrace platonic and neoplatonic writings, the sayings of the desert fathers, and the debates of the medieval thinkers, among others—they are anchored in his Jesuit training and insights. Lilburn's tastes constitute a veritable gallimaufry of sources and influences both conventional and recondite. In fact, his early verse is occasionally weighed down by his erudition, the dense allusions cluttering his luminous understanding.

Nevertheless, in spite of its multitiered complexity and periodic opacity, Lilburn's first volume of poetry, *Names of God*, underscores his graced and passionate celebration of the "body," of created matter, of the radical intermingling of eros and agape, of flesh and spirit:

> And if, then, the frumpy, / peppermint breathed, hymn-gargling dead, / their eyes eagled with Pharisee fire, / tisk still, Baptist-lunged, the love-stained bed / with a psalmic curse, / heave open the Book, run finger to the verse, / where God fathered love in matter, / where triple light feathered into flesh / in a womb whorled like a forming star / and the bashful genes tambourined / and calypso jumped / because the seeded Word was the lingo of chromosomes, / the hosanna of cells, / syllables of bone / linking in the blood thud and warm brine. ("Jeremiad For The Body")

The created order is the theatre of the divine, and the body of desire for transcendence.

In his later volume, *Tourist to Ecstasy*, Lilburn maps out the geography of eros in contradistinction with that of commercialized sex: "There the lust-a-rama of the shopping malls humiliates eros" ("Sermons: 1. Fervourino to a Barn of Milking Doe Goats Early Easter Morning"); and he excoriates those who seek shelter from the body in the etherealized spirituality of the pious:

> Forget, too, the lamb-y, metaphor-male, the groinless, bourgeois Jesus, / with his Easter-egg, candy-store-window eyes / ogling the cruciform crosspiece of his eyebrows. / If you meet such a Christ on the way, / kill him." ("Elohim Mocks His Images for the Life of the World")

Although Lilburn is indebted to Hopkins, in both poetic and spiritual terms, now that he has mapped out a poetic and spiritual terrain of his own, a divorce is necessary, but, he prays, not a rupture. In "It's Like This" he makes his case for a new poetics with its more robust and mundane spirituality:

> Gerard Manley Hopkins, you with a mouth like a brassiere strap showing, / do not hate me. / Not with the Maginot Line of your moral headbone hate me. / You would not have done what I / did: given. / Take your eye out of my left shoulder. / Stop the tieing and untieing of your cassock sash, clipped huffing / through nostril, the metronome walk back and forth, / the lion sweep of your beautiful head. / I have gone into matter / and seen new tribes: teenagers and cars / beneath the bull-roarer of the city's spirit tongue. / . . . . Gerard Manley Hopkins do not hate me. / This is a new place / with the lingua of matter and matter's Columbus ambitions, / and war plans of matter and the love-looking of matter at matter's / own juvenile face. / Among the lawnchairs and chocolates, revolutionary light / jerks up like Ahab's calling arm.

In the biblical manner, Lilburn must leave Hopkins, but not without first securing his father's blessing. Lilburn has passed his Gorgon at the gate. And now, to change the metaphor, he must wrestle with the demons within.

Lilburn's personal history—"speculation on dreams, my early relationship with my mother, my tattered Jesuit calling"—is recounted with poignancy and arresting self-disclosure in his 1990 essay, "Breakdown as School." In this moving prose piece he outlines the spiritual as well as the psychological consequences of a breakdown in language that draws less upon a Freudian glossary of psychotherapeutic terms and concepts than upon the ascetic insights of Carmelite (John of the Cross) and Ignatian spirituality:

> The dark experiences of breakdown are likewise purgative and enlightening. They, too, mark an alternation in life, the passage from a way of being where one is "nursed" by the enervating delights that reward those who strive to please others. You are torn from the nourishment of such approbation in collapse—you are lost, then, a failure—and are made to eat "bread with crust" which is "the food of robust persons." You learn to desire the fulfilment of God's promise in your life, the word that will sanctify you, bring you full expression, and to ignore the more modest demand to be "good." At first you

> feel sharp nostalgia for the easy praise of others, your taken-for-granted inclusion in the order, the family, the group. You experience terror at your inability to imagine what will replace what you seem to have lost. You live less by your eyes now—watching your effect upon others, tinkering with yourself until you see the glow of recognition rise in them—and more with your passion; you are turned inside out for the sake of your soul, for the greater glory of God.[29]

Lilburn is still engaged, and will always be so, in pursuing his writing and his inner journey *ad majorem Dei gloriam*, for such is at the heart of his very self-definition. It is utterly Jesuit. And to that end, Lilburn struggles to know the relationship of spirituality with sexuality, of contemplation with poetry, of earthly desire with heavenly. And that in turn brings him back to Hopkins, to the poet who understands

> what fires astonishment, shards of a cosmic grace stressed into singular things. Hopkins calls this "inscape," his word for describing what intimations of Scotus's *haecceitas* felt like on the palate of the keen eye, the elegance of the universal eased incredibly into this and that as idiosyncratic individuality. . . . Poetry seems to be the speech of a desire, a love, an eros for union with the world building from awe. . . . Poetry is the rearing in language of a desire whose end lies beyond language. . . . Poetry gestures to contemplation and contemplation feeds the poetry, modifying language by letting awe undermine it, pare it back, lending the poems a humility, compunction. . . . Poetry is where we go when we want to know the world as lover.[30]

Poetry "yearns beyond [the] barrier of intelligibility to know the withinness of things." This is vintage Hopkins. To know the withinness of things Lilburn returns to his native Saskatchewan, to a scrubland, "a large rise of hummocky aspen land on either side of the South Saskatchewan River," and out of this contemplative experience comes his collection of poems, *Moosewood Sandhills*. And in his "cave in the earth / room of knowing, room of tears" ("Rest") he will "Love the earth as felt and grease, love it, / heavy bread of leafmould, deer shit and moon light" ("From An Anchorage"). He will love the earth and he will know it, his desire to see God, his transcendental yearning, articulated and shaped by words.

The Jesuit poets are the supreme wordsmiths, their desire to know the withinness of things a political as much as a theological statement. They understand the fecund silence of the Word.

VI

Jesuit as Modern Savant

THE TERMS "JESUIT" and "learned" are for many people synonymous. The much-celebrated investment in schooling by the Society of Jesus, the arduous and lengthy training of the Jesuit candidate for the priesthood, the Ignatian openness to all branches of human investigation—the natural, human, and divine sciences—and the extensive range of Jesuit publications, all bear ample testimony to the persistent image of the Jesuit as savant. Willing to explore and master every area of legitimate intellectual activity, Jesuit intellectuals can be found scattered throughout a wide range of professions and research interests: astronomy, chemistry, theology, physics, medicine, law—both civil and ecclesiastical—history, sociology, ethics, political science, accountancy, psychology, economics, philosophy: in short, the gamut of human inquiry.

The contemporary Jesuit is engaged in a series of multivalent conversations with the proponents of theories profoundly critical of the Christian tradition. The Jesuit scholar and educator is called to dialogue and informed judgement, in the spirit of the Second Vatican Council and GC32, and not to the easy triumphalism and isolationism of the most recent past.

Jesuit philosophy professors like Joseph Godfrey of St. Joseph's University in Philadelphia have no choice but to explore common areas of concern with their non-Catholic and non-Christian colleagues in an atmosphere of mutual regard if they are to have any positive impact on the important questions of the day.

> The American Philosophical Association has become more pluralistic in the past fifteen years and as a consequence more and more viewpoints are welcome in the Association. I think, however, that there is still a native suspicion that people who have religious convictions cannot think very well, that they cannot in fact be reasonable. I think that the only way to counter this bias is to show how it is possible to both think and be religious. Surely that, if anything, is a Jesuit undertaking. There is a kind of practical atheism, if you want, whereby people treat each other badly and unfairly because they do not recognize other people as worthy of respect, as having dignity simply by being a human person. My work in ethics in the classroom deals with this practical atheism, examining the ways in which we are appropriately suspicious of certain practices, policies, and motivations in our social structures and ideologies. We must be critical of the interests of power and domination both in the structures that we have erected to govern us and in the language we use to define us. We must develop an intellectual habit that is suspicious of the categories and discourse of power. And for a Jesuit this entire enterprise is grounded in hope and in justice.

Jesuits like Godfrey appreciate the necessity for an intelligent and critical conversation with contemporary culture and its historical antecedents. They understand the temper of the times; they acknowledge the widespread disaffection with institutional religious authority; they recognize the current backlash against an uncritical reception of the faith that has been characteristic of most Catholics who have not accepted their responsibility for self-appropriation of the tradition. In the words of the Munich-based theology professor and Jesuit priest Albert Keller, they realize only too poignantly that

> before the church can teach, it must listen, not only to the revealed word but to the contemporary world as well. . . . Otherwise, we bar our own access to the world for which our proclamation is intended, and with it inevitably our access to Christians as well, insofar as they live in and are a part of the world. The end result must be that, since we, too, are people of

> this world and time, we ourselves will no longer understand what we are saying.[1]

The Jesuit savant's task is clear: the critique/proclamation must be intelligible and credible to all partners in the conversation.

The Jesuit as intellectual pioneer is not a new species. As builders of systems of thought, as arch apologists of a meaningful and relevant Catholicism, Jesuits have been at the forefront of the Roman Church's intellectual *engagement* with history and culture—non-Christian, Christian, and post-Christian. Such Jesuit thinkers include: the sixteenth-century Pedro da Fonseca, known as the "Portuguese Aristotle," a philologist, logician, and metaphysician of preeminent stature in the Iberian Peninsula; the sixteenth-century Spanish thinker Francisco Suárez, author of twenty-three volumes of erudite scholastic thought; the eighteenth-century French Enlightenment editor and intellectual Guillaume Berthier, an investigative reporter who unearthed the true source—none other than his fellow Jesuit Claude Buffier—of several entries in the first volume of the *Encyclopédie*, the great work of the *philosophes*, men such as Diderot, d'Alembert, and Voltaire who were pledged advocates of the "new reason" and sworn enemies of clericalism and the church; the three eighteenth-century German Jesuits Heinrich Kilber, Thomas Holzklau, and Ignaz Neubauer who produced the *Theologia Wirceburgensis*, a fourteen-volume theological work without equal in the age; the nineteenth-century Italian political theorist Luigi Taparelli d'Azeglio, an esteemed nationalist and editor of the powerful Jesuit publication, *La Civiltà Cattolica*; pioneering twentieth-century French Jesuits such as patristics scholars Jean Cardinal Daniélou and Claude Mondésert, ecclesiologists Henri Cardinal de Lubac, and the dangerously inventive geologist and paleontologist Pierre Teilhard de Chardin; and philosophy historian Frederick Copleston, sparring partner of Bertrand Russell and A. J. Ayer, and author of the widely used nine-volume *History of Philosophy*.

The modern Jesuit savant has an impressive pedigree; the role of thinking *for* the church and *in* the church is not foreign to him and the tightrope he must occasionally walk has been trod before. Loyalty to the institutional church is a cardinal maxim of the Jesuit ethos, but at the same time the injunction to "find God in all things" can lead to unsettling explorations and, to the official eye, disturbing conclusions. The Laurence J. McGinley Professor of Religion and Society at Fordham University, and highly productive Jesuit ecclesiologist, Avery Dulles provides a fine definition of the Jesuit thinker's vocation when he says that "commitment to the Church is a normal prerequisite for competently criticizing the Church."[2]

Perhaps no twentieth-century Jesuit more ably epitomizes the bipolar tensions of critical fidelity and critical dissent than the German Karl Rahner, who speaks with Meinold Krauss, Lutheran pastor and journalist, in the following interview excerpt:

> *Meinold Krauss:* Professor Rahner, you said once: "Even a definitively binding dogma proclaimed by the Church is essentially open to the future. A dogma must always be interpreted anew to remain alive, and this always permits even diverse interpretive possibilities in the contemporary situation."
>
> Such a statement from your lips may indeed help the faith of some people; for others, it may be rather a hindrance to faith, because it could lead to error, perhaps even to disturbing the faith. Does it bother you that your statements are indeed a help to faith for some, but for others are more of an obstacle to faith?
>
> *Karl Rahner*: Well, show me the theologian in the whole history of the Church of whom this was not unavoidably the case. The bishop of Paris objected to the saintly Thomas Aquinas. Obviously, Aquinas's theology unsettled him. And so with Suárez, the great baroque theologian of the Jesuit order—he also had troubles with Rome. Things like this cannot be avoided. It is self-evident to me that a dogma ought not to be distorted or denied in its real, originally intended meaning. But it is also self-evident that through new theological effort, every dogma can always be thought anew, made new, and considered in other connections, and so to that extent every dogma is open to the future. That is something self-evident.[3]

The boldness and clarity of the above is characteristic of Rahner the man and the theologian. Theology, intellectual integrity, openness to intelligent and justified change, radical loyalty to the tradition, and a keen appreciation of the historicity of truth are all fundamental features of the Rahner enterprise.

Rahner's life was very much the life of a twentieth-century citizen. He was born in 1904 in Freiburg, Germany, and died in Innsbruck, Austria, eighty years later. The church at the time of his birth was a defensive church, a citadel bravely withstanding the assaults of modernity, a redoubt for the legions of reaction, a fortress society resolved to proclaim the unalterable truths of the Holy Roman Church in a time of general apostasy and heresy. It was a church that bore the seemingly ineradicable stamp of the sainted pontiff, Pius X. With his face set firmly against the modern world, Pope Pius defined Catholic Christianity in the most vigorously defensive terms. He saw the taint of modernism everywhere. He hunted down its sympathizers and supporters from within the ranks of the church and had them censured, silenced, or exiled. His zeal for the truth was unchecked. In Rahner's historical perspective, however, St. Pius X stands at the midpoint of what he calls the "pian era." This period, which roughly covers the reigns of Pius IX (mid-1800s) through to Pius XII (mid-1900s), was a period of pronounced Roman monolithism with a heavy emphasis on ecclesiastical absolutism and eurocentricity. The dominant philosophical school, nay the *only* official, authoritative one, was neoscholastic Thomism, established as *the* philosophy of the Roman Catholic Church by Pope Leo XIII in 1878. Interestingly, Leo turned to the Jesuit-run Gregorian University in Rome as the future centre of a Thomist revival, installing the chairs of philosophy and theology with bona fide Thomists, and eventually summoning the distinguished French theologian Louis Billot to its ranks. Not all Gregorian Jesuits were Thomist, however, and, as a consequence, they found themselves shifted elsewhere.

Neoscholasticism—the revived philosophy of the medieval schoolmen—was the orthodoxy of the day when Rahner began his philosophical studies in 1922, and he argues it remained such until the Second Vatican Council (1963–65). The principal architect of its dismantling was Rahner himself.

While working towards his doctorate in philosophy at the University of Freiburg, Rahner studied for four semesters under the great existentalist philosopher Martin Heidegger, who profoundly influenced Rahner's two philosophical works, *Spirit in the World* (1939) and *Hearers of the Word* (1941). Heidegger's "philosophy of Being" and method of thinking influenced Rahner, not in the area of his theological investigations, but

> in my manner of thinking, in the courage to question anew so much in the tradition considered self-evident, in the struggle to incorporate modern philosophy into today's Christian theology.[4]

Following his philosophical studies, Rahner turned his attention to theology and completed his doctorate at the University of Innsbruck, subsequently beginning his own teaching career in theology at the Jesuit faculty at the same university in 1937. He remained there until 1964—with the exception of those years when the Jesuit faculty was closed, and the Canisianum, the diocesan seminary conducted by the Jesuits, was expropriated by the Nazis. He spent most of the war years in Vienna, serving in the local curia. Although highly critical of the Nazis' ideology and supportive of the activist witness of such church figures as Delp, Rösch, Grimm, Gröber, and von Galen, Rahner remained anxious and unsure about the right response: "But how should one have actually behaved, worked, protested, and taken to the barricades in those days? That I don't know even today [1979]."[5]

Within a year of the restoration of the Jesuit faculty at Innsbruck, Rahner was appointed Professor of Dogmatics. He now began a prolific and taxing regimen as a writer that remained unabated until his death. He was driven by the simple illumination that the essence of Christianity is reducible to a few meaning-crammed sentences, but that the act of rendering Christianity credible, of exploring points of interconnection with modernity, religious pluralism, and interfaith developments necessitates a radical and comprehensive articulation of Christian symbols, creedal formulas, and the philosophical underpinnings of theological concepts like sacrament, grace, nature, freedom, salvation, and spirit.

> For Karl Rahner theology must not just talk about God, but must introduce people to the experience of those realities from out of which talk about God emerges. He calls this process of introduction "mystagogy," a strange-sounding mediaeval

> term, but its meaning is clear. It is the process of learning what faith and theology mean from within one's own experience, and not merely by indoctrination from without. It is only when one is in touch with the realities that theology is talking about that one can really see what theology means. Hence Rahner quotes with approval the remark of Hans Urs von Balthasar that part of theology must be done on "one's knees."[6]

Theology is not an archaic science for Rahner, an intellectual divertissement; it draws on the very depths of human meaning and mystery, of the constitutively human in the very presence of Absolute Mystery. And this is why, to Rahner's thinking, atheism is a "horrible deformation of the person and of human consciousness." The denial of the numinous, the transcendent, the holy, is ultimately the denial of the real, of the truly human. Rahner's "theological anthropology" is predicated on an understanding of God's dynamic relationship with humanity, an active relationship that is trinitarian, free, sovereign, historical, and yet fully respectful of divine Otherness. At the same time that Rahner affirms the utter uniqueness of the Christian religion—"the culmination of the graced relationship of humanity to God"—and of the irreplaceable reality of the church—"the institutional constitution of the religion of the absolute mediator of salvation"—he also speaks of the dignity of the "anonymous Christian," whereby he means the person who, acting in the light of conscience, cannot be excluded from God's love and salvation on the grounds of *not* confessing an explicit faith in Christianity.

In every sense, however, Rahner is a Christian theologian, fully rooted in the Roman Catholic tradition and fully persuaded of the ecclesial nature of Christianity:

> The concreteness of Jesus Christ as something which challenges me must confront me in what we call the church. It is a church which I do not form and which is not constituted only through my wishes and religious needs, but rather it is a church which confronts me in a mission, a mandate and a proclamation which really make the reality of salvation present for me.[7]

Rahner remained at Innsbruck until his appointment as chair of the philosophy of religion department at the University of Munich in 1964, a position he held for three years until he began his final academic posting at the University of Münster. He stayed at Münster until his retirement from teaching in 1971. These years at Munich and Münster were especially important for Rahner and the church because they coincided with the Second Vatican Council and the theological and ecclesiastical ferment that immediately followed the Council's closure in 1965. Rahner had been chosen by both Franz König, the Cardinal Archbishop of Vienna, and Julius Döpfner, the Cardinal Archbishop of Munich, to be their *peritus* (theological expert) at the Council. In this role he was to exercise an unequalled influence amongst *periti* on the drafting and evolution of key conciliar documents, although in a more indirect way than that of many of his celebrity-ranked confreres. There were few leading bishops or contemporary theologians who had not been influenced by Rahner through his numerous writings on church sacraments, episcopacy, revelation, and the diaconate, but it is arguable whether the introduction of any specific passage or idea into the body of a conciliar text is attributable to him.[8]

He also served as an unofficial confidant to many a zealous, well-intentioned, and bewildered bishop. What the Council did *for* Rahner was nothing short of confirming what his own experience as a philosopher-theologian, professor, and writer had taught him, namely, that the

> *Roman* Catholic Church [must] become the Roman *Catholic* Church, that is, a truly universal Church. . . . It must shed the exclusive trappings of European culture to allow Christian faith to find roots and come to expression in all the cultures of the world [and] it must discover God's Spirit at work in every genuine effort to humanize the world both in our individual and social lives.[9]

Rahner saw Christians as the "true humanists of the age." To the degree that the liberating power of the Jesus message atrophies within church walls, covetously contained by canons and clerks, circumscribed by institutional interests, and mediated to the world through the channels of ecclesial correctness, Rahner saw himself poised in opposition. He was the loyal dissenter in the ranks of the faithful. He manifestly refused to dehistoricize Christianity and the church, to idealize the structures in such a way that they are unrecognizable in their human context. Rahner was also concerned that the declericalization of our conception of the church, so bravely articulated in the Vatican Council's *Lumen gentium* (the Dogmatic Constitution on the Church), continue as a dynamic for structural change as well.

> [W]e ourselves are the church, we poor, primitive, cowardly people, and together we represent the church. If we look at the church from outside, as it were, then we have not grasped that we are the church. . . . A Christian . . . is obliged . . . to recognize the church of God and the assembly of Jesus Christ in this concrete church with its inadequacies, with its historical dangers, with its historical refusals, and with its false historical developments. For the victory of God's grace on us. . . who together are the church is won right here in the form of this servant and under the cross of its Lord, and under the ongoing shadow of the powers of darkness.[10]

Although Rahner occasionally ran afoul of the authorities in Rome—he had been canonically forbidden to write, had been partially silenced, was once investigated by a Roman visitor while at Innsbruck, and was assigned a Roman censor for his writings—these strictures were soon withdrawn or never seriously applied. Rome clearly valued Rahner more than it feared him; Rome appreciated the fact that he was thoroughly Jesuit in sensibility, training, and spirituality: "the spirituality of Ignatius himself . . . has become more significant for me than all learned philosophy and theology inside and outside the Order."[11]

Like Aquinas, Rahner saw his considerable writings as so much straw when compared with the fundamental value of an encounter with Jesus of Nazareth, the starting point of all true theology. And like Ignatius, Rahner saw the incarnational principle of "finding God in all things" as the theological foundation upon which to build. In fact, Rahner's indebtedness to Ignatius finds creative expression in his 1978 experiment, "Ignatius of Loyola Speaks to a Modern Jesuit." In this work, Rahner dons the persona of Ignatius and has him render an account both of himself and of the challenges that he sees facing the modern Jesuit. This piece of fiction is bold theology and applied autobiography. By having Ignatius revisit the Society in the turbulent '70s—with its large numbers of departures from the Society, particularly in the Western world; confusion and anxiety following the 32nd General Congregation with its social justice and faith thrust; and severe conflicts between the Society and the Vatican in various quarters of the globe—Rahner reminds his fellow Jesuits that their charism is grounded in the Ignatian mission, a mission that is both ecclesial and mystical.

> Great stress is put upon the fact that I am a man of the Church; Marcuse calls me a soldier of the Church. . . . And when I am called a man of the Church, and I readily admit to it, then it is precisely the Church in its tangible hard institutionalism that is meant, the official Church, as you term it today with the not altogether pleasant nuance that the word has. . . . But my devotion to the Church is totally misunderstood, if it is understood as the egotistic, fanatically and ideologically restrictive love of power which triumphs over the conscience or as a form of identification with a "system" which does not have any vision beyond itself. . . . I loved the Church as the realization of God's love for the physical body of his son in history. In this mystical union of God with the Church—in spite of the radical difference between them—the Church itself was and remained a way to God for me and the point of my inexpressible relationship to the eternal mystery.[12]

This is the voice of Ignatius of Loyola; but it is also the voice of Karl Rahner. Loyalty to the church is not slavish deference but a critical posture, informed, self-effacing, and conscience-driven. The task of the theologian is not to think in opposition to the church but with the church, probing, reassessing, expanding, and explaining. Throughout his long and industrious life Rahner experienced firsthand the countless friction points that mark the terrain of modern theological investigation. Fully conversant with the major philosophical trends of the century, a theologian cognizant of the disjunctiveness of institutional religion with the authentic spiritual yearning of many, Rahner pursued increasingly encyclopedic undertakings that were perceived by him "as the strictest theology, that most passionately devoted to reality alone and ever on the alert for new questions, the most scientific theology . . . itself in the long run the most kerygmatic."[13]

And, one might add, the most Ignatian.

Contemporary with Rahner—even his chronology coincides nicely (1904–84)—the Canadian Jesuit Bernard Lonergan is often compared with the German theologian: "The range of his interests, the depth of his analyses, and the integrative power of his understanding have given him an influence on Catholic theology comparable only to that of Karl Rahner."[14] Like Rahner, Lonergan was schooled in Thomism and like him, too, he sought ways of breaking out of the stranglehold of neoscholasticism, of breathing new life into the official philosophical and theological structures of understanding.

Newsweek noted that Lonergan set out to do for his century what St. Thomas Aquinas had done for his; and scholar Philip McShane observed in a commemorative article:

> One may gather that the shift initiated by Lonergan is a deep cultural shift transformative of the mediation of meaning in human life reaching into areas as diverse as genetic chemistry, the psychology of management, the philosophy of law, the theology of play. It is a pivotal contribution to an axial shift in history initiated primarily in the Greek and Hebrew traditions.[15]

A partial measure of Lonergan's immediate importance can be gauged by the flourishing state of the Lonergan Industry: the University of Toronto Press project to publish the collected works of Lonergan in twenty-two volumes, an enterprise comparable in scope only to their complete Erasmus and John Stuart Mill publishing ventures; the establishment since his death of a number of "Lonergan Centres" throughout the world; the annual Lonergan Workshop held at Boston College; the Lonergan Research Institute in Toronto with its Lonergan archives and library; the University of Toronto Press Lonergan Studies series; the quarterly publication, *Method: Journal of Lonergan Studies*; and a deluge of masters' and doctoral dissertations in various disciplines.

It all began in Buckingham, Quebec, where Lonergan was born on

December 17, 1904. Educated by the Jesuits at Loyola College in Montreal, he entered the novitiate in Guelph, Ontario, in 1922 and remained there for his juniorate. Then, in 1926, he proceeded to study philosophy at England's Heythrop College and classics at the University of London. This was followed by his regency at Loyola in Montreal for three years. He was then sent to the Gregorian to do a doctorate in theology. He wrote his dissertation on Aquinas's thought on *gratia operans*. From Thomas he would learn much, perhaps most importantly the discovery of God as mystery, a discovery that would remain with him to the end.

> In the welter of words that with other theologians it was his vocation to utter, Lonergan never lost what Thomas above all theologians could teach, that theology can be done, must be done, that when it is done, we are confronted with mystery and bow our heads in adoration.[16]

From 1940 to 1965 Lonergan taught theology at Regis College in Toronto, at the Collège de l'Immaculée-Conception in Montreal, and at the Gregorian. He considered the conditions under which he worked antiquated and impossible, but managed nonetheless to write several books, including his seminal study *Insight: An Essay in Human Understanding* (1957), in which he said, "the root or key from which results intelligibility in the ordinary sense . . . and the intelligible in the profounder sense . . . cannot be understood without understanding what understanding is."

Epistemology, the study of human knowing, and metaphysics, the study of being, are at the heart of *Insight*, but Lonergan was also engaged in something new, something revolutionary in fact:

> Here was an existentialist stress on the value of freedom purged of the irrationality with which it is so often associated; an enthusiasm for the achievements of science without the slightest tendency to "scientism" with its neglect of the human subject as such; a political philosophy which clearly placed both liberalism and Marxism as partial viewpoints; an ethics which adroitly steered through the shoals of scepticism and relativism without capitulating to dogmatic authorita-

> rianism; and finally a stringently rational philosophy of religion which issued neither in atheism nor in fideism.[17]

In spite of the multidisciplinary sweep of *Insight* and his later work, Lonergan maintained his defining interest in the act of knowing and its relationship to subjective interiority.

> Freely the subject makes himself what he is; never in this life is the making finished; always it is still in process, always it is a precarious achievement that can slip and fall and shatter. Concern with subjectivity, then, is concern with the intimate reality of man. It is concern, not with the universal truths that hold whether a man is asleep or awake, not with the interplay of natural factors and determinants, but with the perpetual novelty of self-constitution, of free choices making the chooser what he is.[18]

Lonergan's concern with the knowing subject involves a formal repudiation of those static, constricted conceptions of human behaviour, of human meaning, that are the sad inheritance of centuries of neoscholastic anthropology. At the same time, Lonergan has little patience for the easy nihilism of those who despair of the human subject's ever knowing what is true, and beautiful, and good.

What Lonergan was prepared to face, and most of his contemporaries were not, was nothing short of that massive shift in human consciousness that has come to define the crisis of our age:

> What breathed life and form into the civilization of Greece and Rome, what was born again in a European Renaissance, what provided the chrysalis whence issued modern languages and literatures, modern mathematics and science, modern philosophy and history, held its own right into the twentieth century; but today, nearly everywhere, it is dead and almost forgotten. Classical culture has given way to a modern culture, and, I would submit, the crisis of our age is in no small measure the fact that modern culture has not yet reached its maturity. The classical mediation of meaning has broken down; the breakdown has been effected by a whole array of new and more effective techniques; but their very multiplicity and complexity leave us bewildered, disorientated, confused,

> preyed-upon by anxiety, dreading lest we fall victims to the up-to-date myth of ideology and the hypnotic, highly effective magic of thought control.[19]

Freed of our secure moorings, cut adrift without our reliable navigational instruments, without even a compass to know our general direction and a map to define our destination, we must come to appreciate the historical significance of our time of crisis or remain vulnerable to every system, ideology, and manifesto that offers firm anchor in the turbulent seas of modernity.

To move from a classicist mentality, in which a culture and system of belief is normative, to a modern culture, with its historical consciousness and fluidity of culture, is more than unsettling. It is traumatic. And it is especially so within the ranks of the clergy, those professionals faithfully schooled in a neoscholastic framework and instructed to bring to the multitudes a "truth" that is invariable, fixed, and intelligible. In Lonergan's mind the Society of Jesus, an organization conceived in a time of crisis and for whom a principal function is to respond to cultural upheavals, the shift from the classicist mentality to the modern mentality is a "crisis of the first magnitude":

> Classicist philosophy was the one perennial philosophy. Classicist art was the set of immortal classics. Classicist laws and structures were the deposit of wisdom and prudence of mankind. This classicist outlook was a great protector of good manners and a great support of good morals, but it had one enormous drawback. It included a built-in incapacity to grasp the need for change and to effect the necessary adaptations. . . . If I am correct in assuming that the Jesuits of the twentieth century, like those of the sixteenth, exist to meet crises, they have to accept the gains of modernity in natural science, in philosophy, in theology, while working out strategies for dealing with secularist views on religion and with concomitant distortions in man's notion of human knowledge, in his apprehension of human reality, in his organization of human affairs.[20]

With the possible exception of Rahner, no Roman Catholic thinker has worked out quite so comprehensive a strategy of dealing with modernity as Lonergan has. Robert Doran appreciates this fact better than most. Co-founder of the Lonergan Research Institute in Toronto and co-editor of Lonergan's *Collected Works*, Doran wrote his doctoral dissertation on Lonergan and Carl Gustav Jung at Marquette University in Milwaukee, and relied on Lonergan's thought for his own significant and weighty *Theology and the Dialectics of History*. Doran has known his mentor as a scholar, as a disciple, and as a friend.

> I had started studying Lonergan's work in 1967, and became convinced almost immediately that it was a work of utmost importance for the church and for theology itself. In the course of writing my dissertation, I came to Toronto to spend several months at Regis College, mainly to get Lonergan's reaction to what I was doing. I had met him on several occasions prior to that, but I didn't really develop any kind of close or intimate knowledge of him until these months at Regis. I found a propitious moment to give him some materials that I was working on, but I had chosen to wait until he seemed more relaxed because he was giving lectures at Trinity College and I didn't want to bother him. When the lectures were over, I handed him about five pages that were really more of a dissertation abstract than anything. He got back to me the same evening and with tremendous encouragement told me that he had long hoped that someone would undertake the kind of critique that I was embarked on. I asked him—tentatively and timidly—if I interpreted him correctly, and he answered "yes." It was a great moment for me to get that kind of affirmation as a young scholar of thirty-five.
>
> He became very interested in my work and asked me to keep him abreast of my thinking and publications. And so I dutifully sent him articles over the years and I would get back a note acknowledging receipt or commenting on the content. Eventually he left Toronto to assume the position of Distinguished Visiting Professor at Boston College—he had previously been in the Boston area as Stillman Professor at Harvard—and he remained at B.C. until a year before his death.
>
> Shortly after I had moved to Regis College to teach in 1979,

> I received a call from him asking me if I would be one of the executors of his literary estate. He wanted to get a younger person to help edit his work—his close friend, collaborator, and amanuensis Fred Crowe was of advanced years—and he alighted on me. I was floored. I realized then that he really meant what he had said so many years ago when he told me that what I was doing, the direction I was taking, was important and right.
>
> During the last year of his life, after he had moved to the Jesuit infirmary in Pickering, I went to visit him on New Year's Day and told him that every weekend that I'm in Toronto I would come to visit him. I was unsure at the time whether this registered with him or not. The week before he died, when he was not all that lucid, I was sitting with him and holding his hand when he said: "You have been faithful to your promise." He died three weeks short of his eightieth birthday.

In Doran's mind, Lonergan is the modern midwife par excellence. He is the one who rightly apprised us of the irreparable breakdown of the old controls of meaning, of the fact that theory and logic, because of the development of modern science, can only offer hypotheses in need of verification and that historical consciousness itself has brought us to the recognition that all is inescapably relative. This, in turn, can breed nihilism and various forms of intellectual terrorism like postmodern deconstructionism. Lonergan, however, does not argue for the restoration of some overarching theoretical structure that can guarantee once again the security of absolutism. Rather, he argues for the discovery of norms for authentic behaviour in subjective interiority, with the human spirit's desire for meaning, truth, goodness, and love perceived as orientations open to God.

> What he has attempted to do with rigorous precision is to help people discover these orientations within themselves. What is it in your consciousness that manifests your desire for meaning? What are the operations that you perform to test the meanings that you have arrived at to see if they are true? What are the operations that you perform when you have to make a decision? What is the process that you go through because you want to make a good decision, a responsible decision? Given

that you are innately endowed with the desire to be responsible, what is it that you do in order to fulfill that desire? What are the operations? What are the questions you raise, the things you take into account, the feelings that influence your decision?

What is this orientation to God, what Lonergan calls "the shrine for ultimate holiness," our interiority?

These are the "basic" questions Lonergan attempted to answer, and he did so by spelling out the desires of the interior life of human beings with the conviction that those desires will provide the norms that they need: be attentive to the experience of data of sense and consciousness; be intelligent about inquiring into the meaning of this experience; be critical in one's judgements; be responsible in one's decisions. And all of this is possible as the fruit of God's love inundating the human heart.

No culture, then, is normative and no philosophy perennial. One can only turn to intentionality analysis and human interiority to discover the perduring, the constant: "implicit in human inquiry is a natural desire to know God by his essence; implicit in human judgement about contingent things there is the formally unconditioned that is God; implicit in human choice of values is the absolute good that is God."[21] The divine sustains and suffuses the concrete, historical reality of human experience and consciousness. The divine is not abstract, remote, ahistorical, or disengaged. Lonergan's God is like the God of Augustine, Ignatius, Pascal, Kierkegaard, and Newman, an affective God who responds to the yearnings and desires of the human heart: "His theology is a love that thinks and a thinking that loves. What Dame Edith Sitwell [the English poet] wished for, Lonergan has shown to be true: 'the fire of the mind and the heart are one'."[22]

The mind's fire for Bob Doran, disciple of Lonergan's method and insight, is to forge a new systematics out of a history and context that begins as the twentieth century comes to a close: a century of mass slaughter, racial genocide, cultural cleansing, genetic experimentation of a variety and sophistication Huxley and Orwell would shudder to consider, and new and virulent diseases. But it is also a century that has given birth to an iconoclastic anthropology, a stripping down of the old order and the laying of new foundations, radical breakthroughs in consciousness, and global strategies designed to preserve the integrity of creation. For a Christian, and particularly for an Arrupe-generation Jesuit, there are new calls for justice and solidarity with the poor. In Doran's mind

> there are resources in Lonergan for a theology constructed out of such solidarity, and that kind of theology brings those resources to their richest fulfillment as historically-catalytic elements of meaning. Without that fulfillment the resources can be left hanging, as it were, in a never-never land of heuristic possibilities for an *intellectual* but not a reasonable and responsible, that is, *factual* constitution of the human world. Lonergan means and intends primarily praxis, and by forcing the meaning of his scale of values we can begin to satisfy his profound practical intentions.[23]

And where there is praxis there is the heart. In Doran's own life the fire of the heart works closely in tandem with the fire of the mind.

> I have been engaged since the summer of 1988 in a pastoral ministry among persons who are living with HIV infection and AIDS. It was the same summer when the desire to become involved in this area first began to arise within me and I tested it every way that I knew, concluding that it was a genuine desire and that I should act on it. In the fall of 1990 we began a monthly healing service at the Toronto Jesuit parish of Our Lady of Lourdes, not only for those living with HIV infection and AIDS, but the whole HIV-affected community—partners, families, and care-givers. In the last four years some one thousand individuals have been at the service at least once.
>
> Before the healing takes place there has to be a transcendence of the stereotypes that have been imposed on the HIV community, stereotypes that have been internalized making it hard for them to believe in God's unconditional love for them. And yet, if you go to the apartment of someone with AIDS and see the love and care they are receiving, you will see the compassion, the love, of Jesus.

As Doran struggles to integrate the mind and the heart—the new systematics with praxis—he is acutely aware that a culture torn from its classicist mentality and uncomfortable with the new historical consciousness is going to be a culture wildly veering from right to left, often intolerant, and fearful. And this is true of both church and society, as Lonergan sagely observed:

> There is bound to be formed a solid right that is determined to live in a world that no longer exists. There is bound to be formed a scattered left, captivated by now this and now that new possibility. But what will count is a perhaps not numerous center, big enough to be at home in both the old and the new, painstaking enough to work out one by one the transitions to be made, strong enough to refuse half-measures and insist on complete solutions even though it has to wait.[24]

However, being in the centre is sometimes the same as being in the vanguard. It depends on one's historical perspective. And for the Jesuit priest-scientist Marie Joseph Pierre Teilhard de Chardin, the vanguard proved uncompromising.

Like Lonergan, Teilhard laboured to embody a new vision of things, a new cosmology, a new humanity, but unlike Lonergan he repeatedly ran afoul of the Roman authorities. He was refused permission to publish his writings, and it was only after his death in 1955 that the world truly became aware of the breadth and daring of the Teilhardian vision.

Jesuit, palaeontologist, evolutionist, religious philosopher and mystic, Teilhard dreamt of a great synthesis between science and religion. This passion would occupy centre stage for most of his life. He was born on May 1, 1881, in the Auvergne region of France, near the city of Clermont-Ferrand. The landscape near his home is severe, the rocky soil literally veined with crystals.[25] The Auvergne has been called a "geologist's paradise," and one cannot imagine a more fitting environment for one who was to become a scientist of the earth's mysteries.

The young Teilhard came by his love of science not only through the natural wonders of his immediate setting—the conical summit of the Puy de Dôme in the distance—but through the influence of his father Emmanuel, who was a gentleman farmer with a taste for the natural sciences, onetime permanent secretary of the Academy of Sciences, Letters and Arts of Clermont-Ferrand. He encouraged his son to explore the mountains near his home.

But if Teilhard took his scientific orientation from his father, he took from his mother the very French and Jesuit devotion to the Sacred Heart of Jesus. Berthe Teilhard de Chardin was a woman of extraordinary piety and charity, self-sacrificing and indifferent to social conventions. In Teilhard we can find her resoluteness of character, simplicity of faith, and generosity of temper.

In 1892, at the age of 11, Teilhard was admitted to the Jesuit college of Notre Dame de Mongré, Villefranche-sur-Saône, and there he began his lifelong association with the Society. Following the completion of the necessary five years at the college, he was presented with seven awards, including the coveted Prix d'honneur. He was then admitted to the Jesuit novitiate at Aix-en-Provence and passed to the juniorate at Laval shortly after. Because of the anticlerical government in France and its expulsionary legislation regarding the Jesuits, Teilhard had to continue his training on the Channel Islands where he pursued his first love, his "jealous and absorbing passion—stones."

From 1905 to 1908, however, Teilhard had the opportunity to examine a quite different terrain from that of the Channel Islands or the Auvergne: the desert. He was appointed to teach chemistry and physics at a Jesuit secondary school in Cairo and he used the opportunity to study the marvels, ecological and mystical, of the desert.

In 1908 he returned to Europe and continued his theological studies in Hastings, England. He was ordained in 1911. He was then assigned to graduate studies—the anti-Jesuit legislation having been rescinded—at the Museum of Natural History in Paris. When the Great War broke out in 1914 Teilhard served with considerable distinction as a military chaplain and medical orderly. But he was not content to stay in the wings. He longed to be part of the action, and so he volunteered as a *brancardier* or stretcher-bearer. He was subsequently awarded the Médaille Militaire for his bravery.

The spiritual shock of the war sharpened Teilhard's capacity to transcend the immediate and narrow conditions of history. And it also sharpened his understanding of the fusion of science and religion. In *Note sur le progrès* Teilhard argued that without biological evolution, which produced the brain, there would be no sanctified souls. He also reasoned that "without the evolution of collective thought, which alone can realize the fullness of human consciousness on earth, there would be no consummated Christ." The outline of his thinking on evolution—bold, idiosyncratic, and visionary—was beginning to form.

Following the war, Teilhard resumed his studies in Paris, wrote his dissertation on the mammifers of the Lower Eocene in France, received his doctorate in science in 1922, became President of the Geological Society of France, and was appointed professor of geology at the Institut Catholique de Paris. The following year, on the first of his many scientific expeditions to China, he went to the Ordos Desert in Mongolia and it was again in the desert that he confronted his destiny, not only as a scientist but as a mystic. It was the desert that fed his imagination and steeled his spirit for the burgeoning demands of the future. In *La Messe sur le monde*, a work that he began during the war and finished in China in 1923, Teilhard consecrates himself to the Lord of Matter, the Christ of the Universe: the conjunction of matter and spirit, the sacred tangibility of things, the coming together of God and matter in the Incarnation—these are the thoughts of a scientist at work in the desert, of a mystic in search of God in and through the stuff of the universe.

In 1924, Teilhard returned to Paris to lecture on evolution. However, on November 13 he was summoned by his provincial superior, Kosta de Beauregard, to account for a paper that he had written on the doctrine of Original Sin. Teilhard found himself under the scrutinizing eye of the powerful and aristocratic Roman prelate Cardinal Merry del Val, a man who would not take lightly any trifling with orthodox teaching. The Cardinal applied pressure on the General of the Society of Jesus, Wlodimir Ledochowski, who in turn instructed Beauregard to withdraw Teilhard from his position at the Instiut, to order him to cease writing articles on matters of a theological nature, and to confine himself exclusively to his scientific concerns. Such censure might have destroyed the faith of a less determined person, but Teilhard had come to terms with his feelings towards the official church as early as 1921:

> If there is one thing that I fear less than everything else, it is I believe persecution for my opinions. There are a good many points about which I may be diffident, but when it comes to questions of truth and intellectual independence, there is no holding me. I can envisage no finer end than to sacrifice oneself for a conviction. That is precisely how Christ died. . . . I cannot shut my eyes to the fact that it would be a biological blunder for me to leave the religious current of Catholicism. I believe that the church is still a child. Christ, by whom she lives, is immeasurably greater than she imagines.[26]

Teilhard was sent to China, where he remained for nearly twenty years, engaged in various aspects of palaeontological research, including his involvement with the celebrated discovery of Sinanthropus or Peking Man. His lengthy sojourn in the Far East was more than a liberal gesture on the part of his superiors to provide him with the opportunity for serious scientific research. It was a means of ensuring his silence. Teilhard's commitment to what he called *intégralisme*—"the extension of Christian directives to all the resources of the world"—in marked contrast to the prevailing notion of *intégrisme*—"dogma as a cage"—underscored the fully ecumenical dimensions of his dream of "planetization," by which he meant a process that would lead the human development on the surface of the earth to a critical point of saturation; at which time a new stage of evolution would set in. But such an undertaking smacked as much of theological unorthodoxy as it did of scientific heresy. Teilhard's writings were suppressed by church authorities.

After the Second World War—which he spent largely in the Orient—Teilhard returned to Paris, and now his problems with Rome took a particularly disturbing turn. In his eagerness to serve the cause of Christianity, Teilhard made as many adjustments as he could to his controversial writings in order that they might be published. This was especially the case with his major work, *Le Phénomène Humain*. To no avail. Teilhard's talk of an evolving Christianity, of a Cosmic Christ, of an evolutionary process that embraces all human and natural activities, continued to perplex and alarm the ecclesiastical authorities. His notion of evolution was not so much threatening, however, as it was novel. Christopher Mooney, a Jesuit Teilhard scholar and author of *Teilhard de Chardin and the Mystery of Christ* (1966), identifies the key word of Teilhard's evolutionary system as

> *enroulement*, which comes up continually in his writings and yet is not translated well. In *The Phenomenon of Man*, for instance, it is translated as "involution," which is quite incorrect because involution in a strict sense means reverse volution. In any case, the correct translation is "coiling," a word which Teilhard actually used in some of his English lectures. This *enroulement* is terribly important because it is the image that Teilhard wishes to use when describing evolutionary progress: namely, the fact that evolution consists in the same cycle being repeated, but each time with a slow advance. In other words, a coiling, with each new advance the occasion for a new crisis, with each new crisis the result of a previous achievement. As soon as you have an achievement, you move up the coil to a new crisis. Each new advance increases the temptation to stop, of course, because you have a greater capacity and you have reached a plateau, at which time there is a natural urge to stop and even to regress. Teilhard felt that the human species in the twentieth century had reached this point. It had made an enormous advance, reached a plateau, and the temptation was now not to go on.[27]

Teilhard's fear of human timidity prompted him to write from his observatory in Peking that

> everything strengthens my conviction that the future can be forced and led only by a group . . . united by a common faith in the spiritual future of the earth. "Get behind me," I would make bold to say, "all Godless pessimists *and* all Christian pessimists." . . . After many years of thought it seems to me that I have now the scientific, philosophic, and religious equipment to attack this fiercely contested strong-point: the one vital strategic point standing at the fork which commands the whole future of the Noosphere [Teilhard's term for the "envelope of reflective life embracing the biosphere, though still dependent on it"].

> I feel that at the age of sixty I have at last found or pinned down my true vocation.[28]

Rome was not so sure. They demanded clarification in his writings, and then they required accommodation, and then they imposed censure. But Teilhard was not to be deterred. Throughout his travails he remained confident that the truth of evolution would triumph. For Teilhard, matter and spirit are immersed in a forward-moving process from instinct to reflection to love with all creation engaged in a valiant advance into the future.

In 1947, at the same time as he remained under Rome's shadow of displeasure and suspicion, a string of scientific honours came his way. He was promoted to the rank of Officer of the Legion of Honour, named Director of Research at the National Centre for Scientific Research, elected a Corresponding Member of the mineralogical section of the Academy of Sciences, and nominated as a candidate for the Chair of Geology at the Collège de France.

The following year he went to Rome, eager to persuade any who would listen that his evolutionary ideas were not hostile to or incompatible with Catholicism and that dialogue with modern humanism is essential if humanity is ever to be Christianized. But Rome found his work—especially his theologizing—mystifying and dangerous.

> I think Teilhard would be the first to admit that he was not a theologian in the professional sense. Professionally, he was a geologist and a palaeontologist. But his geology and palaeontology brought him an insight into the development of the human species and of the cosmos. After all, he had a profound spiritual experience of the material world long before he became a scientist. In fact, his scientific training simply gave him a different perspective on matter. What he saw was the importance of an evolving human species, a conclusion he came to as a result of his law of complexity-consciousness, which means that the more developed consciousness will always correspond proportionately to the more complex organic structures. This law led him to the view that the human species is the goal of the evolutionary process now taking place at the level of thought (noogenesis) and spirit (christogenesis).

> For Teilhard all matter evolved and, indeed, the spirit evolved as well. Since the Christian message is that Christ is at the centre of all God's creation, therefore it follows that Christ has to be at the centre of the evolutionary process.[29]

He was forbidden by Rome—with nary a protest from the Jesuit Curia—to publish his manuscripts and was told to decline the Chair of Geology at the Collège de France, not because they feared his palaeontological work, but because they feared that he would use his position as a pulpit for the propagation of his evolutionary ideas. Disappointed by Rome's reception, but not broken, he accepted invitations for expeditions of a scientific nature to both South Africa and parts of South America, and retained his strong conviction that the times were urgent, propitious, and ripe for new breakthroughs of awe-inspiring magnitude. And yet Rome fiddled. In a May 31, 1953, letter to his fellow scientist and Jesuit confrere Pierre Leroy he is at his most biting:

> Again I ask, why is it that in Rome, along with a "Biblical Commission" there is no "Scientific Commission" charged with pointing out to authorities the points on which one can be sure Humanity will take a stand tomorrow—points, I repeat, such as: 1.) the question of eugenics (aimed at the optimum rather than the maximum in reproduction, and joined to a gradual separation of sexuality from reproduction); and 2.) the absolute right (which must, of course, be regulated in its "timing" and its conditions!) to try everything right to the end —even in the matter of human biology; and 3.) the admitted existence (because statistically it's more probable) of Foyers of Thought in every galaxy. All this descends directly on us—for general reasons of universal order and for basic reasons. And while all this is going on churchmen really think that they can still satisfy the world by promenading a statue of Fatima across the continents.[30]

Though tired after years of work and struggle for acceptance, Teilhard's spirit of hope and intelligent optimism never flagged. However, the body had its limits. On April 10, 1955, after attending a pontifical mass at St. Patrick's Cathedral in New York, he suffered a major heart attack and died. He was still largely unknown to the world. But very soon, thanks to the intrepid labours of his secretary Madame Jeanne Mortier, his writings began to see the light of day. Indeed, there was a veritable Teilhard cult in the years following his death.

With these publications "Neo-cosmic," "Ultra-human," and "Pan-Christic" entered our vocabulary. But it was precisely terms such as these that succeeded in alarming or irritating those scientists who preferred their science pure and not admixed with theological metaphor or coloured by what British scientist Sir Peter Medawar called "tipsy euphoric prose poetry." Teilhard's penchant for neologisms, his creative fusion of metaphor with fact, image with statistic, and science with religion did prove disconcerting for many critical readers. And yet Teilhard's revolutionary system requires a mode of expression that is perhaps as disrespectful of syntax as his ideas were of acceptable categories of thinking. Other scientists like Piveteau in France, Dobzhansky in the United States, and Huxley, Needham, and Towers in England considered him a "seminal force of great significance to science."[31] Likewise, theologians of the rank of Henri de Lubac argued vigorously for a critical response to the creative synthesis he posed to the conventional categories of modern theology.

If Jesuit superiors were only too compliant with Roman instructions to silence Teilhard, many Jesuit scientists and theologians were correspondingly forceful in his defence. A kind of restitution was being made. Jesuits are comfortable with science—from the beginning of the Order the studying and teaching of the physical or natural sciences was deemed important—and they are comfortable with theology, the traditional "queen of the sciences," but the mix can be problematic even to them. Still, Teilhard's inventive and poetic mysto-science invited scholars to shed their uniperspectival stance for the multiperspectival stance of a new age. Many were reluctant to do so. Thoroughly trained in their disciplines but not inclined by temperament to the grand synthesis boldly proffered by Teilhard, most scholars and researchers, lay and Jesuit, preferred their science and/or religion straight and not mixed.

Teilhard's cosmic Christianity and his determination to waken a somnolent church to the challenges of a new age struck a raw nerve in the institution he was ordained to serve. Prepared to admit the possibility of the evolution of the species, church authorities had a much more difficult time with the Teilhardian notion of the evolution of the church and, indeed, of Christ. Similarly, scientists had difficulty with his interweaving of mystical concepts and terms with the technical jargon of the discipline. In Teilhard's mind, a world capable of the advanced stage of evolution—noogenesis—is a world also capable of that higher and more perfect expression of Creation's evolutionary destiny, christogenesis: the Total Christ; the Super Christ; the Omega Point. Teilhard's poetic vision can be found at that point of intersection between matter and spirit that highlights the deficiences of our conventional modes of discourse and understanding. It should not be surprising, then, that most scientists, both Jesuit and non-Jesuit, should approach Teilhard with a combination of caution, bemusement, and disapproval. It is the mystical flavour, the interdisciplinary thrust, of Teilhard's thought that vexes them. The science is fine.

After all, Jesuits have been well practised in the scientific arts for centuries. Biology, physics, and chemistry continue to draw Jesuit interest—think only of the pioneering work of the eighteenth-century Dalmatian Jesuit Roger Joseph Boscovich whose 1758 masterpiece, *The Theory of Natural Philosophy*, "anticipated many developments of atomic physics,"[32] or think of the contemporary U.S. Jesuit Timothy Toohig, Deputy Associate Director of the Superconducting Super Collider Laboratory in Texas, whose research endeavours focus on the relationship between high energy physics and Ignatian spirituality.

But it is astronomy more than any other science that has served as an area of high accomplishment for Jesuits from the inception of the Order to the present. For instance, craters and other lunar formations perpetuate the names of over thirty Jesuits, including that of the seventeenth-century Bolognese astronomer Giovanni Riccioli.[33] German Jesuits like Johann Deckers and Albert Curtz, collaborators of the great astronomer Johann Kepler; Austrian court astronomer Maximilian Hell and his confreres Joseph Stepling at Prague and Christian Mayer and Johann Metzger at Mannheim; the Polish Martin Poczobut, who outfitted one of the most advanced observatories in eighteenth-century Europe at the Jesuit Academy at Vilna and who earned for himself an international reputation as an astronomer for his several discoveries; Ignaz Kögler, who presided as President of the Tribunal of Astronomy in Peking; Pietro Angelo Secchi, who provided the first comprehensive spectral classification of the stars; and Hungarian Fenyi Gyula all provide ample evidence of the Jesuit penchant for proficiently and innovatively scanning the skies. And they continue to do so from their many observatories, including the Vatican Observatory, where Director George Coyne recently opined that observatory findings provide some evidence of the existence of many solar systems like our own with possible life forms. For the British Jesuit astronomer Christopher Corbally, who is overseeing the construction of the Vatican's new Advanced Technology Telescope in Arizona, the opinion of his Jesuit brother does not distress him but merely confirms his faith in a God who is personal and full of surprises, although he allows that "the discovery of intelligent life elsewhere in the universe . . . would have serious ramifications for Christianity and would mean a rethinking of some of the theological foundations on which Christianity is built."[34] And not for the first time. Remember Galileo!

The celebrated Galileo affair is very much a Jesuit affair, given the principal players. Galileo Galilei was a seventeenth-century mathematician, physicist, astronomer, and inventor who provided evidence to support the Copernican hypothesis that the earth revolved around the sun (heliocentrism) as opposed to the generally held view that the sun revolved around a fixed earth (geocentrism). Following the publication of his famous work *Dialogue on the Two Great World Systems* in 1632, Galileo found himself enmeshed in a bitter controversy with the Vatican that would last for many years. It wasn't his first experience with the Holy Office of the Inquisition.

At the time of the beginning of the Galileo affair there were three eminent Jesuit astronomers attached to the Roman College: Christoph Klau, also known as Clavius, Christoph Grienberger, and Christoph Scheiner. They agreed with Galileo's support of the conclusions the great Polish canon and astronomer Copernicus had presented in *The Revolutions of the Celestial Orbs*, but they wanted further corroborating evidence before they would jettison the Ptolemaic system or its modified Tychonic variation for the Copernican. Because Galileo's claims appeared to call into doubt various passages of scripture, the theologians and the Holy Office now took an active interest in his writings and publications. Copernicanism was condemned in 1615, and it was the lot of one Robert Bellarmine, cardinal, theologian, and Jesuit, to convey the decision and receive the Italian astronomer's faithful submission. It was not a job he relished. Although he cautioned against advancing as incontrovertible truth what can be only reasonably argued as a hypothesis of great probability, and although he sought a *modus vivendi* between the zealous Galileo and the guardians of the scientific and theological status quo, Bellarmine was forced to communicate to the hapless but devout Galileo the negative judgement of the Vatican. But Bellarmine the theologian hinted at a possible resolution of the seeming impasse in a letter he wrote to the Carmelite Foscarini on April 12, 1615:

> I say that if it were really demonstrated that the sun is at the center of the world and the Earth is in the third heaven, and that it is not the sun which revolves round the Earth, but the Earth round the sun, then it would be necessary to proceed with great circumspection in the explanation of Scriptural texts which seem contrary to this assertion and to say that we do not understand them, rather than to say that what is demonstrated is false.[35]

Unfortunately, Bellarmine's bid to buy time failed. In the words of Canadian Jesuit Joe Mroz, "Bellarmine was born too late to save Aristotelianism and too early to organize a new synthesis."[36] He died twelve years before the famous trial of 1633 when Galileo was condemned by the Holy Office for being "vehemently suspected of heresy," forced to recant, and placed under house arrest until his death in 1642. This is not how Bellarmine would have wanted it to end. He would have heartily approved the recommendation of the papal commission established by Pope John Paul II in 1981 to investigate the Ptolemaic-Copernican controversy wherein the commissioners note

> that Galileo's judges, incapable of dissociating faith from an age-old cosmology, believed quite wrongly that the adoption of the Copernican revolution, in fact not yet definitively

> proven, was such as to undermine Catholic tradition, and that it was their duty to forbid its being taught. This subjective error of judgement, so clear to us today, led them to a disciplinary measure from which Galileo "had much to suffer." These mistakes must be frankly recognized, as you, Holy Father, have requested.[37]

An apology that is 350 years late might impress some, but for Christopher Moss, a member of the department of astronomy at Cambridge University,

> it's not a great hill of beans for a working scientist. In the sixteenth and seventeenth centuries the church was confronted by new knowledge in astronomy which apparently questioned the inerrancy of the bible and challenged the church to deepen its understanding of biblical texts, particularly in the area of Creation. The church reacted by judging science from the perspective of sacred science. They made a mistake that has reverberated down the corridors of history. In my view, they have learned little. For instance, Joseph Cardinal Ratzinger, Prefect of the Congregation for the Doctrine of the Faith, issued his directive on homosexuality in 1985 in which he denounced homosexuality seemingly oblivious of the finest medical evidence showing that homosexuality may well be genetically determined and not a freely chosen life option. Once again the church has allowed sacred science or theology to function like a super science passing quick and easy judgement on complex matters.

Christopher Moss is no anticlerical scientist. He is the former dean of St. Edmund's College, Cambridge, and he is a Jesuit. But he is a Jesuit with a radical edge, the Arrupe edge. The son of a headmaster from Lancashire, and of decidedly lower-middle-class roots, young Moss was sent to the Jesuit school in Preston and not to its prestigious counterpart, Stonyhurst. At the end of secondary school he entered the Jesuit novitiate in Scotland in the '60s and then began philosophical studies at Heythrop. This was succeeded by studies in physics at Oxford where, in his final year, he asked his superiors if he could pursue a doctorate in astronomy. But it appears his provincial had other plans; Moss lamented his plight to his physics tutor, who happened to be a devout Catholic, and she, in turn, promptly phoned his provincial and gave him an earful. Moss was sent to the University of Sussex to do a Ph.D. in astronomy.

> When I went to the University of Sussex as a Jesuit student I lived on my own. When I first arrived I walked the streets of Brighton, found digs, and lived solo persuaded that I was going to be working with atheists and agnostics who would have little appreciation of the religious sensibility. Well, what happened was quite different. There was the student I shared my office with at the university, a fellow doctoral candidate, who was a leading member of the Baha'i; there were two Anglicans who went to daily Eucharist; a fundamentalist who believed the world was created in the year 6000 BCE; and an Emeritus Professor who was an ardent Christian. There were only one or two agnostics or atheists among the lot of them. And that has been my experience as a scientist generally.
>
> All this contributed significantly to disabusing me of my adolescent notion that somehow I needed to re-Christianize the world of science. And when I finished my theological studies and began to do research as an astronomer at the University of Texas in Austin I shared an apartment with a Jesuit from Chicago who was completing his doctorate in economics, alternating his studies with periods of pastoral service in the slums of Peru. This was my conversion. He taught me a great deal about liberation theology and I began to read the work of our fellow Jesuit, the theologian Juan-Luis Segundo.
>
> The key insight I derived from the liberation theologians is the idea that theology is conditioned by the socioeconomic circumstances in which it is formulated. This puts you at odds with others of your community who may not share your theological understanding. It certainly has introduced strains between many of my Jesuit brothers in Britain and myself.

Moss the astronomer has become Moss the liberation theologian. At the same time as Moss pursues his research as an astronomer he struggles for the cause of justice in the manner of a true disciple of the Thirty-Second General Congregation. While working at the

Vatican-owned observatory near Tucson he assisted a local priest on the native reservation, got involved with the Witness for Peace Movement, the Sanctuary Movement, and the Casa Maria Centre for the Homeless. When in England he did likewise:

> During the coal miners' strike I was doing my tertianship and I experimented with living in a hostel for the down and out in Manchester. I did my astronomy work at the University of Manchester for part of the day and then mopped floors in the hostel afterward. I also spoke on behalf of the miners, sometimes in situations of incipient violence. The Thatcher years were with us. It was time to question the structural injustices built into British society. It was the time of the poll tax, civil disorder, and rampant inequity and the British province of the Society, in spite of stunning exceptions like Michael Campbell-Johnston, was and remains too conservative. We Jesuits must, ironically, be on the margins or we will have no future.

Committed though he is to the "justice agenda" of the new Jesuit, Moss remains very much the scientist, occupied with professional questions raised by such cosmologists as Stephen Hawking, questions of meaning, order, causation, entropy, and extraterrestrial life forms, and he knows like every other Jesuit scientist who has come before him and every Jesuit scientist who is his contemporary that "the vastness and coherence of the physical universe revealed by modern scientific cosmology will surely serve as a powerful reminder of the majesty of God."[38]

Ad majorem dei gloriam.

Conclusion

In the year 2040 the Society of Jesus will celebrate its five hundredth anniversary. If it makes it. The Society has, of course, survived persecution at the hands of enemy and friend alike, withstood the assaults of violent change in government and society, faced down oppressor and foe, and known the cost of suppression and the price of restoration.

But the world and the church have altered so profoundly in the last forty years that all the reserves of the Order will need to be called to attention if there is to be a future. The ranks of the Society have been significantly reduced—from some 36,000 in 1968 to 23,000 in 1995—and the numbers could fall more drastically still. In a bulletin issued by the Jesuit Curia in April 1994 stark reckoning was the order of the day:

> If we assume that the current intake of 600 novices a year will remain stable, that the number who leave will continue to be 1.75% each year, and that the number of deaths will gradually increase from 2.1% to 2.3%, a mathematical computation shows that the Society will not reverse its downward trend until it has been reduced to 14,814 members, which will occur approximately the year 2040. This is not a prediction of what will certainly happen, but a projection. If the trend is to be reversed more quickly, then either the number of vocations

> must increase, or the percentage of those leaving must decrease.[1]

It is a time of crisis for the Society of Jesus, itself a microcosm of the turbulence afflicting the universal church. The loss in clerical numbers, the empowerment of the laity, the emergence of an articulate and restive body of Catholic theologians, the postmodern critique of authority, the intense struggles between the local and central powers of religious leadership—these and many other contemporary issues cut to the heart of Jesuit conflict. In addition, liberationist theological and pastoral strategies have called into question the long tradition of Jesuit commitment to structure, system, and sodality. The contemporary Jesuit is more inclined to rugged independence, grassroots networking, and conscientizing than to the maintenance of dying institutional enterprises.

But the future is not bleak; it is inviting. The Jesuits after all have known darker times. They have felt the threat of extinction and tasted the joy of resurrection. They have yet to be cut to the quick.

They survive because they do not conform to that homogeneous block of rigid soldierly virtue that history and polemics have made them. If anything, what we discovered through our research, interviews, and archival forays is the rather simple fact that Jesuits are utterly diverse in their talents, various in their undertakings, increasingly eclectic in their training, but nourished all at the same source: the *Spiritual Exercises* of Ignatius Loyola. The spirituality of the *Exercises* and the persistent appeal of the Order's founder define the Jesuit essence. All else is moot and malleable.

Jesuit seminarians in Nicaragua and El Salvador told us that they freely and consciously chose to follow the path of Ignatius rather than that of the regional guerrilla body, the FMLN or the Sandinistas, but that the latter remained an option. They also argued for the inclusion of women into the ranks of the Companions. In sharp contrast, seminarians in Poland and the Czech Republic told us that the subversiveness of Jesuit witness mingled with traditional priestly service was the immediate challenge of the future. Naturally, an all-male priesthood, Jesuit or otherwise, is not negotiable.

Behold the face of the contemporary Jesuit; behold the mystique.

ENDNOTES

Chapter I

1. The conciliar decree on the religious life is entitled *Perfectae caritatis*. It calls on all "religious," that is, men and women living under the religious vows appropriate to their calling, to examine their role in the modern world and to initiate a process of institutional renewal through "(1) a continuous return to the sources of all Christian life and to the original inspiration behind a given community and (2) an adjustment of the community to the changed conditions of the times." Walter M. Abbott s.j., *The Documents of Vatican II* (Piscataway, New Jersey: New Century Publishers, 1966), p. 468.
2. André Ravier s.j., *Ignatius of Loyola and the Founding of the Society of Jesus* (San Francisco: Ignatius Press, 1987), p. 45.
3. John C. Olin, *The Catholic Reformation: Savonarola to Ignatius Loyola.* (New York: Fordham University Press, 1992), p. xiii.
4. W.W. Meissner, *The Psychology of a Saint: Ignatius of Loyola* (New Haven, Conn.: Yale University Press, 1992), p. 3.
5. Meissner, p. 14.
6. Joseph F. O'Callaghan, trans., *The Autobiography of St. Ignatius of Loyola* (New York: Harper and Row, 1974), p. 22.
7. *The Autobiography*, p. 23.
8. Meissner, p. 41.
9. *The Autobiography*, p. 31.
10. John Donne, *Ignatius His Conclave*, Timothy S. Healy s.j., ed. (London: Oxford University Press, 1969), p. 25.
11. *Ignatius His Conclave*, p. 29.
12. Meissner, p. 106.
13. *The Autobiography*, p. 49.
14. *The Autobiography*, pp. 70–71.
15. *The Autobiography*, pp. 80–81.

16. As quoted by Christopher Hollis in *The Jesuits: A History* (New York: Barnes and Noble, 1968), p. 15.
17. Letter addressed to the townspeople of Azpeitia, in William J. Young s.j., ed. *Letters of St. Ignatius of Loyola* (Chicago: Loyola University Press, 1959), p. 44.
18. Meissner, p. 160.
19. Letter to Carafa in *Letters of Saint Ignatius of Loyola*, p. 29.
20. Letter to Carafa, *Letters of Saint Ignatius of Loyola*, p. 30.
21. *The Autobiography*, pp. 100–101.
22. In the "Rules for Thinking with the Church" that formed part of the closing segments of the *Spiritual Exercises*, items 15–17, Ignatius notes: "We should not make predestination an habitual subject of conversation. If it is sometimes mentioned we must speak in such a way that no person will fall into error, as happens on occasion when one will say, 'It has all been determined whether I will be saved or lost, and in spite of all the good or evil that I do, this will not be changed.' As a result, they become apathetic and neglect the works that are conducive to their salvation and to the spiritual growth of their souls. In like manner, we must be careful lest by speaking too much with too great emphasis on faith, without any distinction or explanation, we give occasion to the people to become indolent and lazy in the performance of good works that are conducive to their salvation and to the spiritual growth of their souls. Also in our discourse we ought not to emphasize the doctrine that would destroy free will. We may therefore speak of faith and grace . . . but in these dangerous times of ours, it must not be done in such a way that good works or free will suffer any detriment or be considered worthless."
23. Antonio M. de Aldama, "Origin and History of the Formula of the Institute," in Antonio M. de Aldama, Georges Bottereau, et al., *The Formula of the Institute* (Rome: Centrum Ignatianum Spiritualitatis, 1982), p. 19.
24. *Letters of Saint Ignatius of Loyola*, p. 40.
25. For a modern English translation, see John C. Olin, *The Catholic Reformation*, pp. 203–8.
26. Thomas Lucas s.j. "The Vineyard at the Crossroads: The Urban Vision of Ignatius of Loyola," (doctoral dissertation), p. 133.
27. George E. Ganss s.j., trans., *The Constitutions of the Society of Jesus* (St. Louis: The Institute for Jesuit Sources, 1970), pp. 66–67.
28. *Letters of Saint Ignatius of Loyola*, pp. 387–88.
29. M. Joseph Costelloe s.j. trans., *The Letters and Instructions of Francis Xavier* (St. Louis: The Institute of Jesuit Sources, 1992), pp. 9–10.
30. *Constitutions*, p. 75.
31. *Constitutions*, p. 68.
32. *Constitutions*, p. 234.
33. *Letters and Instructions of Francis Xavier*, p. 266.
34. *Constitutions*, pp. 248–49.
35. *Letters of Saint Ignatius of Loyola*, p. 295.
36. *Letters of Saint Ignatius of Loyola*, pp. 287–95.
37. *Letters of Saint Ignatius of Loyola*, p. 128.
38. John W. O'Malley, *The First Jesuits* (Cambridge, Mass.: Harvard University Press, 1993), pp. 332–33.
39. Hollis, p. 34.

40. *Letters of Saint Ignatius of Loyola*, p. 300.
41. *Letters of Saint Ignatius of Loyola*, pp. 346–47.
42. A copy of Francis Xavier's *Doctrina christiana* has been reproduced in *The Letters and Instructions of Francis Xavier*, pp. 41–45.
43. *Letters and Instructions of Francis Xavier*, p. 167.
44. Anthony Grafton, "The Soul's Entrepreneurs," *The New York Review of Books*, March 3, 1994, p. 36.
45. *Ignatius His Conclave*, p. 51.
46. As quoted by John W. O'Malley, p. 289.
47. *Letters and Instructions of Francis Xavier*, pp. 43–44.
48. *Letters of Saint Ignatius of Loyola*, p. 248.
49. *Letters of Saint Ignatius of Loyola*, p. 442.
50. "The Vineyard at the Crossroads," p. 85.
51. Translated by Christopher Maurer (Toronto: Doubleday, 1992).
52. *Letters and Instructions of Francis Xavier*, p. 180.
53. *Letters and Instructions of Francis Xavier*, p. 52.
54. *Letters and Instructions of Francis Xavier*, pp. 68–69.
55. *Letters and Instructions of Francis Xavier*, p. 149.
56. *Letters and Instructions of Francis Xavier*, p. 166.
57. *Letters and Instructions of Francis Xavier*, p. 330.
58. *Letters and Instructions of Francis Xavier*, p. 456.
59. *Letters and Instructions of Francis Xavier*, p. 242.
60. William V. Bangert s.j., *A History of the Society of Jesus* (St. Louis: The Institute for Jesuit Sources, 1991), p. 345.
61. Bangert, p. 280.
62. Bede, *The History of the English Church and People*, Leo Sherley-Price, trans. (Toronto: Penguin, 1964), I.27, p. 74.
63. Bede, I.30, p. 86.
64. Bangert, p. 255.
65. John Webster Grant. *Moon of Wintertime: Missionaries and the Indians of Canada in Encounter since 1534* (Toronto: Toronto University Press, 1984), p. 27. Grant's comment refers to the Canadian situation, but the conclusion is hardly limited to Canada even though local circumstances may have provided local variation on the motives.
66. E. J. Pratt, *Brébeuf and His Brethren* (Toronto: Macmillan, 1966), p. 13.
67. *The Hours of the Divine Office in English and Latin* (Collegeville, Minn.: The Liturgical Press, 1964), vol. 3, 1577–78.
68. "Apology to Native Americans for Past Mistakes," *Origins*, June 3, 1993, p. 36.
69. *Ignatius His Conclave*, p. 55. Timothy Healy's footnoted explanation of these principles is quite helpful.
70. Bangert, p. 377.
71. René Fülöp-Miller, *The Jesuits: A History of the Society of Jesus*, p. 390.
72. *On Liberty*, Gertrude Himmelfarb, ed. (Toronto: Penguin, 1985), pp. 69, 71–72.
73. David G. Schultenover s.j. *A View from Rome: On the Eve of the Modernist Crisis* (New York: Fordham University Press, 1993), pp. 131–51.
74. Padberg, John W. s.j., Martin D. O'Keefe s.j., and John L. McCarthy s.j., *For Matters of Greater Moment: The First Thirty Jesuit General Congregations* (St. Louis: The Institute for Jesuit Sources, 1994), p. 465.

75. Hollis, p. 206.
76. *For Matters of Greater Moment*, p. 466.
77. J. C. H. Aveling, *The Jesuits* (London: Blond and Briggs, 1981), p. 350.
78. *Faith and Justice: The Social Dimension of Evangelization* (St. Louis: The Institute for Jesuit Sources, 1991), p. 26.
79. As quoted by Christopher Hollis *The Jesuits: A History* p. 256.
80. Pedro Arrupe s.j., *Justice with Faith Today* (St. Louis: The Institute of Jesuit Sources, 1980), p. 62.
81. *The Documents of Vatican II*, ed. Walter Abbott s.j. (Piscataway, N.J.: New Century Publishers, 1966), p. 468.
82. *Documents of the 31st and 32nd General Congregations of the Society of Jesus* (St. Louis: The Institute of Jesuit Sources, 1977), pp. 318–19.
83. *Documents of the 31st and 32nd General Congregations*, p. 529.
84. *Documents of the 31st and 32nd General Congregations*, pp. 539–40.
85. *Documents of the 31st and 32nd General Congregations*, p. 543.
86. *Documents of the 31st and 32nd General Congregations*, p. 548.
87. Renzo Giacomelli, *Peter-H. Kolvenbach—Men of God: Men for Others* (New York: Alba House, 1990), p. 44.
88. Giacomelli, p. 62.
89. *Documents of the 33rd General Congregation of the Society of Jesus* (St. Louis: The Institute of Jesuit Sources, 1984), p. 45.
90. Giacomelli, pp. 31–32.

Chapter II

1. Harvey D. Egan s.j., "Ignatian Spirituality," *The New Dictionary of Catholic Spirituality* (Collegeville, Minn.: The Liturgical Press, 1993), p. 522.
2. Gerard W. Hughes, "Parables of the Spirit," *The Tablet*, October 8, 1994, p. 1263.
3. Jack Costello s.j., "Ignatian Spirituality: Finding God in All Things," *Grail: an Ecumenical Journal*, March 1992, pp. 27–29.
4. Ignatius of Loyola, *A Pilgrim's Journey: The Autobiography*, Joseph N. Tylenda s.j., trans. (Collegeville, Minn.: The Liturgical Press, 1985), pp. 38–39.
5. W. W. Meissner s.j., *Ignatius of Loyola: The Psychology of a Saint* (New Haven: Yale University Press, 1992), p. 108.
6. See Jesuit Father Augustine G. Ellard's landmark 1952 essay "Ignatian Spirituality," republished in *Review for Religious* 50, no. 1 (January/February 1991), pp. 6–23.
7. Hugo Rahner s.j., *The Spirituality of St. Ignatius Loyola: An Account of Its Historical Development*, Francis John Smith s.j., trans. (Chicago: Loyola University Press, 1980), p. 90.
8. Hugo Rahner s.j., *Ignatius the Theologian*, Michael Barry, trans. (London: Geoffrey Chapman, 1990), pp. 17–18.
9. David Lonsdale s.j., "The Spiritual Exercises: A Popular Path to Personal Wholeness," *International Minds: The Quarterly Journal of Psychological Insight into International Affairs* 2, no. 2 (Winter 1990–91), p. 13.
10. George E. Ganss s.j., trans., *The Spiritual Exercises of Saint Ignatius* (St. Louis: The Institute of Jesuit Sources, 1992), p. 21.

11. *The New Dictionary of Catholic Spirituality*, p. 529.
12. John Padberg s.j., "The Jesuit Question," *The Tablet*, September 22, 1990, p. 1191.
13. Margaret Hebblethwaite, *Finding God in All Things: Praying with St. Ignatius* (London: Collins/Fount, 1987), pp. 13–14.
14. Ganss, *The Spiritual Exercises of Saint Ignatius*, p. 95.
15. Eric Maclean s.j., "Homily/Statement," at Cape Crocker, Ontario, August 30, 1992.
16. Walter Burghardt s.j., "Characteristics of Social Justice Spirituality," *Origins* 24, no. 9 (July 21, 1994): p. 164.
17. Joseph de Guibert s.j., *The Jesuits: Their Spiritual Doctrine and Practice*, William J. Young s.j., trans. (St. Louis: The Institute of Jesuit Sources, 1986), p. 138.
18. Margaret Hebblethwaite, "Can Ignatian Prayer be Taught? An Ignatian Reading of Paolo Freire," *Grail: An Ecumenical Journal* 10 no. 1/2 (March/June 1994), p. 57.

Chapter III

1. Donal Dorr, *Option for the Poor: A Hundred Years of Vatican Social Teaching* (Maryknoll, N.Y.: Orbis Books, 1992), p. 379.
2. Peter-Hans Kolvenbach, *The Changing Face of Justice* (London: CAFOD, 1991), p. 4.
3. Pedro Arrupe s.j., "In His Own Words," *Company: A Magazine of the American Jesuits* 8, no. 4 (Summer 1991), p. 18.
4. "In His Own Words," p. 18.
5. As quoted in Edward Sheridan's "Faith and Justice: Followers of Ignatius," *Compass: A Jesuit Journal* 9, no. 3 (July/August 1991), p. 31.
6. Vincent O'Keefe s.j., "Obituary: Pedro Arrupe," *The Tablet*, February 9, 1991, p. 182.
7. Michael Campbell-Johnston s.j., "Being and Doing," *The Tablet*, August 4, 1992, p. 434.
8. Michael Walsh and Brian Davies, eds., *Proclaiming Justice and Peace: Papal Documents from "Rerum novarum" to "Centesimus annus"* (Mystic, Conn.: Twenty-Third Publications, 1991), p. 270.
9. Peter Hebblethwaite, *National Catholic Reporter*, February 15, 1991, p. 16.
10. Pedro Arrupe s.j., as quoted in Jean-Yves Calvez s.j., *Faith and Justice: The Social Dimension of Evangelization* (St. Louis: The Institute of Jesuit Sources, 1991), p. 27.
11. Article 28, *Our Mission Today: The Service of Faith and the Promotion of Justice (Decree Four)*, as quoted in Calvez (ibid.), p. 174.
12. Peter Rawlinson, *The Jesuit Factor: A Personal Investigation* (London: Weidenfeld and Nicolson, 1990), p. 21.
13. Leonardo Boff and Clodovis Boff, *Introducing Liberation Theology* (Maryknoll, N.Y.: Orbis Books, 1987), pp. 88–89.
14. Gregory Baum, *Compassion and Solidarity: The Church for Others* (Toronto: CBC Enterprises, 1987), pp. 74–75.
15. Pedro Arrupe s.j., *Justice with Faith Today: Selected Letters and Addresses—II* (St. Louis: Institute of Jesuit Sources, 1980), p. 205.

16. *Justice with Faith Today*, pp. 206–7.
17. Pope Paul VI, "*Populorum progressio*": *Proclaiming Justice and Peace*, p. 230.
18. *Justice with Faith Today*, p. 124.
19. Oakland Ross, "Be a Patriot, Kill a Priest," *Saturday Night*, October 1991, p. 50.
20. Jon Sobrino, Ignacio Ellacuria, et al., *Companions of Jesus: The Jesuit Martyrs of El Salvador* (Maryknoll, N.Y.: Orbis Books, 1990), p. 150.
21. Jon Sobrino s.j., "Compassion: The Shaping Principle of the Human and of the Christian," the fifteenth Nash Lecture, delivered at Campion College, University of Regina, Saskatchewan, November 26, 1992, pp. 9, 14–15.
22. Daniel Berrigan s.j., "The Martyrs' Living Witness", *Sojourners: Faith, Politics, and Culture* 19, no. 3 (April 1990), p. 24.
23. Daniel Berrigan s.j., *Steadfastness of the Saints* (Maryknoll, N.Y.: Orbis Books, 1985), p. 124.
24. Quoted from a letter of January 12, 1983, by Paolo Dezza s.j., to Fernando Cardenal s.j.; translated by Robert Foliot s.j.
25. Fernando Cardenal s.j., "A Letter to My Friends," Robert Foliot s.j., trans., December 11, 1984, pp. 3, 12.
26. William R. Callahan s.j., correspondence, April 15, 1991, p. 3.
27. Malachi Martin, *The Jesuits: The Society of Jesus and the Betrayal of the Roman Catholic Church* (New York: Touchstone Books, 1988), p. 449.

Chapter IV

1. John C. Olin, *The Catholic Reformation: Savonarola to Ignatius Loyola* (New York: Fordham University Press, 1992), p. 205. See also John W. Padberg s.j., Martin D. O'Keefe s.j., and John L. McCarthy s.j., *For Matters of Greater Moment: The First Thirty Jesuit General Congregations* (St. Louis: The Institute of Jesuit Sources, 1994), First General Congregation, Decree 138, p. 102 and Second General Congregation, Decree 58, p. 125.
2. William J. Young s.j., *Letters of St. Ignatius of Loyola* (Chicago: Loyola University Press, 1959), p. 67.
3. Allan P. Farrell, *The Jesuit Code of Liberal Education: Development and Scope of the* Ratio Studiorum (Milwaukee: Bruce Publishing, 1938), p. 378.
4. *For Matters of Greater Moment*, p. 198. The theological centrality of Thomas Aquinas is a much-visited topic, reappearing as it does in General Congregations 22 (1853), 23 (1883), 25 (1906), 29 (1942), and 30 (1957). In the post-conciliar and post-32nd General Congregation life of the Society, the centrality of Thomas Aquinas is no longer quite so clear: neither the theologians nor the seminarians with whom we spoke about the topic at the University of Central America, San Salvador, considered the study of Aquinas to be as important as the mastering of the theology of liberation.
5. See William H. MacCabe s.j., *An Introduction to Jesuit Theatre* (St. Louis: Institute of Jesuit Sources, 1983) for a thorough and interesting analysis of the topic.
6. Farrell, p. 319.
7. Christine Temin, "In the priesthood, body and soul," *The Boston Globe*, November 9, 1988.
8. *For Matters of Greater Moment*, p. 306.
9. *For Matters of Greater Moment*, p. 391.

10. As quoted by Allan P. Farrell, p. 375.
11. As quoted by Allan P. Farrell, pp. 388–89.
12. George E. Ganss, *Saint Ignatius' Idea of a Jesuit University* (Milwaukee: Marquette University Press, 1956), p. 76.
13. *Saint Ignatius' Idea of a Jesuit University*, p. 136.
14. Frei Betto, *Fidel and Religion: Castro Talks on Revolution and Religion with Frei Betto* (New York: Simon and Schuster, 1987), pp. 121–22.
15. *Fidel and Religion*, p. 140.
16. Pierre Elliott Trudeau, *Memoirs* (Toronto: McClelland and Stewart, 1993), p. 21.
17. "Address by Reverend Giuseppe Pittau s.j., July 28, 1991," delivered at the University of Guelph, Guelph, Canada and reprinted by the Canadian Institute of Jesuit Studies in Toronto in a booklet entitled *Companions of Jesus, Pilgrims with Ignatius: Congress '91*, p. 25.
18. *Documents of the 31st and 32nd General Congregations of the Society of Jesus* (St. Louis, Missouri: The Institute of Jesuit Sources, 1977), p. 403.
19. *Documents of the 31st and 32nd General Congregations*, 58, p. 413.
20. *Documents of the 31st and 32nd General Congregations*, 109, p. 432.
21. Washington, D.C.: The Jesuit Secondary Education Association.
22. Thomas E. Muir, *Stonyhurst College: 1593–1993* (London: James and James, 1992), "Foreword."
23. *The Stonyhurst Magazine*, 45 (1987), 68.
24. "Stonyhurst Remembered," *The Tablet*, May 22, 1993, p. 649.
25. *Documents of the 31st and 32nd General Congregations of the Society of Jesus*, p. 427.
26. Amanda Hopkinson, "Martyrdom and the Academy," *The Tablet* (June 1, 1991), 671–72.
27. Amanda Hopkinson, p. 672.
28. Ignacio Ellacuría, "The Task of a Christian University," in Jon Sobrino, Ignacio Ellacuría, et al. *Companions of Jesus: The Jesuit Martyrs of El Salvador* (Maryknoll, N.Y.: Orbis, 1990), p. 150.
29. *Ex corde ecclesiae* (Vatican City: Libreria Editrice Vaticana, 1990), item 32, p. 26.
30. *Documents of the 31st and 32nd General Congregations*, p. 410.
31. *Documents of the 31st and 32nd General Congregations*, p. 432.
32. Giuseppe Pittau, in *Companions of Jesus, Pilgrims with Ignatius*, p. 18.
33. *Documents of the 31st and 32nd General Congregations*, 457, p. 217.

Chapter V

1. Appendix I, "The Founding Text," in Simon Decloux s.j., *The Ignatian Way* (Chicago: Loyola University Press, 1991), p. 131.
2. Andrew Hamilton s.j., "Keeping Company," *Eureka Street: A magazine of public affairs, the arts and theology* 4, no. 4 (May 1994), p. 50.
3. Renzo Giacomelli, *Peter-H. Kolvenbach—Men of God: Men for Others* (New York: Alba House, 1990), pp. 96–97.
4. Pedro Arrupe s.j., "International Collaboration and Investigation," *Other Apostolates Today* (St. Louis: The Institute of Jesuit Sources, 1981), p. 134.
5. As quoted in Notebook editorial "Prisoner no. 1442," *The Tablet*, July 30, 1994, p. 955.

6. René Fülöp-Miller, *The Jesuits: A History of the Society of Jesus*, F.S. Flint and D.F. Tait, trans. (New York: Capricorn Books, 1963), p. 420.
7. Anthony D. Cousins, *The Catholic Religious Poets From Southwell to Crashaw: A Critical Study* (Westminster, Maryland: Christian Classics, 1991), pp. 16–17.
8. Louis L. Martz, *The Poetry of Meditation: A Study in English Religious Literature of the Seventeenth Century* (New Haven: Yale University Press, 1978), p. 28.
9. Norman White, "Poet and Priest: Gerard Manley Hopkins, Myth and Reality," *Studies: An Irish Quarterly Review* 79, no. 314 (Summer 1990), p. 148.
10. Robert Bernard Martin, *Gerard Manley Hopkins: A Very Private Life*, (London: HarperCollins, 1991), p. 194.
11. Gerard Manley Hopkins, *Poems and Prose*, W. H. Gardner, ed. (Harmondsworth: Penguin, 1972), p. 146.
12. Gerard Manley Hopkins, letter to R. W. Dixon, October 5, 1878, *Poems and Prose*, p. 187.
13. *The Month* 136, no. 1299 (December 1975).
14. John F. X. Harriott, "Making Theology Beautiful," *The Tablet*, June 17, 1989, p. 686.
15. Desmond Egan, "The Hopefulness of Hopkins," *The Tablet*, July 23, 1994, p. 920.
16. Martin, p. 223.
17. Daniel Berrigan s.j., *Consequences: Truth and. . .*, (New York: Macmillan, 1967), p. 91.
18. Daniel Berrigan s.j., "Thomas Merton," *Daniel Berrigan: Poetry, Drama, Prose*, Michael True, ed. (Maryknoll, N.Y.: Orbis Books, 1988), p. 90.
19. "Not Feeling Poetic," *Daniel Berrigan: Poetry, Drama and Prose*, pp. 343–44.
20. Daniel Berrigan s.j., *The Dark Night of Resistance*, (New York: Doubleday, 1971), pp. 56–57.
21. Daniel Berrigan s.j., *To Dwell In Peace: An Autobiography* (San Francisco: Harper & Row, 1987), p. 325.
22. Peter Levi, *The Flutes of Autumn* (London: Harvill Press, 1983), p. 65.
23. *The Flutes of Autumn*, pp. 64–65.
24. *The Flutes of Autumn*, p. 61.
25. *The Flutes of Autumn*, p. 140.
26. Peter Levi, "Visionary Poets," *The Art of Poetry: The Oxford Lectures 1984–1989* (New Haven: Yale University Press, 1991), p. 94.
27. Levi, "Goodbye to the Art of Poetry," *The Art of Poetry*, p. 312.
28. William Blissett, *The Long Conversation: A Memoir of David Jones* (Oxford: Oxford University Press, 1981), p. 111.
29. Tim Lilburn, "Breakdown as School," *Grail: An Ecumenical Journal* 6, no. 3 (September 1990), p. 100.
30. Tim Lilburn, "How to Be Here?" *Brick: A Literary Journal*, no. 49 (Summer 1994), pp. 22–23, 25.

Chapter VI

1. Albert Keller, "Analytical Philosophy and the Magisterium's Claim to Infallible Authority," *Journal of Ecumenical Studies* 19, no. 2 (Spring/1982), p. 89.

2. Avery Dulles s.j., *The Craft of Theology: From Symbol to System* (New York: Crossroad, 1992), p. 66.
3. Karl Rahner s.j., *I Remember: An Autobiographical Interview with Meinold Krauss*, Harvey D. Egan s.j., trans. (New York: Crossroad, 1985), pp. 67–68.
4. *I Remember*, p. 46.
5. *I Remember*, p. 53.
6. William V. Dych s.j., *Karl Rahner* (Collegeville, Minn.: Liturgical Press, 1992), pp. 28–29.
7. Karl Rahner s.j., *Foundations of Christian Faith: An Introduction to the Idea of Christianity*, William V. Dych s.j., trans. (New York: Crossroad, 1987), p. 344.
8. Herbert Vorgrimler, *Understanding Karl Rahner: An Introduction to His Life and Thought*, John Bowden, trans. (New York: Crossroad, 1986), p. 100.
9. William V. Dych s.j., "Karl Rahner," *The Modern Catholic Encyclopedia*, Michael Glazier and Monika K. Hellwig, eds. (Collegeville, Minn.: Liturgical Press, 1994), p. 716.
10. *Foundations of Christian Faith*, p. 390.
11. Karl Rahner s.j., *Theological Investigations* (New York: Seabury/Crossroad, 1961–1991), vol. 16, pp. 130ff.
12. Karl Rahner s.j., *Ignatius of Loyola*, Rosaleen Ockenden, trans. (London: Collins, 1979), pp. 26–27.
13. *Theological Investigations*, vol. 1, p. 7.
14. Vernon Gregson, "Preface," *The Desires of the Human Heart*, Vernon Gregson, ed. (New York/Mahwah: Paulist Press, 1988), p. v.
15. Philip McShane, "The Historical Reach of Lonergan's Meaning," *Compass: A Jesuit Journal* (Spring 1985), p. 15.
16. Frederick C. Crowe s.j., *Lonergan* (Collegeville, Minn.: Liturgical Press, 1992), p. 48.
17. Hugo Meynell, "Lonergan and the Future of Philosophy," *Compass* (Spring 1985), p. 17.
18. Bernard Lonergan s.j. "Cognitional Structure," *Collected Works of Bernard Lonergan*, Volume 4, Collection (Toronto: University of Toronto Press, 1993), p. 220.
19. Bernard Lonergan s.j., "Dimensions of Meaning," *Collected Works*, Volume 4, p. 238.
20. Bernard Lonergan s.j., "The Response of the Jesuit as Priest and Apostle in the Modern World," *A Second Collection: Papers by Bernard J. F. Lonergan s.j.*, William F. J. Ryan and Bernard J. Tyrrell, eds. (London: Darton, Longman & Todd, 1974), pp. 182, 186–187.
21. Bernard Lonergan s.j., "*Existenz*" and "*Aggiornamento*," *Collected Works*, Volume 4, p. 230.
22. Harvey D. Egan s.j., "Bernard Lonergan and the Future of Spiritual and Mystical Theology," *Compass* (March 1985), p. 19.
23. Robert M. Doran s.j., "Prolegomenon for a New Systematics," *Grail: an Ecumenical Journal* 10, no. 3 (September, 1994), p. 86.
24. Lonergan, "Dimensions of Meaning," *Collected Works*, Volume 4, p. 245.
25. Robert Speaight, *Teilhard de Chardin: A Biography* (London: Collins, 1968), p. 21.

26. Pierre Teilhard de Chardin, "On My Attitude to the Official Church," *The Heart of Matter* (London: Collins, 1974), pp. 115–18.
27. Christopher Mooney s.j., as quoted in Michael W. Higgins, *Pierre Teilhard de Chardin: The One-Hundredth Anniversary, 1881–1981* (Toronto: CBC Enterprises, 1982), p. 18.
28. Pierre Teilhard de Chardin, *Letters from a Traveller: 1923–1955* (London: Collins/Fontana, 1973), pp. 224–25.
29. Mooney, in *Pierre Teilhard de Chardin: The One-Hundredth Anniversary (1881–1981)*, p. 20.
30. Pierre Leroy, *Letters from My Friend Teilhard de Chardin, 1948–1955*, Mary Lukas, trans. (New York: Paulist Press, 1980), p. 172.
31. Teilhard de Chardin: *A Biography*, pp. 273–74.
32. Bangert, *A History of the Society of Jesus* (St Louis: The Institute for Jesuit Sources, 1991), p. 288.
33. Bangert, p. 188.
34. As quoted by Michael McAteer, *The Toronto Star*, December 26, 1992.
35. Paul Cardinal Poupard, "Galileo: Report on Papal Commission Findings," Press Office of the Holy See.
36. Joe Mroz s.j., "Robert Bellarmine: Able Defender of a Crumbling Synthesis," *Compass: A Jesuit Journal* (September/October 1993), p. 33.
37. Poupard, "Galileo: Report on Papal Commission Findings."
38. Christopher Moss s.j., "A Glimpse of Creation," *The Tablet*, May 2, 1992, p. 540.

Conclusion

1. As quoted in Alain Woodrow's "The Jesuits Take Stock," *The Tablet*, January 7, 1995, p. 10.

Sources

Interviews

(Unreferenced quotations derive from the following interviews)

Altilia, Len s.j.: interviewed at Montreal on January 14, 1994.
Berrigan, Daniel s.j.: interviewed at New York on July 25, 1992.
Bordes, Laetitia, s.h.: interviewed at San Salvador on June 25, 1992.
Brackley, Dean s.j.: interviewed at San Salvador on June 26, 1992.
Brennan, Margaret, i.h.m.: interviewed at Toronto on January 29, 1993.
Bull, George: interviewed at London on November 8, 1991.
Callahan, William R. s.j.: interviewed at Washington on June 8, 1992.
Campbell-Johnston, Michael s.j.: interviewed at London on November 7, 1991.
Caraman, Philip s.j.: interviewed at London on November 8, 1991.
Cardenal, Rodolfo s.j.: interviewed at San Salvador on June 26, 1992.
Carranza, Salvator s.j.: interviewed at Santa Tecla, El Salvador on June 25, 1992.
Carter, Samuel s.j.: interviewed at Kingston, Jamaica on June 29, 1992.
Casia, Michael: interviewed at Montreal on January 14, 1994.
Chaning-Pearce, James s.j.: interviewed at Stonyhurst on February 17, 1993.
Costello, Jack s.j.: interviewed at Toronto on December 22, 1992.
Dardis, John s.j.: interviewed at Dublin on November 12, 1991.
Darowski, Roman s.j.: interviewed at Krakow on May 17, 1994.
Davis, Eamon, Bro. s.j.: interviewed at Dublin on November 11, 1991.
Desai, Evan: interviewed at Montreal on January 14, 1994.
De Sivatte, Rafael s.j.: interviewed at San Salvador on June 26, 1992.
De Vera, José s.j.: interviewed at Rome on October 24, 1994.
Doran, Robert s.j.: interviewed at Toronto on July 7, 1994.
Drinan, Robert s.j.: interviewed at Washington on February 3, 1992.
English, John s.j.: interviewed at Guelph on October 17, 1994.
Faron, Kazimierz: interviewed at Krakow on May 17, 1994.
Fessio, Joseph s.j.: interviewed at San Francisco on July 24, 1991.
Franke, Bernd s.j.: interviewed at Munich on May 11, 1994.
Gallagher, Michael s.j.: interviewed at Dublin on November 12, 1991.
Gervais, Marc s.j.: interviewed at Toronto on December 20, 1991.

Godfrey, Joseph s.j.: interviewed at Philadelphia on August 15, 1991.
Gomez, Jose Luis Rocha s.j. : interviewed at San Salvador on June 26, 1992.
Gorski, Isidore : interviewed at Regina on November 27, 1992.
Gudgeon, Philip s.j. : interviewed at Rome on November 10, 1991.
Healy, Timothy s.j. : interviewed at New York on October 16, 1991.
Hebblethwaite, Margaret : interviewed at London on November 7, 1991.
Hebblethwaite, Peter : interviewed at Oxford on February 19, 1993.
Hehir, Bryan : interviewed at Toronto on February 2, 1993.
Hogan, Paul : interviewed at Montreal on January 14, 1994.
Hyland, Ted s.j. : interviewed at Toronto on April 30, 1992.
Hylmar, Frantisek : interviewed at Krakow on May 17, 1994.
Jutras, Fernand s.j. : interviewed at Montreal on January 14, 1994.
Kaputska, Pawel: interviewed at Krakow on May 17, 1994.
Keller, Albert s.j.: interviewed at Munich on May 11, 1994.
Kerber, Walter s.j.: interviewed at Munich on May 11, 1994.
Kolvenbach, Peter-Hans s.j.: interviewed at Buffalo on May 10, 1993.
Leach, George P. s.j.: interviewed at Toronto on October 2, 1992.
Levi, Peter: interviewed at Frampton-on-Severn on February 16, 1993.
Litva, Felix s.j.: interviewed at Waterloo, Ontario, on January 24, 1994.
Llanos, Chris s.j.: interviewed at Kingston, Jamaica, on June 30, 1992.
Llasera, Francis Xavier s.j.: interviewed at Managua on June 27, 1992.
Locatelli, Paul s.j.: interviewed at Santa Clara, California, on July 22, 1991.
Lucas, Tom s.j.: interviewed at Washington on February 3, 1992.
Mandziak, Aleksander: interviewed at Krakow on May 17, 1994.
Massie, Brian s.j.: interviewed at Kingston, Jamaica, on June 30, 1992.
McCarthy, Douglas s.j.: interviewed at Toronto on July 7, 1994.
McGuckian, Allan s.j.: interviewed at Dublin on November 12, 1991.
McKevitt, Gerald s.j.: interviewed at Santa Clara, California, on July 22, 1991.
McLean, Eric s.j.: interviewed at Toronto on April 22, 1992.
McPolin, Jaime s.j.: interviewed at San Salvador on June 25, 1992.
Mercer, Giles, Dr.: interviewed at Stonyhurst on February 17, 1993.
Mittelholtz, Robert (Brother) s.j.: interviewed at Toronto on August 19, 1991.
Monet, Jacques s.j.: interviewed at Toronto on August 29, 1991, and at Notre Dame University on August 3, 1994.
Moss, Christopher s.j.: interviewed at Cambridge, England, on February 15, 1993.
Musial, Stanislaw s.j.: interviewed at Krakow on May 17, 1994.
Obirek, Stanislaw s.j.: interviewed at Krakow on May 17, 1994.
Obrigewitsch, Frank s.j.: interviewed at Montreal on January 14, 1994.
O'Halloran, Michael s.j.: interviewed at Stonyhurst on February 17, 1993.
O'Hare, Joseph s.j.: interviewed at New York on October 17, 1991.
Ong, Walter s.j.: interviewed at St. Louis on September 21, 1991.
Orsy, Ladislas s.j.: interviewed at Toronto on March 31, 1992.
Padberg, John s.j.: interviewed at St. Louis on September 21, 1991, and on December 22, 1992.
Padzerka, Josef s.j.: interviewed at Prague on May 15, 1994.
Pendergast, Terry s.j.: interviewed at Toronto on November 24, 1993.
Pitawanakawat, Isaac: interviewed at Toronto on October 2, 1992.
Pittau, Joseph s.j.: interviewed at Rome on November 10, 1991.

Popiel, Jan s.j. : interviewed at Krakow on May 17, 1994.
Popowycz, Stefan: interviewed at Montreal on January 14, 1994.
Privett, Steve s.j.: interviewed at Santa Clara, California, on July 22, 1991.
Pungente, John s.j.: interviewed at Toronto on May 3, 1993.
Purcell, Desmond s.j.: interviewed at Dublin on November 12, 1991.
Rawlinson, Peter: interviewed at London on February 20, 1991.
Reites, James s.j.: interviewed at Santa Clara, California, on July 22, 1991.
Reyes, Victor Manuel Guerra, s..j.: interviewed at San Salvador on June 26, 1992.
Rixon, Gordon s.j.: interviewed at Toronto on April 30, 1992.
Rye, Winston s.j.: interviewed at Montreal on January 14, 1994.
Schade, Marty s.j.: interviewed at Kingston, Jamaica, on June 29, 1992.
Schner, Joe s.j.: interviewed at Regina on November 26, 1992.
Senkewicz, Robert s.j.: interviewed at Santa Clara, California, on July 23, 1991.
Smith, Francis R. s.j.: interviewed at Santa Clara, California, on July 22, 1991.
Sobrino, Jon s.j.: interviewed at Santa Clara, California, on July 22, 1991, and at Regina on November 26, 1992.
Sowa, Krystian: interviewed at Krakow on May 17, 1994.
Starkloff, Carl s.j.: interviewed at Toronto on January 29, 1993.
Steinmetz, Franz-Josef s.j.: interviewed at Munich on May 11, 1994.
Thuringer, Rune s.j.: interviewed at Stockholm on September 30, 1992.
Turner, Frederick s.j.: interviewed at Stonyhurst on February 17, 1993.
Walsh, Michael: interviewed at London on February 18, 1993.
Webb, Jim s.j.: interviewed at Kingston, Jamaica on June 29, 1992.
Williams, Monty s.j.: interviewed at Regina on November 27, 1992.
Wren, Richard s.j.: interviewed at Stonyhurst on February 17, 1993.
Ziemianski, Stanislaw s.j.: interviewed at Krakow on May 17, 1994.
Zubizarreta, Inaki s.j.: interviewed at Managua on June 28, 1992.

Selected Books and Articles

Abbott, Walter s.j. *The Documents of Vatican II*. Piscataway, N.J.: New Century Publishers, 1966.
Aldama, Antonio M. de s.j. *Constitutions of the Society of Jesus*. St. Louis: The Institute of Jesuit Sources, 1989.
Aldama, Antonio M. de s.j., Georges Bottereau s.j., et al. *The Formula of the Institute*. Rome: Centrum Ignatianum Spiritualitatis, 1982.
Arrupe, Pedro s.j. *Justice with Faith Today*. Jerome Aixala s.j., ed. St. Louis, Missouri: The Institute of Jesuit Sources, 1980.
———. "In His Own Words." *Company: A Magazine of the American Jesuits* 8 (4 Summer 1991).
———. "International Collaboration and Investigation." *Other Apostolates Today*. St. Louis: The Institute of Jesuit Sources, 1981.
Aubert, A. "Pope Pius IX." *The New Catholic Encyclopedia*. Vol. XI. Toronto: McGraw Hill, 1967.
Aveling, J. C. H. *The Jesuits*. London: Blond and Briggs, 1981.
Bangert, William V. s.j. *A History of the Society of Jesus*. St. Louis: The Institute of Jesuit Sources, 1986.

Baum, Gregory. *Compassion and Solidarity: The Church for Others*. Toronto: CBC Enterprises, 1987.

Bede. *A History of the English Church and People*. Leo Sherley Price, trans. Toronto: Penguin, 1964.

Berrigan, Daniel s.j. *Consequences: Truth and . . .* New York: Macmillan, 1967.

———. *The Dark Night of Resistance*. New York: Doubleday, 1971.

———. *Jubilee*. New York: Hudson View Press, 1991.

———. "The Martyrs' Living Witness." *Sojourners: Faith, Politics, and Culture*. 19 (3 April 1990).

———. *Steadfastness of the Saints*. Maryknoll, N.Y.: Orbis Books, 1985.

———. *To Dwell In Peace: An Autobiography*. San Francisco: Harper & Row, 1987.

Betto, Frei. *Fidel and Religion: Castro Talks on Revolution and Religion with Frei Betto*. New York: Simon and Schuster, 1987.

Blissett, William. *The Long Conversation: A Memoir of David Jones*. Oxford: Oxford University Press, 1981.

Boff, Leonardo, and Clodovis Boff. *Introducing Liberation Theology*. Maryknoll, N.Y.: Orbis Books, 1987.

Bullen, Andrew s.j. *Ignatius the Pilgrim: Poems for Prayer*. Richmond, Australia: Jesuit Publications, 1992.

Burghardt, Walter s.j. "Characteristics of Social Justice Spirituality." *Origins* 24 (9 July 1994).

Burns, Jimmy. "Stonyhurst Remembered." *The Tablet*, May 22, 1993.

Calvez, Jean-Yves s.j. *Faith and Justice: The Social Dimension of Evangelization*. John E. Blewett s.j., trans. St. Louis: The Institute for Jesuit Sources, 1991.

Campbell-Johnston, Michael s.j., "Being and Doing." *The Tablet*, August 4 , 1992.

Caraman, Philip s.j. *Ignatius Loyola: A Biography of the Founder of the Jesuits*. Toronto: Harper and Row, 1990.

Carlen, Claudia, i.h.m., ed. *The Papal Encyclicals, 1903–1939*. New York: McGrath Publishing, 1981.

"Characteristics of Jesuit Education." *The Stonyhurst Magazine* 45 (Autumn 1987).

Chardin, Pierre Teilhard de s.j. *Letters from a Traveller: 1923–1955*. London: Collins/Fontana, 1973.

———. "On My Attitude to the Official Church." *The Heart of Matter*. London: Collins, 1974.

Costello, Jack s.j. "Ignatian Spirituality: Finding God in All Things." *Grail: An Ecumenical Journal* 8 (1 March 1992).

Cousins, Anthony D. *The Catholic Religious Poets From Southwell to Crashaw: A Critical Study*. Westminster, Md.: Christian Classics, 1991.

Crowe, Frederick C. s.j. *Lonergan*. Collegeville, Minn.: Liturgical Press, 1992.

Decloux, Simon s.j. "The Founding Text." *The Ignatian Way*. Chicago: Loyola University Press, 1991.

Dictionary of Jesuit Biography: Ministry in English Canada, 1842–1987. Toronto: Canadian Institute of Jesuit Studies, 1991.

Documents of the 31st and 32nd General Congregations of the Society of Jesus. St. Louis: The Institute of Jesuit Sources, 1977.

Documents of the 33rd General Congregation of the Society of Jesus. St. Louis: The Institute for Jesuit Sources, 1984.

Donne, John. *Ignatius His Conclave*. Timothy S. Healy s.j., ed. London: Oxford University Press, 1969.

Doran, Robert M. s.j. "Prolegomenon for a New Systematics." *Grail: An Ecumenical Journal* 10 (3 September 1993).

Dorr, Donald. *Option for the Poor: A Hundred Years of Vatican Social Teaching*. Maryknoll, N.Y.: Orbis Books, 1992.

Dulles, Avery s.j. *The Craft of Theology: From Symbol to System* New York: Crossroad, 1992.

Dych, William V. s.j. *Karl Rahner*. Collegeville, Minn.: Liturgical Press, 1992.

———. "Karl Rahner," *The Modern Catholic Encyclopedia*. Collegeville, Minn.: Liturgical Press, 1994.

Egan, Desmond. "The Hopefulness of Hopkins." *The Tablet*, July 23, 1994.

Egan, Harvey, D. s.j. "Bernard Lonergan and the Future of Spiritual and Mystical Theology." *Compass: A Jesuit Journal* (March 1985).

———. "Ignatian Spirituality." *The New Dictionary of Catholic Spirituality*. Michael Downey, ed. Collegeville, Minn.: The Liturgical Press, 1993.

Ellard, Augustine G. Ellard. "Ignatian Spirituality." *Review for Religious* 50 (1 January/February 1991).

Farrell, Allan P. *The Jesuit Code of Liberal Education: Development and Scope of the* Ratio Studiorum. Milwaukee: Bruce Publishing, 1938.

Feeney, Joseph J. s.j. "Can Jesuit College Education Survive in a New Century? A Historical Initiative." *America*, May 28, 1994.

Fülöp-Miller, René. *The Jesuits: A History of the Society of Jesus*. F. S. Flint and D. F. Tait, trans. New York: Capricorn Books, 1963.

Ganss, George E. s.j., trans. *The Constitutions of the Society of Jesus*. St. Louis: The Institute of Jesuit Sources, 1970.

———. *The Jesuit Educational Tradition and Saint Louis University: Some Bearings for the University's Sesquicentennial 1818–1968*. St. Louis: St. Louis University Press, 1969.

———. *Saint Ignatius' Idea of a Jesuit University*. Marquette, Wisconsin: Marquette University Press, 1956.

———, trans. *The Spiritual Exercises of Saint Ignatius*. St. Louis: The Institute of Jesuit Sources, 1992.

Giacomelli, Renzo. *Peter H. Kolvenbach—Men of God: Men for Others*. New York: Alba House, 1990.

Go Forth and Teach: The Characteristics of Jesuit Education. Washington, D.C.: Jesuit Secondary Education Association, 1987.

Gracián, Baltasar. *The Art of Worldly Wisdom*. Toronto: Doubleday, 1992.

Grafton, Anthony. "The Soul's Entrepreneurs." *The New York Review of Books*, March 3, 1994.

Grant, John Webster. *Moon of Wintertime: Missionaries and the Indians of Canada in Encounter since 1534*. Toronto: University of Toronto Press, 1984.

Gregson, Vernon. *The Desires of the Human Heart*. New York/Mahwah: Paulist Press, 1988.

Guibert, Joseph de s.j. *The Jesuits: Their Spiritual Doctrine and Practice*. William J. Young s.j., trans. St. Louis: The Institute of Jesuit Sources, 1986.

Hamilton, Andrew s.j. "Keeping Company." *Eureka Street: A magazine of public affairs, the arts and theology* 4 (May 4, 1994).

Harriott, John F. X. "Making Theology Beautiful." *The Tablet*, June 17, 1989.
Hebblethwaite, Margaret. "Can Ignatian Prayer be Taught?: An Ignatian Reading of Paolo Freire." *Grail: An Ecumenical Journal* 10 (1/2 March/June 1994).
———. *Finding God in All Things: Praying with St. Ignatius*. London: Collins/Fount, 1987.
Hebblethwaite, Peter. *National Catholic Reporter*, February 15, 1991.
Hollis, Christopher. *The Jesuits: A History*. New York: Barnes and Noble, 1968.
Hopkins, Gerard Manley. *Poems and Prose*. W. H. Gardner, ed. Harmondsworth: Penguin, 1972.
Hopkinson, Amanda. "Martyrdom and the academy." *The Tablet*, June 1, 1991.
Hours of the Divine Office in English and Latin. Vol. 3. Collegeville, Minn.: The Liturgical Press, 1964.
Hughes, Gerard W. "Parables of the Spirit." *The Tablet*, October 8, 1994.
Hull, Robert R. *The Syllabus of Errors of Pope Pius IX*. Huntington, Ind.: Our Sunday Visitor Press, 1926.
Jencks, Christopher and David Riesman. *The Academic Revolution*. New York: Doubleday, 1969.
John Paul II. *Ex corde ecclesiae: Apostolic Constitution of the Supreme Pontiff John Paul II on Catholic Universities*. Vatican City: Libreria Editrice Vaticana, 1990.
Johnston, William s.j. *Letters to Contemplatives*. Maryknoll, N.Y.: Orbis Books, 1991.
Keller, Albert. "Analytical Philosophy and the Magisterium's Claim to Infallible Authority." *Journal of Ecumenical Studies* 19 (2 Spring/1982).
Kolvenbach, Peter-Hans s.j. "Apology to Native Americans for Past Mistakes." *Origins* 23 (June 3, 1993).
———. *The Changing Face of Justice*. London: CAFOD, 1991.
Labrie, Ross. *The Writings of Daniel Berrigan*. Lanham: University of America Press, 1989.
Leroy, Pierre. *Letters from My Friend Teilhard de Chardin, 1948–1955*. Mary Lukas, trans. New York: Paulist Press, 1980.
Levi, Peter. "Visionary Poets." *The Art of Poetry: The Oxford Lectures 1984–1989*. New Haven: Yale University Press, 1991.
———. *The Echoing Green*. London: Anvil Press, 1983.
———. *The Flutes of Autumn*. London: Harvill Press, 1983.
———. *The Frontiers of Paradise*. London: Anvil Press, 1988.
———. *Private Ground*. London: Anvil Press, 1981.
———. *Shadow and Bone*. London: Anvil Press, 1989.
Lilburn, Tim. "Breakdown as School." *Grail: An Ecumenical Journal* 6 (3 September 1990).
———. "How to Be Here?" *Brick: A Literary Journal* 49 (Summer 1994).
———. *Moosewood Sandhills*. Toronto: McClelland and Stewart, 1994.
———. *Names of God*. Lantzville, B.C.: oolichan books, 1986.
———. *Tourist to Ecstasy*. Toronto: Exile Editions, 1989.
Lonergan, Bernard s.j. *Collected Works of Bernard Lonergan: Volume 4, Collection*. Toronto: University of Toronto Press, 1993.
———. "The Response of the Jesuit as Priest and Apostle in the Modern World." *A Second Collection: Papers by Bernard J. F. Lonergan s.j.* William F. J. Ryan and Bernard J. Tyrrell, eds. London: Darton, Longman & Todd, 1974.

Lonsdale, David s.j. *Eyes to See, Ears to Hear: An Introduction to Ignatian Spirituality*. London: Darton Longman & Todd, 1990.

———. "The Spiritual Exercises: A Popular Path to Personal Wholeness." *International Minds: The Quarterly Journal of Psychological Insight into International Affairs* 2 (2 Winter 1990–91).

Lucas, Thomas s.j. *Saint, Site, and Sacred Strategy: Ignatius, Rome, and Jesuit Urbanism*. Rome: Biblioteca Apostolica Vaticana, 1990.

———. *The Vineyard at the Crossroads: The Urban Vision of Ignatius of Loyola*. Doctoral dissertation, Jesuit School of Theology, Berkeley, California, 1991.

Martin, Malachi. *The Jesuits: The Society of Jesus and the Betrayal of the Roman Catholic Church*. Toronto: Simon and Schuster, 1987.

Martin, Robert Bernard. *Gerard Manley Hopkins: A Very Private Life*. London: HarperCollins, 1991.

Martz, Louis L. *The Poetry of Meditation: A Study in English Religious Literature of the Seventeenth Century*. New Haven: Yale University Press, 1978.

McAteer, Michael. *The Toronto Star*, December 26, 1992.

McCabe, William H. *An Introduction to the Jesuit Theatre*. St. Louis: The Institute of Jesuit Sources, 1983.

McShane, Philip. "The Historical Reach of Lonergan's Meaning." *Compass: A Jesuit Journal* (Spring 1985).

Mealing, S. R., ed. *The Jesuit Relations and Allied Documents*. Toronto: McClelland and Stewart, 1969.

Meissner, W. W. s.j. *The Psychology of a Saint: Ignatius of Loyola*. New Haven: Yale University Press, 1992.

Meynell, Hugo. "Lonergan and the Future of Philosophy." *Compass: A Jesuit Journal* (Spring 1985).

Mill, John Stuart. *On Liberty*. Gertrude Himmelfarb, ed. Toronto: Penguin, 1982.

Mitchell, David. *The Jesuits: A History*. Toronto: Franklin Watts, 1981.

Mooney, Christopher s.j. As quoted in Michael W. Higgins, *Pierre Teilhard de Chardin: The One-Hundredth Anniversary, 1881–1981*. Toronto: CBC Enterprises, 1982.

Moss, Christopher s.j. "A Glimpse of Creation." *The Tablet*, May 2, 1992.

Mottola, Anthony, trans. *The Spiritual Exercises of St. Ignatius*. Toronto: Doubleday, 1964.

Mroz, Joe s.j. "Robert Bellarmine: Able Defender of a Crumbling Synthesis." *Compass: A Jesuit Journal* (September/October 1993).

Muir, Thomas E. *Stonyhurst College: 1593–1993*. London: James and James, 1992.

O'Callaghan, Joseph F., trans. *The Autobiography of St. Ignatius Loyola*. New York: Harper, 1974.

O'Connor, F. M. "George Tyrell." *The New Catholic Encyclopedia*. Vol. XIV. Toronto: McGraw Hill, 1967.

O'Keefe, Vincent s.j. "Obituary: Pedro Arrupe." *The Tablet*, February 9, 1991.

Olin, John C. *The Catholic Reformation: Savonarola to Ignatius Loyola*. New York: Fordham University Press, 1992.

O'Malley, John W. s.j. *The First Jesuits*. Cambridge, Mass.: Harvard University Press, 1993.

Padberg, John s.j. "The Jesuit Question." *The Tablet*, September 22, 1990.

Padberg, John W. s.j., Martin D. O'Keefe s.j., and John L. McCarthy s.j. *For Matters of Greater Moment: The First Thirty Jesuit General Congregations*. St. Louis: The Institute of Jesuit Sources, 1994.

Piderit, John J. s.j. Inaugural Address as 22nd President of Loyola University Chicago in *Building New Traditions: From Small Steps to Great Strides*. Chicago: Loyola University Press, 1994.

Pittau, Giuseppe s.j. "Address by Giuseppe Pittau, S.J., July 28, 1991." In *Companions of Jesus, Pilgrims with Ignatius: Congress '91*. Toronto: Canadian Institute of Jesuit Studies, 1991.

Poupard, Paul Cardinal. "Galileo: Report on Papal Commission Findings." Press Office of the Holy See.

Pratt, E. J. *Brēbeuf and His Brethren*. Toronto: Macmillan, 1966.

"Prisoner no. 1442." *The Tablet*, July 30, 1994.

Rahner, Hugo s.j. *Ignatius the Theologian*. Michael Barry, ed. London: Geoffrey Chapman, 1990.

———. *The Spirituality of St. Ignatius Loyola: An Account of Its Historical Development*. Francis John Smith s.j., trans. Chicago: Loyola University Press, 1980.

Rahner, Karl s.j. *Foundations of Christian Faith: An Introduction to the Idea of Christianity*. William V. Dych s.j., trans. New York: Crossroad, 1987.

———. *Ignatius of Loyola*. Rosaleen Ockenden, trans. London: Collins, 1979.

———. *I Remember: An Autobiographical Interview with Meinold Krauss*. Harvey D. Egan s.j., trans. New York: Crossroad, 1985.

———. *Theological Investigations*. Volume 16. New York: Seabury/Crossroad, 1961–1991.

Rawlinson, Peter. *The Jesuit Factor: A Personal Investigation*. London: Weidenfeld and Nicolson, 1990.

Regimini militantis ecclesiae. In Arturus Codina s.j., ed. Monumenta Historica Societatis Jesu, Vol. 63. Rome: Gregorian University, 1934.

Ross, Oakland. "Be a Patriot, Kill a Priest." *Saturday Night*, October 1991.

Rowntree, Stehpen C. s.j. "Ten Theses on Jesuit Higher Education." *America*, May 28, 1984.

Schultenover, David G. s.j. *A View from Rome: On the Eve of the Modernist Crisis*. New York: Fordham University Press, 1993.

Sheridan, Edward s.j. "Faith and Justice: Followers of Ignatius." *Compass: A Jesuit Journal* 9 (3 July/August 1991).

Sobrino, Jon s.j. "Compassion: The Shaping Principle of the Human and of the Christian." The fifteenth Nash Lecture; delivered at Campion College, University of Regina, Saskatchewan, November 26, 1992.

Sobrino, Jon, Ignacio Ellacuría, et al. *Companions of Jesus: The Jesuit Martyrs of El Salvador*. Maryknoll, N.Y.: Orbis, 1990.

Speaight, Robert. *Teilhard de Chardin: A Biography*. London: Collins, 1968.

Spence, Jonathan D. *The Memory Palace of Matteo Ricci*. New York: Penguin Books, 1985.

Temin, Christine. "In the priesthood, body and soul." *The Boston Globe*, November 9, 1988.

Trudeau, Pierre Elliott. *Memoirs*. Toronto: McClelland and Stewart, 1993.

Tylenda, Joseph N. s.j., trans. *A Pilgrim's Journey: The Autobiography*. Collegeville, Minn.: The Liturgical Press, 1985.

Vorgrimler, Herbert. *Understanding Karl Rahner: An Introduction to His Life and Thought*. John Bowden, trans. New York: Crossroad, 1986.

Walsh, Michael and Brian Davies, eds. *Proclaiming Justice and Peace: Papal Documents from* Rerum novarum to Centesimus annus. Mystic, Conn.: Twenty-Third Publications, 1991.

White, Norman. "Poet and Priest: Gerard Manley Hopkins, Myth and Reality." *Studies: An Irish Quarterly Review* 79 (Summer 1990).

Woodrow, Alain. "The Jesuits Take Stock." *The Tablet*, January 7, 1995.

Young, William s.j., trans. *Letters of St. Ignatius of Loyola*. Chicago: Loyola University Press, 1959.

Copyright Acknowledgements

The authors express their gratitude to the following for permission to reprint previously published material. Every effort has been made to obtain applicable copyright information. Please notify the publisher of any errors or omissions.

Excerpts from "The Soul's Entrepreneurs" reprinted with permission from *The New York Review of Books*. Copyright © 1994 Nyrev, Inc.

Excerpts from "The Vineyard at the Crossroads: The Urban Vision of Ignatius of Loyola" reprinted with permission of Thomas M. Lucas s.j.

Excerpts from *A History of the English Church and People* (page 86) by Leo Sherley-Price, revised by R. E. Latham (Penguin Classics 1955, revised edition 1968) copyright © Leo Sherley-Price, 1955, 1968, reproduced with permission of Penguin Books Ltd.

Excerpts from E. J. Pratt's *Brébeuf and his Brethren*, © The Macmillan Company of Canada, Limited 1966 and from "Cognitional Structure," by Bernard Lonergan in *Collected Works of Bernard Lonergan: Volume 4 Collection*, reproduced with permission of University of Toronto Press Incorporated.

Excerpts from *Fidel and Religion*, copyright © 1987 by Frei Betto, reprinted with permission of Simon & Schuster, Inc.

Excerpts from Ganss/*The Spiritual Exercises of St. Ignatius*; Arrupe-Calvez/*Faith and Justice*; Arrupe/*Justice With Faith Today*; Ignatius Loyola-Ganss/*The Constitutions of the Society of Jesus*; Xavier-Costelloe/*The Letters and Instructions of Francis Xavier*; Bangert/*A History of the Society of Jesus*; Padberg/*Documents of the Thirty-first and Thirty-second General Congregations of the Society of Jesus*; Padberg, O'Keefe, McCarthy/*For Matters of Greater Moment* reproduced with permission of The Institute of Jesuit Sources, St. Louis, Missouri, USA.

Excerpts from *Letters From My Friend Teilhard de Chardin, 1948–1955* by Pierre Leroy, published by Paulist Press, New York, 1980 reproduced with permission of Paulist Press.

Excerpts from *Letters of St. Ignatius of Loyola*, selected and translated by William J. Young s.j. (Copyright © 1959 Loyola University Press) used with permission of Loyola University Press, Chicago.

Excerpts from *The Catholic Reformation: Savonarola to Ignatius Loyola*, © 1992 by Professor John C. Olin, Fordham University Press, reprinted with permission of Professor Olin.

Excerpts from *The Documents of Vatican II* reprinted with permission of America Press, Inc., 106 West 56th Street, New York, NY 10019 © 1986, all rights reserved.

Excerpts from *The Formula of the Institute Centrum Ignatianum Spiritualitatis*, Rome, 1982 reprinted with permission of The Secretariat for Ignatian Spirituality (SSI), Rome.

Excerpts from *The Month*, 1975, volume 136, number 1299, December reproduced courtesy of *The Month*.

Excerpts from *The New Dictionary of Catholic Spirituality* by Harvey D. Egan, *Karl Rahner*, by William V. Dych, *A Pilgrim's Journey: The Autobiography* by Ignatius of Loyola, "Karl Rahner" by William V. Dych in *The Modern Catholic Encylopedia*, and *Lonergan* by Frederick C. Crowe, reproduced with permission of The Liturgical Press.

Excerpts from *The Psychology of a Saint: Ignatius of Loyola* by W. W. Meissner, Yale University Press © 1992, reproduced with permission of Yale University Press.

Excerpts from *The Spiritual Exercises of St. Ignatius*, translated by Anthony Mottola, Ph.D., and *The Dark Night of Resistance* by Daniel Berrigan, reprinted with permission of Doubleday.

Peter-Hans Kolvenbach s.j., *Men of God: Men for Others*, An Interview with Renzo Giacomelli (Alba House, New York, 1990), pp. 96–7.

Excerpts from the following HarperCollins Publishers Limited books reproduced with permission: Karl Rahner, *Ignatius of Loyola*, Norman White, *Poet and Priest*, Margaret Hebblethwaite, *Finding God in All Things*.

Excerpts from *One Jesuit's Spiritual Journey* by Pedro Arrupe s.j., used with permission of The Institute of Jesuit Sources, St. Louis, Missouri, USA.

Excerpts from *Introducing Liberation Theology* by Leonardo and Clodovis Boff, reprinted with permission of Maryknoll: Orbis Books; Tunbridge Wells: Burns & Oates © 1987.

Excerpts from *Option for the Poor: A Hundred Years of Vatican Social Teaching* by Donal Dorr, reproduced with permission of the publishers, Gill & Macmillan, Dublin.

Excerpts from *The Documents of Vatican II*, general editor Walter M. Abbott s.j., translation editor Msgr. Joseph Gallagher, reprinted with permission of America Press, Inc., 106 West 56th Street, New York, NY 10019 © 1986 All Rights Reserved.

Excerpts from *A Second Collection: Papers by Bernard J.F. Lonergan s.j.*, (London: Darton, Longman & Todd, 1974), quoted with the permission of the Trustees of the Bernard Lonergan Estate.

Excerpts from *To Dwell in Peace: An Autobiography* by Daniel Berrigan, copyright © 1987 Daniel Berrigan, reprinted with permission of HarperCollins Publishers, Inc..

Excerpts from *The Autobiography of St. Ignatius Loyola* by John C. Olin, ed., and Joseph F. O'Callaghan, trans., copyright © 1974 J.C. Olin and J.F. O'Callaghan, reprinted with permission of HarperCollins Publishers, Inc..

Thanks to George Bull, editor of *International Minds: The quarterly journal of psychological insight into international affairs* and David Lonsdale, author, for permission to reprint excerpts from David Lonsdale's article, "The Spiritual Exercises: A Popular Path to Personal Wholeness".

Index